The Struggle for

DEMOCRACY

The Struggle for DEMOCRACY

Patrick Watson & Benjamin Barber

KEY PORTER BOOKS

Canadian Cataloguing in Publication Data available upon request

THE CANADA COUNCIL | LE CONSEIL DES ARTS
FOR THE ARTS | DU CANADA
SINCE 1957 | DEPUIS 1957

The publisher gratefully acknowledges the support of the Canada Council for the Arts and the Ontario Arts Council for its publishing program.

We acknowledge the financial support of the Government of Canada through the Book Publishing Industry Development Program (BPIDP) for our publishing activities.

Key Porter Books Limited
70 The Esplanade
Toronto, Ontario
Canada M5E 1R2

www.keyporter.com

All photographs courtesy of CP Picture Archives.

Cover design: Peter Maher
Electronic formatting: Heidi Palfrey

Printed and bound in Canada

00 01 02 03 04 05 6 5 4 3 2 1

Contents

Introduction to the First edition

THIS IS THE STORY OF THE STRUGGLE FOR DEMORACY
—of the endless striving for liberty, for justice, and for power that has
been the history of peoples everywhere and in all times. It is a struggle as
ancient as human will, reflecting our wish to master our own immediate
world, to be free of tyranny from without and within.

But if the struggle for democracy is as old as human consciousness, if
we can find evidence of natural co-operation and a rudimentary equality
among the earliest tribes, the political quest for formal democratic institutions began in earnest only about 2,500 years ago, on a barren, rocky out-
cropping reaching into the Mediterranean. That was when Greek tribes
wrested control of their cities from the rule of kings and blood clans and
set up the foundations for communities to govern themselves—eventually
creating one of the most splendid civilizations the world has ever seen.

The spirit of that civilization endures today in the established democracies of the West, where citizens struggle to preserve their old freedoms in
the face of complacency and bureaucracy, of oppression and terrorism,
and where they labour to accommodate those freedoms to new technologies and new economic conditions. Today we may wonder, as puzzled voters, how our one vote can matter when millions are being cast, or whether
the choice is really a choice at all if the alternatives are not of our own
making. At the same time, we are apt to think that the battle for true citizenship has largely been won, and that democracy is universally recognized as the ideal system of government.

But is that true? And how will democracy fare in the twenty-first century? Can the civic spirit born in Athens in 430 B.C. deal with the microchip? Is the multinational corporation, which defies the very idea of national sovereignty, compatible with the old-fashioned democratic republic? There are many new questions that suggest continuing perils to democracy, even in those advanced countries where the struggle to establish it is over. And in the newer nations of the Third World, the struggle for democracy has just got under way. There, fledgeling communities battle against land owners, professional armies, demagogues flushed with unaccustomed powers, crippling old colonial attitudes, and poverty and ignorance. Many people are still hoping to win the first victories of emancipation and equality.

This book is published in conjunction with the television series of the same name, and we have tried to keep faith with our intent in the series: to lift the abstract science of democracy off the shelves of academia and took at it in the context of our daily lives and the lives of our forebears—wherever they may have come from. The television series began as a global quest, and we have followed the series as closely as possible, while taking advantage of the additional scope a book allows us to explore more deeply, and gather additional illustrations from sources around the world. Each chapter, like each television show, is a journey into an aspect of democracy; we travel from continent to continent, from era to era, searching for the people and the stories that tell us of democracies progress—and its setbacks—over the centuries, and help illuminate our own world. Our text is filled with the observations of very different people in very different countries, and in all walks of life, across the globe. Our approach is that of the filmmaker and reporter as well as that of the scholar, because this is a subject that touches us all on a daily basis—in the rules and behaviour we set ourselves in the family, as children at school, as adults. It is a fundamental element of our rights and freedoms, and our responsibilities—and so it is, inevitably, involved in many of our most controversial issues. As we discovered, it is impossible to open a newspaper almost anywhere in the world without seeing the word "democracy" and wondering: "What does it really mean to me? To the people around me?"

Our aim has been not to tell the story of democracy itself, in chronological, historical fashion—such histories exist and some are noted in the bibliography at the end of the book for those who wish to pursue the quest further—but to explore the nature of the struggle for democracy that has illuminated the human race since the beginning of time. The challenge in undertaking such a global series, and then bringing it to life again in words and pictures, has been very great—and enormously stimulating. For our theme has been human freedom—and there is no theme more crucial to the future of our race.

"Freedom," warned the great French philosopher of democracy, Jean Jacques Rousseau, "is a food easy to eat but hard to digest." For democracy is not simply an ideal to be realized once and for all, or a blueprint to be produced and then reproduced around the world. It is not a destination— it is a journey, a road men and women walk that may traverse many different terrains. Achieving freedom in the first instance may not be so difficult, whether it comes suddenly by violence and revolution (as it did in France), or slowly through an accretion of institutions that extend and protect liberty (as it did in England). Preserving, enhancing, and securing it against its myriad and tireless adversaries is much harder. Governments are no less mortal than people. Winston Churchill's jest—"Democracy is the worst form of government in the world—except for all the other forms"—is no joke. It is hard to conceive of a more chaotic design for government than one that invites absolutely everyone to participate in fashioning it. Deference to authority sometimes seems more comfortable than living with the responsibility of freedom.

We found that to tell the story of democracy is also to explore the fundamental human urge towards self-mastery and liberation: the inclination to speak openly, communicate freely, pray according to one's beliefs, dance to one's own tune, think as one pleases—but to do so in the company of other men and women in a spirit of co-operation. There are people who insist that democracy is an acquired skill that depends on very special circumstances: that it must be taught. That what Thomas Hobbes called "the war of all against all" is the human condition: we are born as enemies and pursue only our own interests with zeal; democracy becomes the cautious experiment in co-operation by which we try gingerly to challenge the terrible reality of our natural condition. But Hobbes was writing during the English civil war in the seventeenth century. A hundred years later, Rousseau argued that our natural condition is one of peace and harmony, and that democracy is the way we make our social life reflect our egalitarian nature. And if freedom is won only by artifice and human invention and is not to be found in nature, what are we to make of the early tribal council that made equals of tribesmen, and encouraged participation in council meetings? What does it mean to say—as Thomas Jefferson says in the American Declaration of Independence—that men are free and equal by nature, and that government serves only to guarantee those natural rights? The old argument is between those "idealists", like Rousseau, who think we are born neighbours and those "realists", like Hobbes, who think we are born adversaries. It is when we turn to look at people from the inside that we find both Hobbes and Rousseau are right. As we discovered, the struggle for democracy also turns out to be a struggle within ourselves: it is a tension we see quite clearly in children between the yearning for freedom and the yearning for security, the need to govern ourselves and the need to be taken care of by others, the need to give and the need to take.

When we set out to make the television series and write this book, we deliberately tried not to define democracy in advance: as a result we found it in the most unexpected places, and found it wanting in many places we expected to find it. We watched democracy at work in the schools and in tribes and looked at formal democracy in the legal constitutions of nations, republics and so-called peoples' republics, constitutional monarchies and one-party democracies, American towns and African villages, face-to-face democracies where almost everyone knows everybody else and bureaucratic democracies where the governors are faceless—democracies all, if we take people at their word, however bizarre it may sometimes seem; yet impostors all, if we set our standards too high.

Westerners, it seems, have a rather proprietary attitude to democracy; after all, they claim, political democracy began in the West. And "one-party democracies" or "peoples' democracies" in which a single strongman claims to rule "in the name of the people" do seem to be contradictions in terms. Yet there are reasons to believe that styles of government other than the typical multiparty parliamentary systems *may* qualify as democratic. The one thing we have become sure of is that there is no consensus on what democracy is or what it requires.

Big states using representatives who are elected by the masses often seem to think they own democracy, and countries like the United States, Canada, France, England, and Mexico make of their size a democratic strength. Yet in such remarkable countries as Iceland, New Zealand,

Switzerland, Holland, Israel, and Papua New Guinea, democracy and smallness go hand in hand, and in some of these accountability depends more on the participation of citizens than on the conduct of leaders.

Socialists and capitalists argue about which of their rival systems is more "democratic", disagreeing about the meaning of democracy itself at every step. The socialist argues that capitalism nourishes poverty and inequality in the name of freedom. How can "one man, one vote" be meaningful if some are millionaires and others paupers? Capitalists say that, in pursuing equality, socialism limits political freedom. Today we find capitalist democracies trying to become more egalitarian in the name of social justice, and we find socialist dictatorships aspiring to more competition and market freedom in the name of *glasnost* and *perestroika*.

Democracy is deeply rooted in talk. It seems to prefer talk to force, deliberation to whim, good reasons to powerful arms, consensus to conflict, peace to war, co-operation to competition. But no sooner do we define democracy as "reasonable discussion" than someone reminds us that it can also mean the politics of conflict as well as the politics of co-operation; or that through the power of today's media, the government of public opinion we call democracy can enthrone whim rather than deliberation.

Democracy is not tidy. It is a rough, obstreperous, messy form of political life. Montesquieu, that thoughtful and ingenious French predecessor of both the French and the American revolutions, observed that where you find an orderly silence, there you will find tyranny. Wherever we find spirited voices raised in debate, where there is tumult and faction and unceasing talk, where men and women muddle their way to provisional solutions for permanent problems—and so clumsily do for themselves what tyrants or bureaucrats might have achieved much more neatly and efficiently for them—there we can feel assured that we are on the precious turf of democracy. Because democracy is finally—more than any other form of government—about people, just plain people. To be democratic is to disagree about what democracy is.

The research, our travels, the making of the television series, and the writing of the book have taken several years. But one unexpected and moving result, for us, was that if we emerged from our long immersion anxious about the power of tyranny, we also emerged exhilarated by the power of democracy. Because we found that the struggle for democracy is intensifying in many places around the world, even if it is shrinking in some. Menaced though it often is by complacency, indifference, corruption, and self-centredness, it has none the less built enormously powerful institutions for the healing of its self-inflicted wounds. And it is propelled into what looks like an expanding and challenging new century by the passionate determination of men, women, and children, who once having eaten of liberty, never forget its taste.

Benjamin Barber and Patrick Watson
New York and Toronto, September 1988

Democracy through the Looking Glass

THE FIRST EDITION WAS TIMED FOR THE CHRISTMAS market of 1988 and the first broadcast a few weeks later, beginning in January 1989, of the television series upon which the book was based. Although both book and television series confidently forecast the irresistible spread of democracy around the world (despite certain pockets of very long-term resistance), nobody connected with the enterprise foresaw how rapidly one of the great totalitarian political structures would begin to come unbuttoned. And so when the Berlin Wall came down a year later, and our British producing partners at Central Independent Television plc had not yet broadcast the television series in the U.K., I had to take leave from my new responsibilities as Chairman of the Canadian Broadcasting Corporation; rapidly assemble a crew under Senior Producer Ted Remerowski; and head off to Russia, Romania, and Poland to make a twelfth program on the dramatic changes in Eastern Europe.

It was a heady fifteen-day video blitzkrieg through three capitals still half stunned and staggering from shock. We met and interviewed political leaders from all the major countries whose fate had suddenly changed because of political events: Ion Caramitrou in Bucharest, Lech Walensa in Gdansk, Boris Yeltsin and Vaclav Havel in Moscow.

We expected, even before we set off for Moscow, that we would find a deeply wounded political culture, a profoundly riven group of peoples, and the confused beginnings of a long voyage whose shaken travellers would spend a lot of time on troubled waters before anything resembling a stable civil democracy could emerge out of the ashes of the old tyrannies. This turned out to be the case.

I recall a lot of romantic optimism in the media, where correspondents and columnists and letters to the editor rejoiced in the brave new democratic worlds bursting into creative flame in every direction. But if we had learned anything in the six very full and fascinating years it took to produce the television series and its accompanying book, one of the great lessons was this: that democracy cannot happen overnight. The creation of a civil society in which the contradictory objectives of majority rule and respect for individual liberties can co-exist depends upon generation after generation of trial and error. The face of each such society will be different from every other one according to the underlying culture. And ultimately this unlikely democratic phenomenon, this messy, difficult, laborious unpredictable thing we hold up to each other as an ideal, works only when its participants have had enough time at it to be at ease with its institutions, tolerate its messiness and other flaws. People become *citizens* only when they have come to accept at a deep and instinctive level that it is possible to trust in the structures (and in the other citizens) sufficiently to keep on at the endless task of building towards an ideal that will never be reached.

The democracies of Western Europe and the English-speaking world had gone through centuries of advances and retreats, carnage and the re-emergence of tyrants, revolutions and evolutions. Individual liberty, justice, and accountability—the underpinnings of the democratic civil society—had been worked at for several hundred years. But it was not until the middle of the nineteenth century that anything really resembling contemporary democracy was effectively in practice. And, with a few transient exceptions, it was not until well into the twentieth century that the rights of citizenship were in the hands of anyone other than male landowners. The uncomfortable idea that democracy is not a destination but a journey is the recent result of the discussion of democracy having been taken out of the hands of elites and become the property of everyone who lives in a functional, more-or-less democratic civil society.

The people who have been slaughtering each other in Chechnya or the former Jugoslavia, or in Malawi or the Congo or Malaysia, have not lived through that kind of evolution. The tribal rivalries released into active violence in parts of the former Soviet Union had been held down by a repressive police state; they had not had the opportunity to be transformed into traditions of tolerance and working things out, the way they briefly did among the Athenian tribes (the *demes*) in their short-lived democratic experiment 2,500 years ago. And in every modern such experiment, from India to Iceland, these same rivalries, the same old competition for a place in the sun based upon birth and ethnicity, still demand the patient labour of convinced democrats, and perhaps they always will.

So nobody should be surprised at the horrors of Bosnia or Grozny or the Sudan or Kenya, or at the explosion of organized Mafia-like crime in Russia. These catastrophes are not proof, as some would have it, that democracy doesn't work, that "They were better off under the USSR." Which you hear a lot. The old regime was a stable society. Life was predictable. The vast criminal activity was the province of the State and was "legal". People could be and were dragged off to slavery and death at the whim of a commissar. Corruption was endemic. It should surprise no one that, upon the removal of the heavy hand of the Police State, a resentful and confused people should look for every chance to get back at old enemies and get what they can while they can. It took the West a very long time and it is going to take the East a very long time. And democracy, when it finally arrives in, say, China, as the result of prosperity, travel and trade, increased communications, will still look more like China than it does like, say, America or Canada. That shouldn't be surprising either, given how closely in most ways the Communist regime, with its centralism and mandarinate, resembles the political culture of the China of the Emperors. What is surprising in China is the rapidity with which a nation still firmly under the control of a determined and skilful totalitarian government is, well, loosening up. Cellular phones, international travel, a central government's discovery of the value of prosperity, the pressures and opportunities of international trade, and of course the computer and everything that goes with it—these have changed the face of this huge country more than anything that has happened to it since the first Republican revolution of Sun Yatsen that began in 1911. It now seems likely that the twenty-first-century face of China will be determined far more by commercial and technical innovation than by political movements, and that political change will follow those innovations rather than lead them.

And what about the astounding success of Poland, which, according to some observers, has the best civil society, law and order, and political process of all the former Warsaw Pact countries except Hungary? Poland suffered terribly as a police state under the Nazis during the Second World War, and then for forty-four more years under the Russians. How it recovered so much better than its former master is only partly clear. But it had to have something to do with the survival of the Catholic Church—not itself a model of democracy, but in this case an effective countervailing force against the State. Part of its effectiveness was to give moral legitimacy to the substantial underground anticommunist movement. So, during the whole period of oppression, the State never had the monopoly on authority that a totalitarian regime requires. (Ironically—given the Church's opposition to some elements of republican civil rights—it has been argued that the success of the Irish Republic may have been helped by its never succeeding in displacing the Church as a second national authority.)

Poland had a tradition of republican politics. Poles knew from experience that you could at the same time oppose the government and be loyal to the Nation; Russians never knew that and still have trouble with it. Poland had the first real parliament in continental Europe, going back to the early post-mediaeval period.

Poland's coalition government didn't purge the old regime, but made room for old Communist officials (in itself an interesting expression of the peculiar democratic uses of tolerance, which frustrate the hell out of doctrinaire purists!) while at the same time the country was building a consumer economy and opening the way to what will probably become full membership in the European Union.

In any case, throughout the West especially, there is a huge appetite for to know more about democracy, the hows and whys of it. That this is no longer primarily the province of academics, leaders, or pundits is demonstrated by the history of the television series upon which this book is based. Filmed in more than thirty countries around the world, it has also been broadcast in at least that many, including Poland, Israel, Zimbabwe, Algeria, Morocco, and—especially interesting for us the producers—Czechoslovakia before partition. In 1992 associate producer Caroline Bamford and I were invited to a world conference on democracy in Prague, jointly hosted by UNESCO and by President Vaclav Havel. We discovered that *The Struggle for Democracy* was playing in Czechoslovakia when we arrived at the conference. I was recognized on the street and invited to take part in television programs. Late in the conference Caroline and I were asked to fly to Bratislava and appear on television with a group of Slovakian independantists. That was seen as daring, at the time. And it was apparent from a number of experiences—the autographs requested by the cabin staff on the flight from Prague to Bratislava and the eager if naïve approaches we received from the independence movement about helping them make a television special to promote *their* particular version of democracy—that the ideas and experiences conveyed by the films were accessible to a far wider audience than the Canadian, American, and British viewers whom we had originally set out to serve.

In fact, evidence of the wide appeal of the ideas and stories on which the series was based had come in very dramatically within months of the original telecast. A phone call came in from Beijing, from Ma Qiang, a young official in the international film co-production office there. He told me that he had acquired a copy of the book and was using it as a text in classes he was holding on documentary filmmaking, and that he was hoping to soon acquire a set of the films themselves for use in those same classes. He very excitedly then told me that he had somehow acquired a copy of my 1964 film about China itself, *The Seven Hundred Million*. He had persuaded senior officials in his office that it would be a very good idea if the creator of that film, and of *The Struggle for Democracy,* should come back to China for a twenty-five-years-later retrospective, covering the same ground and looking at many of the same issues raised in the 1964 film.

To be invited by Official China was extraordinary in those days. I set about the difficult task of enlisting a broadcaster and raising money for the project. The discussions—including my somewhat unorthodox proposals to Beijing about using home video cameras and coming into communities and institutions unannounced to pursue the search for my long missing interpreter Lu Yiching, which was to be the central line of inquiry of the new film—took weeks. One day Ma Qiang phoned in great excitement. "You should see these huge crowds of students in Tian an Men Square!" he said. "Something wonderful is happening. It's all about democracy! President Zhao Ziyang is down there, among the students right now, talking with them openly. I have never seen anything like it in my life. I have to go right back there, but I just had to let you know."

A few days later some of those students were dead, any illusion that something important about democracy was happening in China had been swept away, and so had the possibility of my going back for that quarter-century retrospective. And yet we had learned again that the kind of investigation of the nature and colour and flavour and challenge of democracy that both the films and the books had tried to open up was able to make its way in unexpected parts of the world.

When History Television (Canada) bought the series for rebroadcast, Caroline Bamford and I, and Executive Producer Michael Levine, found ourselves wondering if, a decade having passed, we shouldn't take a long look at the original one-hour programs and see if they might profitably be broken up into thematic segments of, say, twenty minutes, followed by a brief update taking account of the vast changes in the world since the original production. However, screening the films with this in mind, we soon decided that our original intention to create a series whose narrative core would be relatively timeless had, in fact, been achieved, and breaking them up would damage both the integrity of each program and the ideas it conveyed.

So despite the fact that the seemingly impossible challenge of peace in Northern Ireland, a central issue in our program subtitled "The Tyranny of the Majority", seems to be painfully moving towards resolution, the underlying issues that made the history of that troubled land a *locus classicus* for the great democratic issues entailed in Majority Rule and Minority Rights are still dramatically conveyed by the events as we have recounted them, and people reading their newspapers today and sniffing the hope of peace in our time will not be disserved to be vividly reminded on the television screens and here in these pages of the powerful anguish out of which that bloom of peace has grown.

The making of the series contained interesting lessons in democratic collaboration and tolerance. From the beginning we exposed the process of building the series to the scrutiny of experts, as well as to the judgment of "ordinary people". At the very beginning we convened a weekend panel of historians and filmmakers and broadcasters to tell us what they knew—or wondered—about democracy, its origins and its challenges. And a year into production, with only a few segments assembled as rough edits, we convened another such group from around the world to look at what we were doing and assess it. And while I and my producers were nervous about what such luminaries as the great historian Henry Steele Commager would say to us, this second colloquium turned out to be an exhilarating combination of resounding approval and encouragement, plus sound and rigorous advice about gaps in the fabric and weaknesses in the presentation here and there.

But I think another kind of convocation was even more important. We instituted the routine of inviting a ten to twenty people to sit in when we were screening rough-cuts. And not just people working on the series. We asked strangers, other producers we chanced on in the hall, film editors working in another field, the mail boy or a receptionist—a variety of backgrounds and tastes and outlook—from whom we asked only that they say frankly what they found in the film at that stage and whether it seemed worthwhile. A lot of obscurities and stumbling blocks got cleared away through these screenings. And one of them was particularly instructive in the matter of the cultural particularity of different national concepts of democracy. The program in question was subtitled "The Last Citizens". It was one of the episodes that Senior Producer Ted Remerowski produced, wrote and directed personally, and it dealt with the late acceptance of women, in all the major democracies, as full participants. We were screening the dramatic story of Clause 28 in Canada's 1982 Charter of Rights and Freedoms, the gender equity section. This had been achieved in its present form only after an enormous battle by a group of women who came together within a few weeks and fought to a standstill the patronizing condescension of the male officials and politicians who had convinced themselves, wrongly, that the first draft contained everything necessary to, if not genuinely recognize the rights of women, at least to placate them.

The story was told in terms of personalities and institutions that had been very much in the news over the previous five or six years, but we were a little uncertain, as it was an intricate set of events, whether we had it not only right, and dramatically engaging, but clear and comprehensible.

To our delight, when the lights went up after the screening there was a round of vigorous applause from our fifteen or twenty ad-hoc "virgin viewers". Managing Producer Nancy Button looked beatific. Caroline Bamford (known as The Feminist Police) was nodding happily; and indeed we were all grinning and congratulating ourselves until a voice from the back of the room punctured our complacency. It was Professor Benjamin Barber, co-author of this book and our principal academic consultant. Ben is a knowledgeable political philosopher and author (*Strong Democracy, MacWorld vs. Jihad*). He is an American: he had not lived our constitutional struggles. And he said wryly and bluntly, "I am sorry to tell you, but I was completely baffled." All the concrete references to people and institutions that were part of our ongoing journalistic world were totally opaque to him, and it was suddenly clear that if this segment were to be accessible to the international audience for whom the series was intended, we had to get back to the editing bench and the typewriter. (Yes, some of us were still on typewriters in 1988.)

Of course the talent and dedication of the producers and writers and crews, the almost forty people who contributed directly to the making of those programs, was the core of its strength. But I now feel that one of the most important things we did was to institutionalize those Screenings For The Folks, so that we could hear as we went how well we were reaching and serving our constituents. And it seems to me that that process has quite a lot to do with the nature of democracy.

This volume was intended as a kind of handbook to the television series. It would allow viewers to go back through the films without having to stick a cassette in the VHS machine (although that continues to happen in hundreds of classrooms, to this day). It would provide an elaboration of some of the ideas that could be dealt with only briefly on the screen. It would be a tool for reflecting upon and visiting again the vivid and sometimes dramatic experiences of the documentary. So we have left it largely as it was. The television series continues to be rebroadcast; people continue to buy or rent the cassettes for personal study or for school use; so a fresh low-cost edition of the book was needed. But what about all the changes that have taken place, the political and social earthquakes described in this chapter? We have decided that the book should remain largely as it was, still a kind of snapshot reference to the films. From time to time, however, where strong statements, photographs, or captions in the original book might be confusing if not emended, because of especially significant historical changes since that first edition a dozen years ago, we have added brief notes in the running text.

And some of the most dramatic changes are in the world of technology, especially information technology. Professor Barber, who has kept a close eye on those changes especially as they affect the progress of democracy, has done a completely new final chapter, in some cases noting with wry humour the difference between what he forecast in 1988 and what actually happened.

Readers may find it interesting to check the Introduction to the first edition, which preceeds, and ask themselves how much of consequence, in the world's great march towards a civil society in which liberty and justice prevail, has really changed since it was written.

The Birth of Democracy

A Day in the Life of Democracy

PHIDIAS—NEPHEW TO THE CELEBRATED SCULPTOR, and himself an energetic Athenian silversmith—rises before dawn. It's once again a day for the Assembly. So unsettled are the times that there have been five of these raucous gatherings of the neighbourhood demes— Athens' local civic parishes—in as many weeks.

Phidias has to pay a brief visit to his journeyman silversmith at his small factory some distance from the marketplace, the busy agora where so much of the life of the city unfolds, before continuing on to the Assembly. His business is prospering; indeed, he sometimes wishes that silver had never been discovered at Laurium, that his father had remained a simple ironmonger and armourer. With all this work there's less time for politics—the true vocation of every Athenian.

After concluding his business at the foundry, Phidias makes his way to the agora at the foot of the Pnyx. Before climbing the steep hill to the Assembly he takes a moment to check his wicker stall where his brother-in-law, the family merchant, is selling goblets and bracelets. The stall is close enough to the centre of the marketplace that Phidias can follow the informal speeches there while he conducts business. Today he's actually more interested in Haemon's harangue against the Spartans than in his brother-in-law's grumbling about how the Assembly will steal yet another day's business from their flourishing trade.

The clear dawn promises a sunny morning—it seems to Phidias that in this parched year Athens has had even fewer than the forty days of rain the farmers count on. In fact, these are unpleasant days all round. The plague has returned, and the rivalry with Sparta is inflaming civic passions. From the underground of easy talk, gossip, and jesting in the market he hopes to excavate some sense of whether the Assembly's deliberations later today are likely to result in war.

By the time he arrives at his stall the morning pandemonium is well under way and he can hear little of Haemon's rhetoric above the roar. The new iron foundry is clanking nearby; musicians are beginning to play; customers are complaining over the price of drygoods; the cries of fish-mongers, grocers, and other tradesmen are ringing in the air; and the stentorian voice of the herald is already urging the populace to ascend the Pnyx—as if they couldn't see the signal flag flying from the hill. The market is enveloped in the productive chaos that makes it the vortex of Athens' churning civic life.

Phidias loves the noise and tumult of the great agora. It's the heart of Athenian democracy—just as the Assembly is its head. Whatever happens up on the hill has its beginnings down here in the market, in rumours and arguments, economic exchanges, soapbox lectures, informal schools, and philosophical debates.

Phidias' ruminations are interrupted by the voice of the herald, who is still trying to chase the lingering citizens out of the market and up into the Assembly. A rope dipped in red dye will be dragged through the square, and citizens branded by its scarlet mark (usually only a few drunkards and loiterers) will be fined. Today there are few who wish to miss the war debate anyway—so Phidias and his brother-in-law close up the stall swiftly, and begin the climb to the Pnyx. Behind them the din of the marketplace has all but ceased; there are only the occasional voices of a few women and foreign traders, and the odd curse from one of the uniformed Scythian slaves who serve in the police force. The time has come for Athens' head to take over from its heart.

Seven hours later, the debate ends. Phidias is appalled. The citizens have voted for renewed war with Sparta, and so war it will be—and he himself will have to go into battle. In Athens' bold new democracy, the judiciary are but citizens at the bar; civil magistrates are but citizens in office; and soldiers are but citizens in arms. The Assembly has chosen war over his protests, and now it's up to him to execute that choice.

But he has no complaint against the system. He had his chance to speak his mind. And democracy means obedience to a common will that you've participated in forging, if only by opposing it. If the Assembly wants war, then he'll help secure victory. His shop will again suffer, silver will be diverted to pay the costs of armaments, and he'll again lose his journeyman—he's from a family of fishermen, and he makes a well-muscled oarsman. (And *he* voted for war, Phidias noted with annoyance.) Oh well—as Pericles said not long ago, at a funeral speech for fallen warriors, the business of every Athenian is first and foremost public business. That's the price of self-government.

As he descends from the Pnyx, Phidias comforts himself with the thought—a startling new thought for humankind, in the fifth century B.C.—that he would prefer dying in freedom, from the folly of his neighbours, to living securely under the prudence of tyrants.

Democracy's Slow Birth

There were in ancient Athens nearly 22,000 Phidiases—men who were native Athenian citizens. We have conjured our Phidias up from archaeological and historical records, trying to imagine what his day in the marketplace and the Assembly might have been like sometime between 430 and 420 B.C. Athenian democracy was an astonishing development, and although it lasted only a few centuries, it has remained a powerful example of self-government. It is not easy for modern women and men who have a long history of freedom behind them, and centuries of science and technology to insulate them from superstition and mythology, to appreciate what democracy must have meant for men such as Phidias, whose near ancestors had been tribesmen bound together by blood and ruled by hereditary kings. For them to conceive the bold new idea that all men possessed sufficient wisdom to govern themselves, and then to invent a form of civic relations that allowed them actually to do so—well, this seems something of a political miracle. They were little more than a handful of fishermen, olive-grove keepers, and tradesmen who lived in a shadowy world of irrational gods and vengeful spirits, of pugnacious and arrogant neighbours, of tyrannical invaders from without and tyrannical usurpers from within. They were scarcely to be distinguished from the ignorant soldiers in Homer's *Iliad*, and the superstitious sailors of his *Odyssey*. That such men should emerge so abruptly from darkness to light is a magnificent story of the human spirit.

For democracy was born almost overnight in the *polis*, or city-state, of Athens. Yet the democratic civilization that sprang up there in the fifth century B.C. was the beneficiary of forces that had been at work throughout Greece during the three centuries before Pericles—from the time of Homer, in the eighth or ninth century B.C., to the time of Cleisthenes in the sixth. Hundreds of years before Phidias climbed the Pnyx to watch his neighbours declare war, Chios—which some say was Homer's own island—was experimenting with rudimentary democratic institutions. Just as America's colonists had evolved home-rule legislatures and codes of personal rights well before the Declaration of Independence brought them formal independence from England, just as the English had nourished a parliamentary tradition well before Parliament gained its ascendancy over the throne in the "Glorious Revolution" of 1688, so Athens had walked a long political road before it arrived at its destination.

In fact, a number of Greek city-states—including the military garrison of Sparta and the ancient city of Thebes—were approaching the earliest stages of democracy by the middle of the fifth century B.C. Indeed, when the philosopher Aristotle catalogued some 150 constitutions from this period a century later, he found that most of them placed at least some limits on the powers of their rulers.

But why did Athens evolve into a democracy, when states all over the Mediterranean were to remain locked in dictatorship for another two thousand years? Are there special conditions necessary to democracy's growth, that modern peoples seeking self-government will have to cultivate? Are the tribes of Papua New Guinea wrong to think they can pass directly from being governed by Australia to autonomous democracy? Can a feudal and military society like pre-war Japan's adapt to a democratic structure imposed by the West?

It's easy to assume that democracy results directly from acts of political will—acts that depend only on a people's revolutionary courage. We think of the French tearing down the Bastille and overthrowing a thousand years of feudalism, or the Americans declaring their independence from an abusive English king, thereby casting off the yoke of colonialism. But new democracies sometimes confront conditions that may thwart the strongest democratic will. Hard work, good will, and the aspiration to be free are not always enough. What, then, are the conditions that favour democracy? We cannot know for certain; but ancient Greece did enjoy some conditions that seem to have aided the transition from tribal kingship to democracy.

Our Phidias might have had a grandfather who was in the iron business when kings still governed Athens. Craftsmen and traders like these gave the *polis* (the Greek word is the source of our words policy, politics, and police) a cosmopolitan commerce that energized it and brought its citizens into contact with other cultures, so that their political ideas became broader and more sophisticated. Even under the kings, the army's phalanxes of hoplites (heavily armoured warriors) were drawn from more than just the noble classes. A similar broadening of the soldiering class helped make Sparta (the chief city of the Peloponnese) and other warrior cities particularly good candidates for self-government. Men who fight regularly to defend or expand their king's realm soon want to share in the decision-making. Even slavery—the blight of the ancient world—helped to free the slaves' masters from the onus of perpetual labour, and thus, ironically, created the precious leisure required for democratic political life. From the beginning, democracy was a form of political life that took up a great deal of time.

And then there was the Greek leadership—inspirational founders of the calibre of the legendary law-giver Lycurgus, who gave warlike Sparta its remarkable egalitarian constitution and saved it from being merely a vicious garrison state; or of the stature of Solon and Cleisthenes in Athens—aristocrats who despite their high birth could envision a world where men were equal—and Pericles, who brought democracy to its peak.

After 682 B.C., when the hereditary kings ceased to rule in Athens, a momentous part was played by these "founders"—law-givers, constitution-makers, great legislators, even innovative tyrants—whose vision enabled them to create the framework for a government that would no longer depend on their dominance. Without Solon, his successor Pisistratus, Cleisthenes, and Pericles, Athens could not have made good on its people's aspiration to govern themselves. Sometimes such men were seeking allies among the people in their struggles against rivals; sometimes they were genuinely inspired by a noble, altruistic ideal of equality and democracy. More often, they were responding to the demands of their people. For power is rarely a gift; it must usually be fought for, with or without the help of those who possess it.

Back at the turn of the sixth century B.C., Athens was a town of powerful tribal clans where a man's relatives were his main qualification for political office, where it was illegal to marry a foreigner, where the rich could become still richer by selling off the region's precious grain stores abroad while the poor could only become poorer, and where rich and poor alike were generally buried under a mountain of debt. Into this sombre world of privileged aristocrats and aching debtors came a statesman called Solon, an archon elected by an assembly representing land owners. He was first of all a poet, so his visionary idealism came naturally. Driven by his vision, he enacted a series of reforms that began the transformation of Athens. He cleverly cancelled all debt, and then he used the good will this garnered among the people (debtors, after all, always manage to outnumber creditors) to initiate the breakup of the tribes and clans that had always splintered the city into rival factions.

Solon's reforms fell on Athens like a hard summer rain, uprooting the tribalism which had held the city in blood bondage for so long, and watering a terrain that would eventually support a *polis* of free and relatively equal craftsmen, tradesmen, and farmers. Though there was little that resembled democracy, the ground was being prepared, almost 150 years before Pericles.

Tribalism was not dead, however, and after Solon's death no one was in a position to finish what he had started. It took a usurper named Pisistratus—a non-hereditary ruler the Greeks called a *tyrannos*—to maintain Solon's innovations.

In the era of Pisistratus' reforms, Athenians were not yet voting or serving in public magistracies. But they did participate in a thriving culture that had grown up around poetry and popular religious ritual. Phidias' great-grandfather would not have been able to vote for or against the Persian Wars, but he would have taken part in religious ceremonies, and he might have become a worshipper of the bacchanalian god Dionysus. Inspired by this god from the rural Athenian countryside—and by the fermented grapes imbibed in his name—he might sometimes have found himself raging against his haughty aristocratic rulers with an almost democratic passion. For although aristocrats still ruled in the towns, religion and the exciting new theatrical rituals associated with it were spurring the new sense of equality. Dionysus became the patron god of theatre, and thus the poets who wrote in Dionysus' name became allies of the burgeoning democratic spirit.

In 508 B.C., while all of Greece was still under Persian domination, Athens' last great law-giver appeared—Cleisthenes. Solon and Pisistratus had weakened the power of the clans over the previous hundred years, but Cleisthenes went much further; it was he who dealt the fatal blow to the remnants of Athenian tribalism. He dissolved the traditional connections of tribes and clans entirely, and created in their place a remarkable system of groupings that were artificial tribes, each tribe being divided into demes, or parishes. He gave to each tribe (there were ten in all) the name of a great Athenian military hero, linking it to the mythic past. The demes were scattered throughout Athens' urban and rural districts and membership was hereditary, so that within a generation—as sons and daughters moved to new areas—they became a matter of symbolic rather than familial or geographical identity. Every male born in Athens became a citizen of one of the demes; women, foreigners, and slaves were not included. All citizens were required to participate in the assemblies that overnight had become their chief instruments of self-government—a general Assembly for the whole of Athens (heir to the small aristocratic assembly of the seventh century), and neighbourhood assemblies for each of the 170 or so parishes. As no law could be passed without the Assembly's approval, the citizenry had become the law-giver—and 2,500 years later, the power of the citizens to make or change law remains an essential criterion of democracy.

And so the rule of the blood clans was over. The rule of the hereditary kings was over. The rule of the usurpers was over. The rule of the gifted tyrants was over. Democracy—the *kratos*, or rule, of the *demos*, the people of the deme—was finally born. Athens was not alone in this extraordinary metamorphosis. Just as the democratic temper would make itself felt during the Renaissance two thousand years later, springing up right across Europe, so city-states throughout Greece proceeded to shed their tribal monarchies and emerge as democracies of one kind or another.

Chief among them was Sparta—a *polis* where traditional military virtues persisted, but that had been transformed into what was, ideally, to be a democratic brotherhood of warriors. Spartan society was rough-hewn and highly disciplined, and quickly acquired a reputation for deadly stoicism—like the brutal patriotism of the famous Spartan mother, or the mad self-denial of the Spartan lad who hid a fox under his cloak during military drill, and allowed himself to be gnawed to death rather than reveal its presence.

The Athenians regarded the Spartans contemptuously as narrow-minded, primitive xenophobes who left the productive work to their helot slaves and indulged little other than their lust for war. Sparta offered a model of austere fraternity, where women and men were educated in common and taught to live selfless lives; where commerce was prohibited because it supported softness and inequality; and where a senate of elected ephors (elders) was endowed with powers that in certain cases exceeded those of the king. The Spartans prized their citizenship above all things. Later democrats, more judicious than the Athenians, would retrace democracy's history to Lycurgus as often as to Solon. Great democratic philosophers, such as Jean Jacques Rousseau in the eighteenth century, often found themselves admiring Sparta's austere citizen-soldier democracy even more than the glittering civic culture of Athens.

In both its Athenian version and its more controversial Spartan version, ancient democracy was obviously a vigorous and invigorating form of social organization. Within a generation of Cleisthenes' reforms, seafaring Athens and land-locked Sparta and their allies rose up against Persia's overlordship. At the narrow pass of Thermopylae, three hundred Spartans attempted to hold off the Persian emperor Xerxes' powerful invading forces, bravely dying to the last man. At Marathon Athenian troops defeated the great army; and at Salamis the novice Athenian navy (paid for with the silver just discovered at Laurium) routed a Persian flotilla; both battles are still the stuff of legend. What the legends fail to say is that it was a *citizen* army of men like the silversmith Phidias, and a *citizen* navy of men like his journeyman smith, that defeated the imperial army of Persia—the world's most powerful tyranny. So it was that when the tragedian Aeschylus died, he had inscribed on his gravestone neither "Author of *Agamemnon* and *Prometheus Bound*" nor "Laureate Tragedian" but simply "He fought at Marathon."

Democracy may be conceived in the vision of statesmen and in the dreams of a struggling people, but it is usually born from the belly of war: as in 1775, when musket-bearing farmers from Lexington and Concord risked their homes and lives for an independent America; in 1789, when shopkeepers in Paris fought to turn Rousseau's utopian theory of a world governed by a "General Will" into a brash (if shortlived) reality; and again in 1917, when sailors from St. Petersburg and factory workers from Moscow offered up their lives to put the czars to rout and secure a Russian democracy (again shortlived). To establish a democratic constitution requires that pen be put to parchment—the job of law-givers. But the pen often writes in blood—the gift of martyrs. Democracy is most often a product of wisdom *and* blood, of reason *and* violence. The struggle for it is always a test of the human spirit.

Making Democracy Work

Real democracy must be more than a desire or a disposition. It depends in practice on a constitution—what the Greeks called a *politeia* and the Romans a *res publica* (public affairs) or republic; and the institutional arrangements it depends on can vary a great deal from nation to nation and epoch to epoch.

The Athenians hardly invented the democratic temper, but they did inaugurate institutions that remain important to many of our modern democracies. These include:

- assembly democracy: citizens participated directly in initiating, deliberating on, and passing legislation—that is, without "representatives" acting on their behalf;

- citizen juries: justice became a responsibility of the people (a practice which was not fully introduced into English common law until long after the birth of parliamentary government); along with elections, trial by a jury of one's peers remains the most powerful emblem of democracy in modern times;

- the appointment of citizens to political office by lot, a practice still used in jury selection but otherwise largely neglected today;

- citizen soldiers: being a citizen and being a soldier were seen as two sides of the same coin. This concept found its way through later writers like Rousseau and Machiavelli, the brilliant student of Renaissance statecraft, into both the theory and the practice of modern democracy—where however the linkage no longer seems secure, in a world of volunteer and professional armies;

- the device of ostracism, a unique instrument that permitted the people to send a too-powerful politician into an honourable but powerless exile—an extreme ancient version of the modern power of recall by which politicians are "de-elected" by the voters who originally chose them, and removed from office.

How did these astonishing innovations in government, that turned subjects into citizens in the course of a single generation, really work? As we saw with our imaginary Phidias, Athens' government by assembly meant that every significant policy issue had to be subjected to popular deliberation, debate, and decision. In the most important cases, there had to be a quorum of at least 6,000 citizens (out of about 22,000 in all), meeting together at a clearing on the Pnyx, a hill just west of the Acropolis. Moreover, no law was presented for debate unless it had been written down and publicly displayed. A "Council of Five Hundred" made up of fifty men (no women, foreigners, or slaves here either!) from each of the ten tribes acted as a kind of ancient civil service, carrying out everyday administrative functions.

But the sovereign legislative body was the Assembly. Normally it would meet at least forty times each year (about the same number of days that Athens could expect rain!)—which would mean roughly one day-long meeting every nine or ten days. The agendas for these meetings, to which citizens could add their own items (an ancient right of "initiative" such as modern Switzerland and a number of American states enjoy), were exhaustive—as well as exhausting. War and peace, treaties and alliances, colonial administration and empire, trade and finance, buildings and waterworks, and the arranging of honours and religious rites all came regularly to the stone floor of the Assembly. To us many of these issues might seem tedious, but to the Athenians they were the matters that defined their public lives and set them apart from unthinking animals.

Any citizen could speak at the general Assembly and many did: the herald sought out participants with the cry "Who wishes to speak?" and those wanting to would be crowned with a myrtle wreath and bidden to do so. After all, these were not abstract or hypothetical decisions. When Athens voted to send a military expedition to Sicily, the resulting débâcle took the lives of a great many of the very men who had voted in favour of it—and presumably of others who had voted against it. When in 412 the Assembly thought it could seduce the Persians into paying the bill for its war with the Spartans by abolishing its democratic procedures, which the Persians abhorred, it paved the way for a shortlived but dreadful tyranny; those who had the most to lose and would have voted against it, Athens' bold sailors from the poorer classes, were out of the city at the time. They could have their revenge, however, for the originator of a legislative proposal could be held responsible for its untoward consequences, and could be made to pay for it through censure, a fine, and even, in extreme cases, exile.

Moreover, these crucial meetings made up only part of the citizen's legislative responsibility, since he was also duty-bound to attend local assembly meetings of the demes. And there were other responsibilities, such as jury duty; Athens employed enormous juries of 501 and 1,001 citizens to try those few great matters that fell under the narrowly conceived criminal law. Pericles took these duties seriously enough to introduce payment for jury service, to encourage even the poor to turn up. Most of what we today call "crimes" (simple felonies and misdemeanours such as theft) fell under the Athenian equivalent of civil law (what we call "torts"). Only treason and blasphemy and the corruption of the young were state crimes, to be tried by grand (very grand indeed!) juries. And it was in fact for the crimes of blasphemy and corruption that Athens' greatest philosopher was subject to Athens' most famous trial.

While it may conjure up a picture of a mob-scene of 501 irascible Athenians crying for the blood of a noble philosopher, the trial of Socrates in 399 B.C. did not in fact pit a lynch mob against an innocent. The citizenry was incensed because Athens' democracy had been imperilled a number of times—first by the so-called "Thirty Tyrants" during the Peloponnesian War and then again in 411 and 404—in every case by students, friends, and relatives of Socrates who appeared to be carrying out his aristocratic principles, and were possibly even acting with his connivance. Socrates was found guilty after a long and deliberate trial—and then only by a small majority of a few dozen on the 501-member jury. Speeches by prosecution and defence had been timed by waterclocks, and the verdict was reached by a semi-secret vote. As Socrates himself acknowledged, his trial was fair and in accordance with the laws; but he protested those laws as being unjust, and went to his death—by drinking a cup of poisonous hemlock—convinced of the folly of democracy.

As if serving in the parish and state assemblies and on a variety of juries was not enough, citizens were also selected at random, by a lottery process, for many of the state's major offices and magistracies. Though certain fiscal officers were elected, as was the board of generals who supervised military operations, the lottery was regarded as a prudent as well as just way to select officials in a republic where every free native male was qualified merely by virtue of being a citizen. Like jurors, office-holders were paid for their responsibilities, whether these occupied a single day (president of the Council of Five Hundred), or an entire year (as might be the case for a juror); thus being poor was no disqualification. It may seem astonishing to citizens of nations where, today, over half the populace cannot find time to vote once a year, that the Athenians could accept and even cherish their unending civic duties. Oscar Wilde once joked that socialism took up too many free evenings. For the Athenians, whose working hours were limited to daylight, democracy took up large parts of every day, every week, every year. But because to them citizenship was the highest form of activity imaginable, it remained an honour and a joy rather than an uncomfortable burden that competed with more profitable endeavours. Indeed, as Pericles had discovered, it was important enough to justify paying those who otherwise might be unable to participate. Economics was mere household business, unworthy of higher beings, and was left to women and slaves (the word comes from the Greek *oikonomos*, "house-manager"). But politics, like war, was the business of the *polis* and its citizens. Pericles said, "We do not say that a man who takes no interest in politics is a man who minds his own business; we say that he has no business here at all."

If to be a citizen was noble, to be a soldier-citizen was noblest of all. It was not just the Spartans who were instilled with that traditional Greek sense of civic virtue that Homer had identified with the virility of warriors (the words for "virtue" and "virile" have the same root in Greek and Latin: as smooth a way to let etymology do the work of sexism as one can imagine!). The Athenians made war no less efficiently and successfully than their chief adversaries, and like the Spartans they saw in military service an honourable calling for the citizen of the *polis*.

The qualities of the soldier—selflessness, courage, teamwork, and a sense of the common good—were precisely the qualities the Athenians demanded of the citizen. Switzerland's citizen army today is rooted in the same connection between civic responsibility and military duty. And nations such as Israel, the United States, and Britain have sent citizen armies into battle under the necessity of war, only to discover that they have in their hands not only a mighty weapon against their enemies, but a powerful source of such public virtues as fraternity, solidarity, and co-operation, as well as political dissent—which is also a democratic virtue. The American philosopher William James was sufficiently moved by these by-products of war to inquire whether there might not be some "moral equivalent of war" that would achieve peacefully that same sense of vital brotherhood kindled between warriors going into battle together. Peace enabled the Athenians to govern themselves democratically; but war helped make them democrats, and the poorer classes of Athens who rowed the heavy ships of the navy found as they laboured at their oars a civic identity that made them the equals of the wealthier and better-educated men who fought in the infantry. Citizenship, like war, ennobled men. War, like citizenship, helped make them equal.

Having invented the word "politics", if not politics itself, the Athenians regarded it as a noble business. But they were not fools. While they could hardly share our own era's cynicism on the subject, they were no less finely attuned to the abuses of human ambition. In these less heroic times, we have come to regard men as "economic animals"—as self-interested seekers of private goods—and to think of politics as a public means to those private ends. Ambrose Bierce's definition of politics as "the pursuit of public interest for private advantage" does not really shock us, and we are willing enough to smile when politics is called "the last refuge of a scoundrel".

Scoundrels are not a modern invention, however, and democratic scoundrels were presumably born into the world along with democracy itself. The Athenians regarded their great rhetoricians—masters of oratory, as our politicians must today be masters of television—with as much suspicion as admiration. Like the later Romans, the Athenians were capable of bringing down not merely the crude abuser of power, but also the potential Caesar who spoke not wisely but too well. Moreover, they equipped themselves with an instrument by which they could rid themselves of potential dictators. It was called ostracism.

A quorum of 6,000 citizens could vote to exile anyone for five or ten years simply by writing his name on pottery shards (ostraka) cast as ballots. After all, this was still essentially an oral society, and so a man cut off from Athens, communicating only by letters, was out of touch, deprived of influence. But the system did not always work out as intended. Plutarch, that marvellous chronicler of the lives of the ancients, tells a story (we needn't believe it to enjoy it) of the great Athenian statesman Aristides the Just, who was ostracized in 482 B.C. He had offended the friends of the military leader Themistocles by proposing that the silver from Laurium be distributed to the populace at large. Themistocles needed the silver to construct a new fleet for the war with Persia. Each statesman tried to ostracize the other, but Themistocles' men outnumbered those of the just Aristides. According to Plutarch, one illiterate citizen—not knowing who Aristides was—asked the great man himself to etch "Aristides" onto his ostrakon. Aristides obliged him, and inquired what he had against this fellow. The irate citizen answered, "I'm sick and tired of hearing him called Aristides the *Just* all the time!"

Whether this is a tribute to democracy's prudent distrust of aristocratic pretentions, as an Athenian might say, or a bitter commentary on democracy's envy-drenched pettiness, as Plutarch believed, we can each decide for ourselves. But a democracy that places too great a faith in leaders can come to grief, and for the Athenians the device of ostracism placed a useful obstacle in the way of dictatorship. Unfortunately the system produced its own problems, and was in time abandoned.

This rich catalogue of Athenian institutions leaves out certain crucial modern democratic devices: *representation*, the system under which citizens elect delegates to govern them, who are accountable to them, rather than trying to govern themselves directly; *party government*, where different economic and class interests can organize themselves into representative groups and compete for public power; and *federalism*, where power is shared by central and regional government units to prevent a dangerous centralization of sovereign authority. None of these played much of a role in Greece, where the small scale of political life and the face-to-face character of political interactions made them seem unnecessary, whereas they are essential in modern large-scale democracies. This is not to say that there were no classes and factions in ancient Athens that exercised a political influence: the philosopher Aristotle in fact talked about them, and warned against them, just as the American founder (and later president) James Madison warned against them at America's constitutional convention in 1787. But government institutions were not organized around them as they are in a modern parliamentary state.

Athens did not invent all of democracy's varied institutions, but it has been the model for democracy from the Romans to the Normans, from the Germans to the Franks, and no nation has achieved democracy without imitating important aspects of the world's first republic.

The Civilization of Democracy—Pericles

Institutions cannot operate in a void. In much of Britain's once-great empire, colonial officers thought they could establish British justice and the common law in lands with wholly different traditions by exporting wigs and robes as well as books and precedents. But democratic forms can only be sustained if they are part of a democratic culture. It was perhaps Athens' greatest victory that alongside its democratic institutions it established a democratic civilization. Other city-states may have engineered certain free institutions, but the Athenians created a free society—if only for the native-born men. Sparta fostered equality among its citizens but it repressed the arts; Athens subsidized them. From the environs of Sparta, called Laconia, we get the word "laconic", whereas the Athenians have always loved to talk. Where Sparta stood there are only bare rocks and empty olive groves; where Athens stood are magnificent ruins testifying still to the wonders of the civilization that produced them. How could two city-states speaking the same language and only two hundred kilometres apart be so different? The answer lies not just in the politics but in the culture of Athens. This is the home of Pericles—and of Sophocles, Euripides, and Socrates—as well as of our imaginary Phidias. It was a culture of monumental aesthetes, of Sophist philosophers who hawked their lawyerlike skills in the marketplace, and wealthy producers who paid to put on plays in the 17,000-seat amphitheatres carved into the hills around the city. But it was also a democratic culture, at least for the 20 per cent or so of the population who were citizens. And this culture was visible above all in the marketplace—the agora. What transpired as high rhetoric up on the mountainside in the Assembly often began down in the agora as whispered gossip. Without a village square, without a town barbershop or general store or petrol station, without the local pub or workers' café or literary coffeehouse where citizens can gather informally, no democratic political business is possible. Citizens exhibit their skills and concerns in the meeting hall or the assembly, but they acquire them on the school board or the bazaar committee or in the beer hall. The final decisions are taken formally, but the opinions are developed around woodstoves or before a communal television set in a village school.

If the marketplace was the vibrant heart of Athens' democratic culture, then the theatre was its soul. In the stadium-like arenas around the *polis*, great civic-religious festivals unfolded, featuring tragedies, and comedies called satyr plays written for the occasion as part of a dramatic competition. In these amphitheatres would gather a great many citizens—again the poor would be paid for their attendance—as well as a number of women, foreigners, and perhaps some slaves. Since the entire population of Athens was likely a few hundred thousand people—even including those from the surrounding countryside—a far larger percentage of the people could gather at these festivals than would ever be possible nowadays.

The enthralled audience would hear poetic retellings of old oral legends in the poignant imagery of Aeschylus or Sophocles, or would be entertained by the biting satires of Aristophanes; the sources were most often stories of ancient blood rivalries, of loyalties betrayed and treasons avenged. There were histories of other Greek towns and the tragedies that befell those who ruled unwisely; or, in the case of comedies, slightly fictionalized accounts of local scandals that, had they been touted about in the Assembly, would probably have led to the indictment and exile of the author. These tales disclosed no plot surprises; they were as familiar to the Athenians as George Washington and the cherry tree to Americans, Guy Fawkes to the English, Wolfe and Montcalm to Canadians, or Danton's death to the French. But they were filled with cautionary moral lessons about the importance of the city, the duties of kings, the fealty of daughters, and the perils of hubris—the dread pride that, in driving men and women to aspire to divinity, sent them and their cities tumbling into chaos and destruction.

Tragedy, always offered as part of civic-religious festivals such as the Olympics, was a function of public instruction and celebration, not something tired merchants watched in the evening to stir their numbed senses. Everything connected with theatre invoked the idea of civic responsibility. This was true for those who produced the plays (rich merchants seeking public glory); Pericles first comes to our attention as a theatrical producer, paying for actors, rehearsals, working lunches, and probably even scripts. It was true for those who wrote them (mostly enemies of aristocracy and tyranny, and dedicated though wary supporters of democracy). It was especially true for those who watched them (theatre attendance was perhaps the most important ritual act an Athenian could perform). Theatre, sculpture, and architecture were all public arts, and honoured the greatness not so much of their individual creators as of the society they reflected and embellished. If Athens was proud of its democracy, it gloried in its civilization—the civilization it produced in the age of Pericles, when the creations of artists, poets, philosophers, and mathematicians shone as brightly as the democratic institutions bequeathed by Solon and Cleisthenes. It was not lost on Athens' neighbours that the Mediterranean's most remarkable culture had been created by the world's first democracy.

The Death of the Birth of Democracy

Modern citizens take note! Democracies are rarely destroyed from the outside. The barbarian Visigoths who came swarming in from the north four centuries after the birth of Christ did not bring Rome tumbling down, though they sacked the city; the Romans had destroyed themselves from within over the preceding centuries. The Weimar Republic effectively self-destructed well before Hitler dispatched its remnants after his "democratic" victory in 1933. And when the great democratic experiment of Athens began to unravel during the disastrous Peloponnesian War with Sparta, it was not only Sparta that was to blame. There were also crucial internal problems.

Many of the same forces that had made Athens great and free—silver, empire, war, slavery, and its fractious, noisy democracy—helped to bring it down. Athens' coin of the realm, which was known throughout the Mediterranean world as a symbol of both power and liberty, was the Attic Owl. This small coin represented the forces that had raised up the *polis* and would bring it down again, for it was mined by slaves whose very existence was an offence to democracy; it underwrote an empire that fuelled Athenian arrogance and ate away at its self-sufficiency by making it dependent on its foreign colonies; and it created rivalries such as the one with Sparta, that drained the material and human resources of the city.

Yet, as important as slavery, empire, and war were in first raising up and then undermining the conditions that favoured democracy, equally important were the self-negating effects of the system itself. Because it both draws on and provokes public passions, democracy is always at risk; the very institutions meant to embody it can also imperil it. The effects of money, birth, and education are mitigated by democracy, but not eliminated; then as now, a wealthy man might have more than his share of influence. And democracy was susceptible to manipulation by glib rhetoricians like Pericles and conniving politicians like Themistocles—as when Themistocles' enemies mounted a campaign of ostracism against him, and he turned the tables on them and had their own populist leader ostracized. Indeed ostracism and the democratic assembly were both vulnerable to the ancient equivalent of modern lobbies, those political action committees and pressure groups by which factions today try to manipulate the electorate. Computer-generated letters used in a mass mailing campaign to influence a legislative vote seem a modern invention, but the Athenians were all too familiar with ostracism campaigns that used mass-produced shards of pottery pre-inscribed with the name of a citizen who had become the enemy of some scheming demagogue. Ostracism could thus become a weapon used to thwart democracy, just as juries could become agents of mass hysteria to try someone whose crime might only have been thinking in unpopular ways—like Socrates.

The most shameful abuses came in the Assembly itself—where democracy also had its greatest successes. For, towards the end of the Golden Age and throughout the years of the Peloponnesian War, the Assembly made a number of decisions that were at best unwise, at worst quite monstrous. In 416, the little town of Melos refused to bend to an Athenian demand for military alliance; its virtuous citizens claimed the right to neutrality, and while promising not to aid Sparta, they insisted on their own independence. The enraged Athenian Assembly, acting with all the prudence of a lynch mob, authorized the razing of the town and the execution of all its citizens; the women and children were sold into slavery. A few months later the influential Alcibiades, who was in time to fall to assassins while travelling abroad, persuaded the Assembly to undertake that disastrous military expedition to Sicily which cost Athens the last of its resources—not least among them its courage and its virtue. Shortly thereafter came the submission to Persian blackmail, with the Assembly dissolving itself in return for foreign revenues, like a snake swallowing its own tail.

Such shenanigans gave a certain legitimacy to all those aristocratic critics who insisted that democracy could never be more than the rude, impulsive will of opinionated ignoramuses elevated to sovereign office through a disordering of nature, and they have helped give democracy a bad name among advocates of prudent and moderate government ever since. And after Socrates' death in 399 B.C., his student Plato beatified him as a victim of the rule of passion and bigotry over wisdom and prudence—though he was certainly guilty of detesting democracy, and may also have conspired with the oligarchs who had ruled while democracy was in abeyance. Perhaps that is why, in those dark and troubled final decades of Athens' democratic civilization, not a single defender of self-government is to be found in the historical records. Or perhaps it is just that the philosophers who left behind records were mostly aristocrats, while the democrats were largely men of action.

In any case, while the intellectuals were writing against democracy, the people continued to practise it, even after the fall of Athens. It was not until late in the fourth century, when Alexander the Great of Macedonia crushed the remaining autonomy of the Greek cities, that the story of ancient democracy was concluded.

The Democratic Legacy of Greece

In democracy's ancient cradle, we can find fearful traces of democracy's modern ills no less than promising seeds of its modern strengths. It was riddled with contradictions, and those contradictions hold out a warning to our own times. Depending on slavery, and treating women as something less than wholly human, it admitted to its heart a form of servitude that ate away at its spirit of equality. In the ancient world the inferior status of women was so generally accepted, and the institution of slavery so widely practised (the philosopher Aristotle wrote a brief for the enslavement of "barbarians" even as he objected to the enslavement of Greeks by Greeks), that these groups were not thought of as candidates for equality. All the same, the great innovation of the Greeks was to render citizens relatively equal, even if they limited who could be a citizen; to prevent great distinctions of wealth; and to try to insulate politics from such economic distinctions as survived. But for modern democracies, to talk about the equality of citizens without talking about who may and may not be admitted to citizenship is to practise hypocrisy. The experiences of nations like the United States in its first seventy-five or one hundred years (democracy for white males only), or South Africa today (democracy for whites only), suggest that much more than mere hypocrisy is involved.

Nor has any modern regime contradicted the conclusion that seems inescapable when we look at Athens' experience with empire-building and war. Although both make power and wealth possible, they erode the conditions of democracy at home. Enhancing the power of money, fomenting an atmosphere of faction, conspiracy, and intrigue, and nourishing intolerance of dissent and disrespect for criticism, both war and empire may over the long term be incompatible with democracy. In peacetime the Athenian Assembly ruled wisely and well; it used its collective legislative intelligence to build a great empire and to conduct that empire's wars with remarkable prudence. But in the end, empire and war overextended the Assembly's capacities, and started to erode the spirit of moderation necessary for democratic government. It is hard to be a democracy and a superpower at the same time. In the end, for Athens, it became impossible. Having picked up the pieces after the Peloponnesian War, Athens did revert to more tranquil times and revive its democracy; but it no longer had the power to defend itself against the Macedonians, who had been waiting a century to seize the greatest prize of the Mediterranean world.

Despite its faults, though, the achievements of the small city-state remain extraordinary. The historian and political philosopher Sir Moses Finley has observed how easy it is to compile "a catalogue of cases of repression, sycophancy, irrational behaviour, and outright brutality in the nearly two centuries that Athens was governed as a democracy. Yet they remain no more than so many single incidents in this long stretch of time when Athens was remarkably free from the universal Greek malady of sedition and civil war."

For a people newly emerged from tribalism, servitude to a foreign empire, and absolute monarchy, it is indeed a political miracle to have been able to create and sustain a democratic civilization for nearly two centuries. And for it to leave behind a legacy of free institutions that have been embraced, emulated, and cherished by nations ever since is a blessing to all those who continue to wage the struggle for democracy. That legacy is at the heart of the modern story—a hundred different stories—of democracy. All the centuries notwithstanding, we are never far from that noisy marketplace where Phidias sold his silver goblets while arguing his views on war, or from the sun-bleached hillside where men first divined the secrets of liberty by learning how to govern themselves.

Reborn in America

III

AFTER THE FALL OF ATHENS, THE GREEK IDEA OF democracy all but disappeared for nearly two thousand years. The idea of law persisted, however, while the fresh notion of Christian brotherhood that spread during the Roman period helped to preserve the ideal of equality. Together, the two kept alive the crucial Athenian concept of *isonomia* (equality before the law) following the fall of Rome, right through to the Renaissance. But the outrageous idea that the people of a nation might rule themselves had little currency in the Roman and Renaissance worlds and, where it did appear in Europe, it often seemed more a threat than a promise, especially in the hands of radical Christians or egalitarians like the Levellers in Oliver Cromwell's seventeenth-century England (see Chapter Six). To property-owners, monarchs, and rulers, democracy— the idea that all people could participate in the affairs of government— seemed to advance the notion that the rabble could rule: government by the ignorant many and the envious poor.

But the desire for democracy, nourished but not yet fully realized in England and Europe, found its way to the wilderness of North America in the eighteenth century, given new life by the quest for personal freedom: life, liberty, happiness—and perhaps property as well. This time, however, democracy took a different form—one that did not derive directly from Athens.

The American story begins, then, not in Athens but in Europe, from which restless adventurers and persecuted minorities fled in the seventeenth and eighteenth centuries to the vast continent discovered by Columbus. For many people in Europe, social status was still determined by birth, and hence fixed throughout their lives and the lives of their children. Your religion was usually your king's religion, your duty was the duty of your forefathers, and your political rank, which had in the feudal era been wholly beyond the reach of will, remained difficult to alter even as feudal distinctions eroded. People had little occasion to think about freedom, and few of them could have conceived of self-government.

The world had been changing since the sixteenth century, however. Movable type, gunpowder, the compass, and other inventions were liberating people from tradition and leading them to question their fixed stations in life. The physical world was being opened up by navigation, the world of the mind by books. Bibles, once available only in Latin or Greek, were being translated into English by William Tyndale and into German by the subversive priest Martin Luther—who persuaded himself, and then much of the German-speaking world, that one might talk to God directly without the mediation of priests and bishops. In God's eyes, Luther argued, each man was worth the same as every other; religious congregations had as much right to rule themselves as princes had to rule them. Here surfaced one of the many curious and sometimes contradictory effects of religion on democracy.

When in 1517 Martin Luther pinned his ninety-five theses to the portals of Wittenberg Cathedral, he began a spiritual revolution known as the Protestant Reformation that would soon become the foundation for a political revolution. Although in many areas the initial impetus of the Reformation was the local rulers' desire to throw off the domination of Rome and the Holy Roman Empire, its ultimate consequence was to displace the traditional feudal hierarchy. If popes and bishops could be challenged, then so too might kings. In Holland, where the Renaissance spirit of adventure had flourished early, the revolt against the tyranny of kings had a forceful start. In 1572, when Holland was under the rule of Catholic Spain, the town of Leiden declared itself Protestant. The King of Spain laid siege to the city, but the townspeople stood fast and established a system of neighbourhood councils that permitted them to govern themselves. Similar rebellions occurred in cities throughout the principalities of Germany and Switzerland—most notably in the Swiss city of Geneva, where Europe's other great Protestant reformer, Jean Calvin, established a self-governing religious community at the beginning of the seventeenth century.

Protestant ideas spread, and with them the spirit of rebellion. But as the Holy Roman Empire collapsed, monarchs enhanced their power in the great new nation-states of England and France, and religious dissenters found themselves persecuted by Protestant rulers as well as Catholic. With Europe suffocating under intolerance, pervasive religious strife, and alternating cycles of Inquisition and counter-Inquisition, a seemingly empty and promising American continent beckoned from across the ocean.

Let John Howland represent an entire generation. Born in the village of Fenstanton in England, young John was drawn by adventure across the high seas. In 1620 he signed on as a servant to Governor Carver, a dissident Protestant who was sailing to America on a ship called the *Mayflower*. The *Mayflower* was to sail from Leiden, that same Dutch town that had revolted against Catholic Spain a half century earlier, carrying a group of English Puritans to the New World. They were not without commercial motives, but they were essentially seeking a second chance—journeying across the sea to what they hoped might be a new Eden.

The group had obtained a royal charter to establish a colony in Virginia, where a colony had been founded at Jamestown in 1607, but the ship was blown off course by autumn gales in the North Atlantic, and in November 1620 they arrived about 150 miles north of their intended destination. Far beyond the pale of their charter and the authority of Virginia's colonial governor, they put in at a rocky cove that became known as Plymouth Rock. There, still aboard ship, forty-one Puritans—a small band among the larger complement of colonists, half of whom were to die that very first winter—signed a compact. It offered no democratic government, and was probably intended above all to maintain order—the Jamestown colony had seen considerable anarchy, and there was a spirit of rebellion brewing aboard the *Mayflower*. Yet, authoritarian and intolerant as the Puritan pilgrims were, they agreed in the charter to "combine ourselves together into a civill body politick, for our better ordering and preservation and futurance of the ends aforesaid." In signing the compact, they swore obedience and submission to "such just and equall lawes, ordinances, acts, constitutions and offices, from time to time as shall be thought most meete and convenient to the general good of the Colonie." John Howland, though only a manservant, affixed his signature to the document with no less assurance than his master, who in this brave new world would quite soon cease to be his master.

Despite the mutual consent of the Mayflower Compact, Pilgrim society began in America as a class society. There was neither freedom of speech nor freedom of trade. Democracy was still a word that signified the very sort of disorder and anarchy the Compact was meant to put down. But the harsh conditions of the New World afforded a levelling unknown to England, and demanded that men govern themselves with a great deal more autonomy than they would have had at home. For England was an ocean away, a good two to three months by ship. With or without royal charters, the English colonists, in practice, had to rule themselves. In time, conventions like the Mayflower Compact became powerful symbols of political power in the New World: sovereignty deriving from the will of the people, under a written social contract establishing the authority of government in the name of those to be ruled. It was a long way from the 1620 Mayflower Compact to America's 1789 federal Constitution, but when the Pilgrims sowed the seeds of their crops at Plymouth, they also planted an idea that would in time spring forth as the sapling of American democracy.

John Howland died at eighty, a prosperous and free citizen. By that time the larger and more powerful Massachusetts Bay Colony to the north had annexed Plymouth, and colonies were strewn along the North American coast from the south of Maine to the Carolinas. Not one of these colonies enjoyed real independence, or complete religious freedom. Dissenters who left England to escape persecution quickly became persecutors themselves, and Quakers, Anabaptists, and others found themselves no more welcome in Virginia or Massachusetts than they had been in Essex or Dorset. It would not be until Roger Williams quarrelled with his Massachusetts brethren in 1635 and left to found Rhode Island, the first American community to call itself a democracy, that colonies emerged— first there and in Maryland, and later in Pennsylvania—that would negotiate freer constitutions founded on genuine religious tolerance. Until that time, the only real democracy in America was practised by the already century-old Iroquois Confederacy, whose unwritten constitution did guarantee equal political rights to men and women (attracting the admiration of Benjamin Franklin). But the Confederacy would be almost wiped out by a later generation of Americans.

The New Constitution

The key to free government in the New World remained the belief in a founding compact expressing the will of a citizenry. From the landing at

Plymouth Rock to this day, towns of New England have perpetuated this ideal by continuing to assemble at least once a year to consider local laws and elect representatives to local offices. The New England town meeting is in fact a living symbol of the social compact: the people renewing their dedication to common goals, electing common officers, manifesting a common loyalty not through representatives but directly. Business is often routine nowadays, and getting a quorum among busy townspeople can be difficult. Larger towns use representative assemblies, where a few citizens are elected to represent the rest at assembly meetings, and critics argue that the complexity and scale of modern society are incompatible with this archaic version of local self-government. Can a village of a few hundred really take on a development corporation hoping to open a major shopping mall within the town's borders? Can the siting of state welfare facilities be left to the parochial anxieties of selfish townspeople?

Yet when the people of a village like Strafford, Vermont, assemble—as happens annually in more than four-fifths of Vermont's 246 towns—they manifest a powerful will to preserve their autonomy. For Vermont not only encourages self-government in its towns, it supports the only state-wide "Citizens' Assembly" in the United States. In Strafford, at least a fifth of the town's nine hundred citizens gather every March to administer their affairs. There is nothing romantic or dramatic about the meeting: just plain folks first electing a moderator to oversee the meeting itself, then choosing other officials such as the town auditor and the town grand juror, and finally debating revenue and spending measures—during our visit, the chief question is how to expend the funds left over from last year. Nobody seems weighed down by seriousness. There is only one candidate for the office of auditor, and he must be talked into the job. Still, like their neighbours in Strafford, most New Englanders have refused to give up this form of town self-government.

There is a sense here in Strafford of people in charge of their own lives, working together to govern themselves, that clearly has origins going all the way back to the parchment signed aboard the *Mayflower* as it lay at anchor in Plymouth bay that morning in late 1620. Perhaps this gathering comes as close to defining the true meaning of American democracy as the great document written in Philadelphia in 1789, the American Constitution.

Still, however intimate America's relationship has been to local liberty and municipal autonomy, it is in the federal Constitution that the principles governing the country's democracy are most powerfully enunciated—and then powerfully curtailed. It was 167 years after Plymouth Rock, and almost a dozen years after the war with England had led to American independence in 1776, that fifty-five disgruntled citizens travelled to Philadelphia, then the national capital. They had had their fill of the squabbling and parochialism of the disunited states of America under the Articles of Confederation—the weak, decentralized arrangements that served as a constitution during the years just after the War of Independence. The Articles afforded so much autonomy to the thirteen states that in many cases the states (and even individual towns) were printing their own money, erecting their own tariff barriers, and raising and paying for their own militias. The liberty won by the war had quickly turned into anarchy, and Americans grew hungry for the common standards a more central government might give them. "Give us a hoop for the barrel!" was the cry of soldiers toasting their victory over the British, but seeking a higher authority that would hold them all together.

The instructions carried by the men who came to Philadelphia called only for the reform of the Articles. But once there they concluded that nothing other than an entirely new form of government could remedy the nation's ills. Locked up together in sweltering Independence Hall, with the windows closed against eavesdroppers, the small band of novice constitution-makers—lawyers, legislators, many of the best and the brightest from all over the thirteen states—deliberated and argued and shouted at one another over four long and hot summer months. Some urged monarchy, a few pushed for a constitution as democratic as the one enjoyed by Pennsylvania, where almost every male got to vote. But most puzzled over democracy's chief conundrums: how to establish a government strong and centralized enough to assure unity and security, but not so strong and centralized that it would infringe on the liberty of individuals; how to police the police when they supposedly spoke on behalf of the people; and how to insulate a government directed by popular will from the frightening spectre of pure democracy. Alexander Hamilton, the New York banker who would be the first Secretary of the Treasury, regarded the people as howling masses, and few others trusted them more. Spare us, they warned, from the "mobocrats and democrats and all the other rats." In fact the democrats and populist farmers who had played such a vital role in the revolution of 1775–76, radicals such as Sam Adams and Tom Paine, were not in Philadelphia that summer. And Thomas Jefferson, the architect of independence, was in Paris, and looked upon the proceedings with some

suspicion. If democracy had any constituency in 1787, it was not represented among the founders.

The men in Philadelphia talked about rights, but property rights were
foremost in their minds. They opted for representative government, where
the popular will might be filtered through the wise judgement of indirect
assemblies such as the electoral college by which, in the early years of the
nation, the president was chosen. Only the House of Representatives would
be directly chosen by the full white male electorate (whose precise qualifi-
cations would be left to the individual states). Native Indians (of whom
there were perhaps a half million in all of North America), women, and of
course slaves (already 400,000 among 4,000,000 whites in the founding
era) would not have the vote. Few of the men in Philadelphia that day were
happy about slavery, and the word was studiously avoided in the
Constitution. But the South relied on a slave economy, and in order to keep
it in the Union a compromise was devised allowing both taxation and representation to be based on population, with a slave counting as three-fifths
of a full human being.

What is remarkable is that from a series of bitter battles and political
compromises came a government that was stable and, if not yet truly
democratic, open to the growth of democracy in subsequent decades. The
new constitution had tamed democracy and made it safe for property
holders; it combined principles of popular government with principles of
elective aristocracy—a government of the "best" men, chosen by the rest;
it gave government certain powers but then curtailed the use of those
powers by dividing the federal government horizontally into competing
branches (the so-called separation of powers) and then dividing it verti-
cally through federalism (by delegating power to state and local governments). What power remained with the central government was hemmed
in by powerful constraints—chief among them the Bill of Rights, which
was added on afterwards as a condition of ratification by some critics of
the Constitution, including Thomas Jefferson.

The object, in James Madison's words, was to "set ambition against
ambition", controlling men—whose natures were not to be trusted—
by unleashing them, one against another. Rather than repressing human
nature, Madison used it.

There was little in the history of ancient republics, of Athens' surprising
democracy or Rome's fractious republic, that could serve as an example
for the experiment in constitution-making that was America in 1787. The

Founders' achievement—giving a republican government to a vast country made up of many separate states and many people of very different religious and cultural backgrounds—flew in the face of two thousand years of history. Perhaps the real genius of the Constitution lay in the breadth and generality, some might even say the vagueness, of its provisions. It was open to a welter of interpretations, and could serve all parties, democratic and anti-democratic, federalist and anti-federalist, the causes of the industrial North and the causes of the agrarian and slave South. The first few presidents were themselves men of the Revolution, but once this generation passed, the Constitution was subject to new interpreters.

The Road to American Democracy

The first president, General George Washington, had led America's armies in the War of Independence, and probably would have been America's first king had the country opted for monarchy. And it was not really until Washington and John Adams and then Jefferson and Madison had taken their turns as president that America's democratic spirit, evident particularly in the new territories west of the original thirteen colonies that made up America prior to its independence, found its way to the capital. The new era was ushered in by the election of Andrew Jackson to the presidency in the 1820s. Born of the kind of rural farmers and small-town independents who had made the Revolution, Jackson came to Washington on horseback, bringing with him hordes of dusty riders and back-country anti-cosmopolitans. On the night of his inauguration, while New York bankers and Boston traders trembled behind locked doors, thousands of his supporters rode through Washington (some even spurring their horses across the lawn and up the stairs into the White House), propelling the nation into a new democratic era.

We have a remarkable eye-witness account of the vitalities and fears of this new democratic epoch. In 1831 a young liberal French aristocrat, Alexis de Tocqueville, arrived in America, ostensibly to study its new prison system. (Prison as punishment in itself was a new-fangled idea; in Europe punishment was largely a matter of torture, corporal punishment, and execution.) Intoxicated by the noisy vigour of the new land, de Tocqueville quickly diverted his attention from prisons to people. In the two volumes of *Democracy in America* he composed over the next twenty years, he gave as brilliant an account of the strengths and weaknesses of the new democracy as it would ever get. He admired America's capacity for vivacious talk and its boisterous local freedoms. But he also saw a conformity, a dangerous spirit of levelling, and he feared that it might portend a new form of tyranny, where self-righteous majorities could crush vulnerable minorities and where mass opinion could ride rough-shod over individual rights just as Andrew Jackson had ridden rough-shod into the White House. Everywhere de Tocqueville went, he saw the country melting into a single class: the same clothes, the same language, the same habits, the same pleasures, the same attitudes. To be different was to be un-American. If this was the land of promise, part of what it seemed to promise was a new tyranny of the majority worse than the tyrannies that had gone before.

But the flexible sweep of the Constitution held the nation back from the extremes predicted by de Tocqueville. Though slavery nearly destroyed the nation, and a great civil war was fought to maintain the Union and, in time, to abolish slavery too, America never came to suffer from too much equality. Too much respect for property, maybe. So much conformity that, at times, to elevate the common man meant to enshrine the mediocre, and to detest rank and privilege was to disdain excellence and uniqueness. But in fact it was too much private liberty and individualism rather than too much equality that eventually emerged as the great problem of the American system of democracy.

In the Gilded Age following the Civil War, oil, steel, and the railways— property in the powerful new guise known as the industrial revolution— came to dominate America's politics. Yet it was not until the twentieth century that government began to take responsibility for the well-being of its citizens, and to create a countervailing force to the power of property. First, President Theodore Roosevelt and, then, in his New Deal, President Franklin Delano Roosevelt moved to check private power with public power, and to use the resources of the federal government to redistribute wealth and provide safety nets for the weak and the disadvantaged.

Even today, American democracy seems less imperilled by the danger of runaway majorities than by the selfishness of unconstrained individuals. Ask any New Yorker nowadays what democracy means, and you will get something like, "Oh, yeah, well . . . freedom, to do what you want. . . . Nobody tells you what to do, when to do it, how to do it, you know?" Freedom. Independence. Your own house. Your own car. Heading west.

Being on the road. Making a buck. Doing your own thing. These are the shibboleths of America's democracy.

The Myth of the Frontier

It sometimes seems that owning a car means more to the average American than owning a house—for in America the car is the symbol of true freedom, the symbol of the frontier, of a new life and moving on and starting over, of all those myths the frontier left behind that continue to play so vital a role in the nation's economic and cultural life. Where a well-watered horse with packed saddlebags once gave access to the real frontier, today an automobile stands for access to the frontier that lives on in the American imagination. In de Tocqueville's day the frontier was still real, a boundary that quite literally moved westward at about seventeen miles a day, pushed forward by the restless tribes of immigrants looking for room to breathe and a second chance at life. The Old West was reached, populated, settled, conquered, over-crowded, and closed down by the turn of this century, but as the frontier meant hope, the automobile still promises optimism. Load up your household goods, put the kids and the dog in the back, and you can set off on an adventure, destiny unknown: it may end up being a baseball game, or a visit to relatives, or a new job, or a whole new life.

When Pennsylvania and Ohio became depression states in the 1930s, the unemployed headed for Kansas and Oklahoma. When Oklahoma dried up into a vast, poverty-ridden dust bowl a few years later, they got back into their cars and headed for California. Not for them the grapes of wrath, though that is what many finally reaped.

Louis L'Amour, who became America's top-selling author and a national myth-maker about the legends of the West, was only nineteen when he headed out to Colorado from North Dakota. The frontier was already a receding horizon chasing an invisible dream. Shortly before his death, he talked with us in the parlour car of a nineteenth-century narrow-gauge railway train heading up into the mountains of Colorado.

His voice was deep and folksy, as if he were practising to be one of the Old West characters in his popular novels. "The history of America is the history of families moving, moving into new country, into pioneer country," he said. But what does the famed frontier have to do with democracy? "A great deal! The cattle barons almost tried to set up a feudal system, but

it didn't work. It was too democratic a situation. A cowboy could be working for somebody, then he could quit tomorrow and ride off into the sun-
set." The great West L'Amour romanticized in his novels was America's
safety valve. It was a place to start over again, with new rules or no rules at
all. Whole towns grew up in Colorado around the allure of cattle or wild
horses or, most poignantly, gold—towns like Cripple Creek that went
from one-horse shantytown to gold-rush metropolis (dozens of hotels, an
opera house, fifty thousand inhabitants) and back to ghost town in a few
short, hysterical decades.

The pioneers were not all adventurers and individualists. Life in the
West was often lived alone, but survival also meant living together, and
the Old West was never as wild as its reputation. The settlers showed an
instinct for rough justice and self-government, and where no government existed they would create their own. First would come a saloon—
"a clearing house for information, a place to drink but also a place to
gather and meet." Then a general store and a church. Common institutions. Streets and a water supply. A mayor and a town council and maybe
a town meeting.

Yet the new, contrived institutions of the West mixed common functions of self-government with a passion for freedom and independence.
The idea of *laissez-faire*—being left alone—was born in crowded England,
but it became a palpable reality in the New World, where every pioneer's
journey west was an exercise in being left alone. What adventurers and
settlers demanded from their government was protection for their freedom: to be left alone by others and by the government itself. Thus the
eternal puzzle of democracy: how to protect people from the government
that is supposed to be the protector of their liberty.

Even today, Americans chase their dreams westward, packing up and
heading to "sunbelt" cities like Houston; leaving Houston for San Diego.
Still believing that if you go far enough, you can find something a little bit
better—perhaps a town called Carefree, which really does exist—an
affluent suburb of Phoenix, Arizona, one of the West's boom towns, with
street signs that say Ho Street and Hum Street and Easy Street. But in reality life is free of care only for the wealthy. In a nation with millions of
homeless, including women with small children and men who suffer more
from joblessness than from alcoholism or mental illness, and a permanent
"underclass" numbering up to thirty million, liberty apparently remains
closely allied with property. The argument at the Founding in Philadelphia

goes on unabated. In 1789, the unpropertied could not vote in the new United States; today they vote, but sometimes feel little less impotent than their forefathers.

Some of these hapless men and women fall back on the old dream of travelling west, lured by vague notions of the golden life they see portrayed in magazines and on television. They live in shacks and tents and trailers alongside the railway tracks of boom cities like Tulsa or Houston or San Diego—restless workers laid off from twenty-year jobs; whole families sleeping in their cars, adults poring over sunbelt-city newspapers for that new position, that special career opening, that will turn their lives around.

Yet even for these victims of modern industrial America—losers, dropouts, the flotsam and jetsam of economic progress—the dream remains powerful. Perhaps this dream has been one of the secrets of America's success in the face of its undeniable economic inequalities: despite the impossible odds, many of the poor and aspiring have preferred the hope of making it *on their own* to the plodding certainty of government-guaranteed economic security. They would rather live poor with Hollywood's dreams to comfort them than come to terms with Detroit's realities. In a tent city on the outskirts of Phoenix, not far from Carefree, we talk with an American busting with dreams—out of work, yes, but with his hope intact. What brought him to Arizona? "Just looking for a dream, that's all," he says, the soul of ingenuousness. "Just gonna follow through with a dream." A buddy at his elbow adds, "It's just a matter of time, we're all going to make it . . . you can't expect to come out here and pick up a job like *that*." His voice rings with the hope of a person who refuses to be influenced by experience; he assures us that "this is better than doing nothing back home in Baltimore."

West of Arizona is California, the end of the line in the U.S.A. We head towards the Pacific coast, looking for dreams in the sad faces of unemployed seekers who have made it to the last frontier. There we find still further proof of the power of the American mythology. A battered Oldsmobile sits below one of the endless freeways that hold together the sprawling suburb that is Los Angeles, making an unlikely garage of an underpass. Clifford Danaghe, his wife, Vanita, and their three children, along with Vanita's brother, have parked their old car there on the recommendation of a state highway patrolman, where it is safe from ambush by unfriendly locals or intrusive lawmen. Leaning over the steering wheel and checking the help-wanted ads in a local newspaper, Cliff tells us without a hint of bitterness, "Well, we ran out of money, and ran out of stuff to feed the kids and everything, and this is the only place you can park without going to jail. We're doing the best we can." He does not despair. "California's a land of milk and honey. It is. There's more money out in this state, I think, than in any other state. But you got to be able to grasp it. You got to figure out how. . . . It's hard to get started but I believe we can do it. A new life, that's what we need."

The new pioneers seem little different from the old: independence remains more important than security, the right to go looking for fortune preferable to the right to a job, making it on your own more noble than accepting handouts from the king, the Congress, or the welfare bureaucracy. This family and many of the other people we talked with pride themselves on "going it alone", making their own way in the world. You win by competing, not by co-operating, and if the cost of the competition is that you end up a loser, so be it.

The Making of American Citizens

Attitudes like these inspire wonder, and even admiration. Yet they reflect a kind of naivety about the power of institutions and economic structures— as if by themselves individuals could climb out of unemployment or do battle with class and elite power that is systematically organized and part of the structure of everyday life. And they suggest a distaste for co-operation and common action that, combined with the traditional American distrust of political power, has undermined the capacity for democratic self-government. This has been costly to politics. America's democracy has rested on representation, on letting the few govern for the many, to whom the few must however remain accountable. This means Americans do not govern themselves at all in the fashion the Athenians did: they keep their governors on a short leash, but otherwise go about their private business protected from political interference by walls of rights and privacy. Little room is left for a sense of civic identity. Where politics is a matter of being left alone, it is hard to get people involved. Where it is a spectator sport, citizens watch rather than do. Where the common good is measured by the pursuit of individual happiness, conflict and competition may create a healthier political environment than co-operation and consensus.

America's founders worried that the majority might run amok, disregarding the rights of minorities and dissenters, and so they imposed significant checks on its potential power. They succeeded perhaps a little too well. They meant to muzzle the loud voice of opinion but in fact silenced the voice of the people, leaving them with only one civic responsibility: voting every year or two. They meant to moderate public passion but instead nearly paralysed it, turning politics into something most Americans *watched* rather than *did*. When de Tocqueville set foot on American soil in the early 1830s he was nearly deafened by what he thought was the roar and tumult of Americans manifesting their civic liberty. Today, the most audible political noise comes from the professional politicians and the sectarian private-interest groups, while too much of America silently watches—mostly on television.

Yet there are few generalizations about democracy that can stand up under close scrutiny. If bureaucracy and representation have sometimes threatened to paralyse citizenship, some citizens are none the less quite busy in America at the neighbourhood level. Public controversies can still catalyse private persons into public action. We came upon two stories on our travels in America that suggest that democratic citizenship remains alive there and can still challenge the passivity of representative government.

Cleaning up California

The citizens of twenty-six American states, many of them in the West, enjoy the right to initiate referenda and have legislation put directly to the public for a vote. This means they not only vote for their representatives but can engage in policy debates and vote on actual bills—which has an invigorating impact on citizens who might otherwise become passive and deferential. Referenda calling for a nuclear freeze have been passed in thousands of localities. In Churchill County, Nevada, prostitution was legalized by referendum; in Michigan and Maine, disposable soft-drink containers have been banned by referendum for environmental reasons. The referendum has been used for conservative and progressive ends, but has always pulled the public into the kind of lively debate usually reserved to their representatives.

The story of California's Proposition 65 began in 1986, when a group of citizens managed to have placed on the ballot an initiative aimed at curbing toxic discharges (mostly from industry) into drinking water. The state government was skeptical and the measure was vehemently opposed by Republican Governor Deukmejian, the California Medical Association, and a well-funded lobby of the affected industries. The debate was pressed in the media, above all television, with Hollywood stars working alongside Los Angeles housewives like Penny Newman to defeat the political and economic elites who were working equally hard to defeat the referendum.

Penny Newman is by her own description an average middle-class housewife with two kids and what Californians like to refer to as a nice lifestyle. She is a member of her local Parent Teachers' Association, a Boy Scout den mother, and a worrier. When her children began coming home from school dizzy and nauseated, she stopped just worrying and started acting. She found that chemicals were being dumped in the hills above Glen Avon, where she and her family lived, and a little research disclosed that tens of millions of gallons of toxic and carcinogenic chemicals were being dumped each year all through California. When it rained, they would run off the dumping sites and come pouring down the gorges from the canyons above Los Angeles, running across front yards, down public roads, into school play areas, the kids playing in the contaminated water and the parents not even knowing, until Penny turned into a citizen— noisy, outspoken, not to be mollified by politicians or "experts".

Despite the formidable opposition, Penny Newman and her fellow citizens got Proposition 65 passed by a margin of two to one, and for many this seemed a great victory. But Penny soon learned otherwise. The referendum victory was the beginning rather than the end of the battle. For it proved difficult to get the government to implement the proposition, and the governor was particularly willing to drag his feet, encouraging media distortions and supporting industry's continuing opposition to the measure. Penny discovered that what was won at the ballot box was easily lost again afterwards: "I think the system has failed the people to some extent, but I think the people have a responsibility in that failure. Too many people are lulled into this idea that all you have to do is to go to the poll and vote for one of these jerks running for an office, and they will take care of everything."

She realized that voting is not enough, that "people have to take the responsibility, have to get involved" in permanent ways, that citizenship begins rather than ends with elections. Civic engagement cannot be a sometime hobby—for the professional politicians, the paid bureaucrats, and the special-interest groups are permanently at work, and in the absence of engaged citizens' action groups and neighbourhood associations and community civic organizations they will always prevail.

In fact, there are a great many Penny Newmans in America engaged in practical politics in their neighbourhoods—what Thomas Jefferson thought of as America's "wards". Even after he had become president, Jefferson worried more about local than about national civic activity. His main quarrel with the Constitution was that it didn't take into account how important it was for people to participate in politics at a local level. "Divide the country into wards!" was a kind of watchword for all of his politics.

During the presidency of Jimmy Carter, a Jeffersonian mood pervaded the White House, with the president himself dedicating significant time to participating in national town meetings meant to give the people more direct access to him. So the ideal of local participation and vigorous local liberty remains entrenched in the otherwise rather passive American political system, even if its practice is uneven and sometimes whimsical.

Bucking the System in Boston

Roxbury, Massachusetts, is a section of Boston that in the early 1980s embarked on a from-the-bottom-up campaign to create an autonomous black community named Mandela (after the black South African hero) by severing its connections to the city surrounding it.

We come to Boston to take the measure of this modern story of rebellion and citizenship, but it feels as though we are returning to where our American story began, just a few miles down the Atlantic coast at Plymouth Rock. If Boston is the American Athens, Roxbury sometimes seems like the American Laurium, where slaves toiled in misery to mine the silver that supported Athens' glory. Much of Boston's racial minority population is packed into the ghetto that is Roxbury, a decaying inner-city township where the scars of the 1960s' racial violence are still visible, like craters on an old battlefield. Black leaders insist Roxbury gets less than its fair share of city services—for example, Boston's old elevated street railway has been "modernized" and replaced by a service that no longer goes into the heart of Roxbury. Activists say its residents have become second-class citizens of a prospering metropolis that ignores them.

With the leadership of a local journalist and musician, Andrew Jones, encouraged by Assemblywoman Gloria Fox and Bob Terrell, who is chairman of the Greater Roxbury Neighborhood Association, Roxbury decided to lay claim to its own destiny. In 1986 the people of Roxbury demanded a referendum on the question of "secession" from Boston—"de-annexation", as it was provocatively called—squaring off against both Boston and the government of the Commonwealth of Massachusetts (which by law had to agree to place the advisory referendum on the ballot). But the outcome in Roxbury was almost the opposite of that of Proposition 65 in California: California won the referendum battle, but lost the ecological war; the Roxbury independence movement lost the referendum, which went down to defeat in the State Assembly, but won a major victory for the morale and civic consciousness of its residents, who found strength and unity in their losing battle to achieve communal autonomy. Indeed, a number of people, including some leading blacks, thought that genuine autonomy might not be economically beneficial to the community, and that it was the symbolic issue of political mobilization that was ultimately most important for Roxbury.

Andrew Jones told us before the referendum's defeat, "I think the essence of democracy is local people who control their day-to-day affairs." Where control is lacking, they "have every right and even an obligation to assume their form of government, and that's what we're trying to do." Bob Terrell concludes, "[they] want to speak for themselves. They're tired of being represented, they want to represent their own point of view."

Thomas Jefferson would have been pleased, but so is Gloria Fox, Roxbury's feisty representative to the State Assembly. She has already been twice elected. A tough realist, a grandmother at forty-five, she shepherded the Roxbury referendum through the political process that brought it to the Assembly. "Democracy is for those who take handle on it," she says with a grin. Her constituents have "a clear handle on how democracy's going to work for them . . . that might mean that they have to take charge and do some things themselves." Representative Fox is adamant: "What we're doing is, we're extending the tradition of democracy for people of colour. We're tired of Boston telling us what to do, we're tired of bigwigs in their little blue suits and ties and white shirts telling us what we have to do with our community and bleeding us dry every day." But these activists are not "burn-it-down" nihilists. Fox's secessionist colleague Andrew Jones, who first conceived the idea of a separate city called Mandela, says, "The tools that we need were placed in the oldest constitution in the world—the Massachusetts constitution—three hundred years ago. Those tools . . . represent the most powerful form of government in the world."

There was a time when the people of Roxbury might have packed their bags and headed west to set up their own community on the edge of the frontier—just as many of Roxbury's blacks left Georgia, Mississippi, and the Carolinas several generations ago to find a new life in Boston. But there is no going back to small-town America, no returning to de Tocqueville's American frontier where most of the population lived in towns with populations under twenty thousand. The local talkshops that once kindled the ardour of citizens—the high school gym, the main street saloon, the local barber shop, the town store, the rural gas pump—are hard to find in the teeming cities and the suburban malls that define the public sphere for most Americans today.

America was born as an experiment, and the experiment continues. The problem facing the United States today is how to rekindle the ideal of participation and citizenship in a pluralistic nation of over a quarter of a billion people. It may be too late to run the country as a town meeting— it was already too late for that in 1789—but it is not too late to revive old institutions and forge new ones that allow people to reconcile property and social justice, privacy and community purposes, liberty and political equality, under the new conditions of mass society. The people of California and Roxbury have pointed the way, reminding us of what Jefferson wrote two hundred years ago: "I know of no safe depository of the ultimate power of the society but the people themselves, and if we think them not enlightened enough to exercise their control with a wholesome discretion, the remedy is not to take it from them, but to inform their discretion."

Pathways to Power IV

"Our" Democracy or Everyone's?

TO MOST WESTERNERS, DEMOCRACY SEEMS SO OBVIOUS and beneficial a form of government that the only question worth asking is why it has not yet become global. They take an almost proprietary interest in the democratic ideal, regarding it as their birthright, an invention of their forefathers, a mark of civilization. They claim it was invented by the Greeks, nourished by the Romans and the Protestant culture of the Reformation, liberated and modernized in revolutions made in England, America, and France. They see its presence in some parts of the Third World as one precious residue of colonialism, however noxious that system may have been, and assume that sooner or later it will come to all peoples everywhere—in the familiar form of parliaments and parties, bills of rights and representative elections, accountable leaders and independent judges. The great economist John Kenneth Galbraith chides us for worrying about the spread of democracy, or trying to force its arrival in those "unfortunate" countries that have not yet acquired the conditions (economic development, wealth, expanded communications) that produce it. And even back in the nineteenth century, Alexis de Tocqueville was confident that there was no stopping democracy.

But can we believe Galbraith and de Tocqueville? Today the global success of Western-style democracy seems less assured. Western forms of democracy are viewed with increasing suspicion in the non-Western world, as election scandals and "dirty tricks" come to light, while the West looks with like cynicism on the self-styled "democracies" and strange hybrids springing up elsewhere. How can Muammar al-Qaddafi call Libya the world's "most advanced" democracy when it's generally regarded as a brutal, terrorist, totalitarian state? Does Ghana's one-party dictatorship qualify as democratic at all? Why is democracy so precarious in Argentina and so shallowly rooted in Brazil? Why does Japanese democracy in some ways seem more feudal than democratic, Indian democracy more Byzantine than modern? Can all these different systems merit the term "democracy"?

In our search for answers to these troubling questions we journeyed to Africa, a vast and varied continent with almost half a billion people spread over four dozen countries, each country divided into dozens or even hundreds of tribes, religions, and languages. In the past Africa was seen as a "dark continent", and the ignorant Europeans who peered at it from across the Mediterranean illuminated it with their own fantasies of monsters, magic, and adventure, uncanny beasts, King Solomon's mines. Today we know that there were great civilizations here long before Solon gave Athens its first constitution; and long before the Europeans set foot in Africa there was a fierce history of intertribal warfare, slavery, and vengeance.

But even in our age of social science Africa remains a mysterious land, resistant to Western styles of democracy and to the "laws of political development" Westerners have tried to apply to it. We might look to Latin America or Asia to learn about the fate of democracy in the Third World, and we would find similar answers. But in Africa, with its great and burdensome colonial past, its thousand distinctive native histories, and its troubled modern history, the range of problems—and attempted solutions—seems exceptionally wide. Clearly the struggle for democracy is no easier here today than it was in Greece 2,500 years ago. If we look at what is happening—if we suspend our own biases and open our minds to other understandings of democracy—we may learn some surprising lessons not just about Africa, but about the democratic Western world as well.

Colonel Anthony Ukpo cuts an impressive figure when he dresses in his smart British-cut military uniform; but when he wears his traditional robes and brocade cap he assumes an almost royal aspect. He regards his appointment as governor of Nigeria's Rivers State (following the coup of 1983, which brought to an end Nigeria's most recent and futile experiment in Western-style democracy) as completely appropriate. Holding political office is to him little different than commanding a brigade or working at staff headquarters. He says, without a trace of cynicism, "I can take a second lieutenant and stand him up in front of a crowd of a thousand people, and he will speak to them with no hesitation at all. It is hard to find civilians who know how to do that, so the military experience is certainly very good training for government."

Like the United States and Switzerland, Nigeria is a federation, and Colonel Ukpo has been able to establish "people's parliaments" throughout the townships of Rivers State. "I discovered [the 'parliament' in the state capital] wasn't really like meeting with the people. . . . I decided it would be better to go meet with them and discuss with them on the spot, to hear their problems." We went along to one of Colonel Ukpo's meetings.

In the upriver town of Yenagoa, a temporary "parliament" has been set up on a parade ground, with a large open tent for the colonel and his ministers and the considerable crowd that has gathered around it under the hot sun. The mood is at once serious and festive, with men and women squatting in the grass or sitting quite grandly on improvised chairs, one man swatting at the flies that besiege him as if they were so many buzzing lobbyists, another batting his eyes in disbelief at a minister who is making excuses for the inadequate water supplies. A vaguely sacred libation of schnapps is poured on the ground, and the meeting begins in earnest. Here the tribal structure is still dominant, so it is not the average man but the chiefs who ask most of the questions of the ministers: exactly what did happen to those announced improvements in the water supply? How are Rivers States educational policies faring? And what of last year's promises? There is little hostility but a good deal of bantering, and the colonel answers the elders with that lack of specificity—"A lot has been done or at least has been planned"—that citizens have come to expect of bureaucrats everywhere, and passes the question to a minister. Few Westerners would call this temporary "parliament" democracy. Yet Colonel Ukpo insists that "even though this is a military administration, we believe it is necessary to consult the people. . . . It isn't an illusion. We go out there, we talk to the people, they ask for certain programs, they ask for reasons why certain things are not being done and they are told, and they are free to challenge it . . . so they can see for themselves they are not just being taken for a ride."

One thousand kilometres to the north across the Sahara desert, in Tripoli—the capital of Libya, the revolutionary Arab state of Qaddafi—a People's Congress is in session. The room is packed, convulsed with noise. At first it is not clear whether the enthusiasts crowding this old movie theatre are conducting a town meeting, a pep rally, or an organized riot. It is in fact one of the two thousand local assemblies that our guide assures us have been the foundation of Libya's democratic order since 1977. "We don't want to diminish the role of government," he explains, "we want to get rid of it altogether. The People's Congresses have abolished the ministry of the interior, abolished the police force. We hope soon to eliminate jails." As people speak up from the floor, addressing the leaders at the head table in impassioned speeches, the walls that normally separate citizen and leader in a democracy seem to tumble. Some speakers are boisterous and excited, others deliberate and thoughtful; the rhetoric is regularly punctuated by ritual chanting and the piercing ululations of the women. As the architect of this novel form of government would say, there remains only the voice of the people and the voice of their leader—the architect himself, Qaddafi.

Although there are few women in the leadership, one is conspicuous at the head table. And while many of the women in the room peer out at the proceedings from the depths of the traditional chador, others are unveiled—and vociferous; one old woman even proclaims poetic verses in praise of the revolution. There is an odour of demagoguery in the air, but many participants speak frankly and with ardour. "You don't have to tell us what the leader says!" a man shouts at the chair at one point. "The leader speaks Arabic, and we understand Arabic as well as you!"

Whether these local congresses, which have replaced formal government, are a genuine expression of grassroots participation or merely a smokescreen, thrown up by unseen leaders, for a one-man totalitarian state, many of those taking part regard them as both progressive and liberating. "Representation is falsification!" bellows one articulate participant into the eye of our movie camera. "No king here, no president, no parliament, no parties. The masses rule!" Or—in the words of our guide—"The state has been cancelled."

These scenes from Nigeria and Libya can be replicated throughout the world. There are people everywhere who act in the name of democracy—who use it, abuse it, modify it, assimilate it, improve it, pervert it. We need only look beyond the borders of the democratic West to discover that the struggle for democracy is global—whether or not that struggle succeeds.

We decided to travel to three nations in Africa—Nigeria, Zimbabwe, and Libya—not because they represent the entire continent (let alone the remarkable diversity of the whole Third World), but because each of them has rich indigenous traditions, a layer of colonial experience, and several decades of post-colonial political experimentation with (and without) democracy. Together they offer a complex tapestry of political patterns, and by exploring them we hoped to learn about the obstacles to democracy in developing countries.

In the course of our exploration, some questions overrode all others: has democracy taken root there in ways that conform to Africa's own traditional culture, or has Africa merely used the language of democracy to conceal new forms of dictatorship? Can the blood brotherhood we find in tribalism breed democratic equality? Or is this just another way of legitimizing traditional notions of the rule of the chiefs?

In short: has the non-Western world failed the West's democratic ideal, and subverted democracy? Or has democracy failed the non-Western world and concealed bold new forms of equality and participation?

Nigeria: Tribalism against Democracy

Drawn to the "dark continent" by untold natural wealth, the lucrative slave trade, and the prospects of vast imperial holdings, Portuguese, Belgian, French, Dutch, German, Italian, Turkish, and British colonialists first began to carve up Africa during the sixteenth century. By the late nineteenth century they had pretty much completed its dismemberment.

When they were finally forced out after the Second World War, they bequeathed their former subjects a set of Western institutions which, while formally democratic, paid scant heed to local hierarchies and traditions. Consider Nigeria: the European explorers who pushed up its rivers almost two hundred years ago found not a nation but a loose collection of over 250 different cultures, each with its own customs, religions, and languages—and literally thousands of villages, ruled by local chiefs. The British welded this diversity into an artificial "nation" by imposing a common language—English, of course—and instituting a British-style parliamentary government, but they were quite unable to turn the vast and fragmented area into an integral democracy.

Nevertheless, for six heady years following independence in 1960 this most populous of African countries (with over a hundred million people) seemed to be making a success of the British democratic legacy. It was a major oil producer, it was potentially self-sustaining in agriculture, and it had a practical form of federal government that appeared to offer ample room, under a rough formula of "separate but equal", to the powerful Hausa and Fulani tribes in the Moslem north, the radically splintered Yoruba in the west, and the pastoral Ibos in the east. It had also inherited from the British all the trappings of democratic government—lots of rival political parties, a dazzling Westminster-style parliament complete with prime minister, cabinet, speaker, an official "loyal opposition" party, and a regular "question period" when cabinet ministers were subjected to intensive queries from that opposition. Just how alien these institutions were can be guessed from the fact that in several native languages the only translation for "leader of the opposition" was "chief enemy", while the idea of a "loyal opposition" was utterly untranslatable. Britain's complicated political system was as out of place in the Nigerian setting as were such British paraphernalia as the speaker's mace, antiquated silk robes, and barristers' wigs.

Furthermore, there was little in the British system to help Nigeria deal with the spectacular corruption that was born along with the new nation—a corruption which seemed to many Westerners a complete betrayal of constitutional principles, but which in the Third World was often the only oil that could keep the rusty bureaucracy moving.

Nigeria's efforts to adapt to these important political institutions came to a tragic and abrupt end in 1966. The tribes quickly lost patience with the contrived parties and the democracy they supposedly embodied. In a pattern now all too familiar in the developing world, five young military officers, all Ibos, assassinated the Hausa prime minister along with several of his fellow tribesmen. They purported to be fed up with the corruption and inefficiency of the politicians, but they were also moved by fierce tribal rivalries. The Nigerian nation, artificially constituted from hostile tribes, came unstuck. Overnight, one of the world's largest democracies went from civilian to military rule.

Within six months of the Ibo strike, the northerners regained control with a coup of their own. They declared their intention to abolish the federation, and fomented what soon became a massacre of Ibos throughout the country. The Ibos retreated to the eastern region—some of them carrying the heads of massacred loved ones in baskets—renamed it Biafra, and seceded from Nigeria. Having barely escaped butchery they were naturally intransigent, and a cruel civil war ensued. In almost three long years of bloody strife, the remnants of Nigerian democracy vanished down a bottomless well of hate. Biafra, as a separate state, was finished.

Following the war a coalition of military men, including representatives of the many tribes, imposed a kind of deadly peace on Nigeria, permitting the surviving Ibos to be reintegrated into national life. In 1975 the charismatic General Murtala Mohammad took control of the coalition, but fell to assassins' bullets before he could complete his work. His successor, General Obasanjo, convened a committee of "wise men" to design a constitution modelled on a strong presidency rather than a strong parliament. In 1979 democracy was briefly restored with the Second Republic, under the leadership of President Shagari. But all in vain: by the time of the 1983 elections there were more polling places (166,000) than there were soldiers to police them, guaranteeing a result rigged by crooked local politicians. Nigerians already took it for granted that doing business meant an add-on cost of 6 to 12 per cent for corruption; the fact that 10,000 candidates were standing for 2,000 offices just proved how lucrative politics had become.

Sam Oni was press secretary to the president of the senate in Nigeria's ill-fated Second Republic; when we interviewed him he had little good to say about it: "[Members of the national assembly manifested] a total lack of sensitivity and awareness, and finally a lack of a sense of responsibility to the needs of the overwhelming majority of the people. Being a legislator became an opportunity for self-aggrandizement. Not only was it an opportunity to get rich and to get rich quick, but it was also an opportunity to throw your weight around. I found the national assembly a monumental exercise in futility, but a very costly one."When the military men stepped in once again in 1983, they were greeted more as redeemers than as usurpers. General Buhari, who led the coup, explained that "Nigeria had been enslaved by a handful of people who had been sharing the wealth among themselves and who were determined to stay in power at all costs." His patriotism did not prevent him from being ousted by still another coup two years later, but the point had been made. Plundered by politicians and ravaged by tribal factionalism, Nigeria had only the military to turn to. It brought its own version of venality and ambition, to be sure, but it also brought intertribal tolerance and an orderliness that the public seemed to crave. Nigeria today is under tight military control. As Jean Jacques

Rousseau predicted, liberty has turned out to be a food easy to eat but hard to digest; Nigerians are finding that they have a larger appetite for security than for freedom.

Like many Nigerians, lawyer Gani Fawehimmi believes that what Nigeria needs is the rule of an iron fist rather than the restoration of democracy's gentle hand. The vehemence with which he responded to our questions belied his neat coat and tie, and made him seem less like a civil rights attorney than a flaming revolutionary: "Nigeria has never produced a leader whose basic interest is the welfare of the people, a leader principled enough, resolute enough, ruthless enough to usher in a progressive Nigeria. . . . We need more than a Gandhi—passive resistance is over. We need a leader strong like Mao Zedong, ruthless like Fidel Castro, resolute like John Kennedy. We need a leader like J. J. Rawlings in Ghana . . . who has a vision, has the clout, the courage, and the ruthlessness of principle." Fawehimmi finishes up with a bang: "People must be executed!" he declares. "They should pay with their lives. And the ill-gotten gains should be taken from their children."

Western democracy has clearly failed Nigeria. But Africans are saying that if democracy is ever to return to this volatile, violent, and corrupted nation, it will have to grow from native roots. "It will have to be African," they say. "We do not need things imported from the West." In fact all of Africa appears to revere things imported from the West—Mercedes Benzes, Uzis, telephones, computers, airplanes, military uniforms and ranks, the formal courtroom and other aspects of criminal law. Yet it is true that the abandonment of deep-rooted customs and cultural patterns may have been the single most critical source of the troubles in Nigeria. Men like Colonel Ukpo in Rivers State appreciate this reality, and nourish tribal forms of consultation and co-operation where they can. Indeed, Sam Oni's final verdict on the Second Republic turns not on its corruption but on its foreign origins: "The system of government that was being attempted was not only too cumbersome, not only too expensive, not only too sophisticated, but above all it was totally un-African and alien." For all his experience with legislature, Sam Oni is another Nigerian who expressly favours a benign dictator as the ideal government for his country.

If Western democracy in Nigeria ended up looking like a sad cross between paternalism and corruption, what are the alternatives? What might an indigenous African form of democracy look like?

Tribalism as Democracy

The equality and participation we expect in Western democracy are found in Africa not in federal institutions but in such native forms as the tribe and the village council. As far back as the nineteenth century, some sociologists were suggesting that tribal society might be considered one of democracy's ancient parents, and were studying the Iroquois in North America and the village mir in Russia in search of the natural fraternity and primitive equality that their own liberal societies seemed to lack. A greater reliance on modern variations of these forms might succeed where Western forms of democracy have failed.

Chief Dagogo Princewell thinks so. Chief Princewell is a village chief in Nigeria's Calabari nation, and is a sagacious statesman poised between two worlds. The Calabari are strategically situated in the Niger River delta, and although they are a "minority" tribe they have played a key role in West African trade for centuries. Chief Princewell was elected to the senate in the 1983 elections and has thus experienced Westminster democracy. But with the December coup that came only a few months after his election, he was banned from the national scene. He resumed his extensive tribal responsibilities as a Calabari chief, and when we talked to him he was in the brightly coloured traditional garb he prefers. On weekends he travels upriver to his home territory to carry out political duties within his tribe that the military have not attempted to interfere with. On this particular weekend he was going to participate in the initiation of a new chief, and he took us with him in his outboard motorboat, talking as we pitched and rolled on the swift current. His strong, lilting voice rose with conviction as he told us how his council of chiefs gathered in the island town of Buguma as "the national assembly of the Calabari nation and its highest court." The chiefs are not elected, but are chosen by their family and clan groups to speak for them in the councils of their king, the Amanyanaba of the Calabari. And while the council has important law-making and judicial powers, the king has the last word—"Whatever he says is final."

Chief Princewell was patient with us. There is plenty of time on Africa's ancient rivers, and the history he was recounting runs in the blood of each of his tribal brothers: "The monarchy has been in existence for a very long time, and the people have the belief that the Amanyanaba cannot do any wrong, and so they all agree that he and his council of chiefs rule them." Then he smiles knowingly. "But if you do not do what they want, then they

drop you. They select someone else. That's a democracy we've been practising for centuries."

Later in the weekend we watched the initiation of the new chief.
Offered a ritual yam and cannonball, he chose the cannonball as a symbol
of his willingness to fight for his people, in a solemn but joyous ritual that
ended with his elevation to full chief. Watching him, we wondered
whether an informal system of "checks and balances"—where there are no
formal elections, but where a chief who does not consult and listen to his
people is soon a chief no more—can be called democratic.

What Chief Princewell told us on the river was confirmed by another
chief, historian Isaac Erekosima. Erekosima is an expert on the Calabari,
and was also head of the council of chiefs for twenty years. He is a learned
and impressive man, and when he lectured us on why the Westminster
model of democracy was not "a natural system for Nigeria", it was easy to
believe him. It was, he says, "merely an alien system. . . . The fact that it
failed showed it didn't have roots here, whereas in Britain it has gone on
for years and they are used to it and know what the pitfalls are. This is why,
before we try it again, we had better think whether we can find things we
understand and have applied that are a bit more suitable to our people and
our conditions here."

But it would be a mistake to think that tribal government means the
same thing throughout all of Nigeria, let alone all of Africa. One of the
most powerful traditional rulers in Nigeria is the Oba (king) of Benin,
who traces his history directly back to the twelfth century and rules with a
far firmer hand than the chiefs of the Calabari. The Oba could once make
or break individuals and families so decisively that he was able to make
every tribal member his own personal subject, and thus break the hold of
his subchiefs over them. While he was regarded as a reactionary ally of the
British in colonial times—he was used by them much as the South African
government today uses tribal chiefs to keep order in the Bantustans—he
has maintained his powers through the period of democracy and coups.
The current Oba studied law at Cambridge and served as a senior government official in Lagos, and he has used the authority he gained when he
ascended to the throne in 1979 to offer his people a kind of justice that is
beyond the capabilities of the military government.

We were admitted to a tribal council and, with some trepidation, in
open session inquired about his idea of government. We had been told that
the Oba employs magicians to warn him of the possible evil intentions of

visitors such as ourselves, so we were gratified when he responded to us with the thoughtful reasoning of a political scientist. He recognizes, he told us, that all Nigerians are "caught up in the web of the modern kind of government" and so are not quite as their ancestors were. Yet tribal customs persist, and may even aid democracy, since while "we do not know what democracy is, [we do know we require institutions that] grow out of the people's own traditions . . . traditions evolved from the heart of the people, from the religion of the people." He feels those who would draw up a new constitution must "give tradition a place."

While tribalism in Benin means powerful kingship, in the regions dominated by the Moslem Hausa and Fulani tribes the social structure is more aristocratic, with power shared by a hereditary elite. Among the neighbouring Yoruba, for example, the king and his chiefs rule together, the king mediating their fractious quarrels while the chiefs are a check on his power.

It is interesting to compare these various systems with the genuine democracy of the small nation of Botswana. Botswana's national democracy leaves much local rule in the hands of the chiefs, who also administer most of the national criminal code, and sit on a council of chiefs that works (not always harmoniously!) with the republican government. The result is a cheerful, peaceful democracy that ranks higher in its observance of human rights than some Western democracies. The tribal forms and traditions that are profoundly important to the people are preserved, and the co-operation between the chiefs and the national government is surprisingly productive.

If by democracy we mean a system where the people do the work of government and accept the credit or the blame themselves, then none of Nigeria's tribal systems is democratic—and a number of them are far from it: consultation is not participation; advice is not consent; approval is not election. Yet a democracy that does not grow out of this tribal context is no more than a rootless weed, to be blown away by the first warm desert wind. Tribalism is not democracy—but a democracy not sustained by tribalism is unlikely to survive, let alone thrive.

One-Party Rule: The Case of Zimbabwe

In Nigeria we encountered the results of failed democracy: a state that is losing the war against corruption—guns everywhere, roadblocks and identity checks on every major highway and, always, the spectre of public executions. In Zimbabwe, a lush country renowned for its splendid game reserves, prosperous farms, and picture-postcard physical beauty, but torn apart by the struggles of rival tribal factions at war with one another and with the white minority, we saw the troubles of democracy as the legacy of an agonizing past.

The colony the British called Rhodesia had a deeply troubled history, and unlike Nigeria it received independence only after a long, violent struggle. Indeed, Rhodesia achieved its "independence" twice. The first time was in 1965, when the white population, under the leadership of Ian Smith, broke with England rather than give up its supremacy; the second was fifteen years later, when the native population finally wrested power from the whites to establish the nation of Zimbabwe. Many whites left at that time; those who remained continue to play a critical economic role in farming and business, and are still represented by a dozen or so moderates in Parliament, but they have become pawns in Zimbabwe's fierce inter-tribal struggles. The two archrivals are the Ndebele tribe, which founded the Zimbabwe African People's Union (ZAPU) under Joshua Nkomo, and the Shona, who split off from the ZAPU and formed their own tribal party, the Zimbabwe African National Union (ZANU), under the leadership of Robert Mugabe, who has been successfully campaigning to create a one-party state under the ZANU party.

Mugabe is now president, but despite his new position as a national statesman, he continues to play the same tune: "As clear as day follows night, ZANU will rule in Zimbabwe for ever. There is no other party besides ours that will rule this country." He adds, in justification, "I don't believe the multiparty state is the best way of going about a democratic system. We must recognize that we are one society, and one country with one government. We must be nationally united and therefore it is necessary that we show this image to our people, the image of being one. The best way of doing it is to have one political umbrella under which all shades of opinion can be accommodated and this can take place only under a one-party state."

Zimbabwe means "burial ground of the chiefs"; Robert Mugabe seems to wish to bury not only the chiefs but their tribes too, in favour of an imposed nationalism. Whether a single-party state is ultimately compatible with the freedoms of genuine democracy is not yet clear. Here in Zimbabwe, it may just be a way station on the road to a one-man dictatorship. Yet to many Zimbabweans, one-party rule is the only way.

Aluis Ndoda Mutandadzi is a believer. Ten years ago he led ten thousand rebel soldiers against the white supremacist government of Ian Smith. When the civil war was over, he and eighteen of his men bought a tobacco farm in the north-east part of the country, where the fighting had been most intense; the farm had previously been owned by whites, who had fled. Today Ndoda runs the farm with his men and their families, as a co-operative; he is chairman of the venture. The co-op is like an extended family, he tells us, and—as in the one-party state—disputes are settled within the family, with one man as boss. That's the African tradition. For Ndoda there is no other way.

Perhaps he is right; on this continent one-party rule may be the only viable alternative to military dictatorship. Throughout the Third World, states resisting one-man rule have been drawn to one-party rule. And no wonder; there have been some spectacular demagogues in Africa's brief modern history of independence. Idi Amin ruled Uganda by slaughter for eight long years before he was deposed in 1979; Jean Bedel Bokassa terrorized the Central African Republic for thirteen years until he was overthrown in 1979; and Flight Lieutenant Rawlings continues to run Ghana with guns in both hands—admired by many in neighbouring Nigeria and elsewhere for his "firmness" and "resolve". Many of Africa's more stable non-military regimes have also shown a yearning for the unifying simplicity of this system; a single party can encompass a broad intertribal (and therefore genuinely national) coalition, and achieve a certain order without wholly sacrificing liberty.

There is another African nation where they claim even one party is too many for genuine democracy. To investigate this claim, we set out for a desert land of nearly four million people that hugs the Mediterranean—a land many Westerners regard as a terrorist state run by a madman—Libya.

"Cancelling the State": Libya's Revolution

It is not easy to get into Libya—the country is off limits to tourists—and the visitor who does overcome the obstacles is greeted by a barrage of rhetoric. The signs and slogans begin at the airport arrival lounge, continue along the modern highway into Tripoli, and persist right into the lobby of our hotel, where the face of Libya's revolutionary leader, Muammar al-Qaddafi, proffers a stern welcome.

Qaddafi was a Bedouin army colonel of twenty-seven when in 1969 he led a bloodless coup against the ineffectual old king and established a revolutionary government in Libya. In his view it is now the most democratic country in the world, a land where Rousseau's "General Will" has been given genuine expression. The French prophet of democracy, who is quoted by visionary tyrants as well as visionary democrats, thought it was possible to discover the shared vision, the common good, of a nation, and turn it into political reality. Qaddafi claims to have done just that. "The most tyrannical dictatorships the world has known have existed under the shadow of parliaments," he says. He insists that Libya now possesses a revolutionary structure where Bedouin traditions of desert hardiness and individual independence are combined with the ancient teachings of the Koran to create a truly self-governed society.

Libya is neither a multiparty nor a one-party state; Qaddafi claims it has ceased to have a state at all. Instead it has over two thousand People's Congresses that supposedly express the voice of the people.

Is Qaddafi a prophet to be taken at his word? Deserts *have* produced more than their share of visionaries and prophets. Or is he a tyrant trying to conceal his true aims? If we examine Libya's reputation as the world's foremost breeding-ground for terrorism; if we look at its isolation from other African and Arab states, and consult Amnesty International's figures on political assassinations and imprisonment; if we note the absence of a free press and the state control of television, the destruction of the economic base of the middle class, the grim propagandizing of the young in schools (now called "barracks") and military camps, and the public hangings, then, for all its democratic congresses, Libya is in fact a frightening tyranny.

Yet, despite our skepticism, Qaddafi's "democracy" is worthy of attention because it illustrates the difficulties of defining what democracy really is, in cultures that lack Western traditions of free government. To those who manage to get into Libya and talk to its messianic leader, as we did, Libya teaches something that we could not learn from Nigeria or Zimbabwe.

Libya bears scant resemblance to Nigeria (though both are oil-rich) or other nations of sub-Saharan Africa, and it is distinctive from its Mediterranean neighbours as well. Indeed, it is the avowed enemy of most of them. It shared a common history with them under the Ottoman empire before the First World War, and it experienced devastating Italian colonialism after the war. But that experience came to an end almost immediately following the Second World War (during which Libya was a battleground for the great tank battles between Rommel's forces and the British army), and in 1951 it received independence.

The timely discovery of vast oil reserves enabled Qaddafi to modernize his sparsely populated nation of desert Bedouin with relative ease. Libya went from being one of the poorest countries in the world to being Africa's most prosperous nation (as measured by per capita Gross National Product)—and with nine hundred miles of accessible Mediterranean shoreline, to boot. Moreover, social conditions were ideal: there were no tribal divisions and no religious cleavages. The four million people come from only nine interrelated and closely knit clans, all of whom possess that dedication to independence for which nomads are legendary.

As an ardent revolutionary, Qaddafi took Egypt's Gamal Abdal Nasser as his idol early in life. A brief study visit to England confirmed his biases against its parliamentary institutions, but he retained an interest in alternative forms of democracy that was much heightened following his 1969 coup. Observers at first saw his "Green Book" as one more version of Third World socialism: a "watermelon", they quipped, because "it's green on the outside and pink on the inside." But Qaddafi was no mere socialist, and he continues to claim that his revolution transcends both capitalism and socialism, reaching for a "third way" that will liberate all the developing world.

In 1974 he resigned his governmental offices, declaring himself the revolutionary leader of a people who no longer required a state apparatus and creating an aberrant form of non-government he calls Jamahiriya, or "the state of the masses". He enunciated the theory of this novel form of people's democracy in his simplistic and polemical little Green Book, and then put it into practice through the creation of the People's Congresses throughout the country.

The great question facing the visitor to Libya is whether the practice reflects or contradicts the theory. As he drove us into Tripoli from the airport, Saad Mujbir, Qaddafi's head of protocol at the time of our visit, bantered about terrorists—"We'll have to keep our eyes open for some!" Still, he was obviously pleased that there were no signs of either terrorists or the police state to trouble us. But for all his friendliness, he was soon wading into familiar revolutionary waters. "Everybody in the world is tired of big governments," he insisted, sounding like an irritated Thatcherite or a Reaganite neoconservative who only wants to get government off the people's back. "Well, we're not just going to limit the powers of government, we are going to do away with government."

As we drove along, Saad Mujbir pointed out the new apartment blocks replacing the shantytowns that had ringed Tripoli before the revolution. Libyans now own their homes, but it is unclear how much they owe their good fortune to the revolution in whose name these flats were built, and how much to the oil revenues that paid for the construction. Qaddafi declares that freedom means home ownership. Yet there are residents who still do not quite understand. Like their leader, who is said to have been born in a goatskin tent, and spends much of his time outside the cities, many of these high-rise Bedouin still long for the desert. Some of them even keep a few sheep on the sun-drenched balconies that are the revolution's gift to them.

The three slim pamphlets in which Qaddafi's revolution is outlined and defended—the Green Book—are bound in luminous green—the colour of Islam. Indeed, as Mujbir enthusiastically pointed out, everything in Tripoli seems to be green; from the auto licence plates to shutters, doors, and flags, to Qaddafi's banners adorning the city, to the pavement in the city's great main square—now renamed Green Square. For Qaddafi's revolution is neither Red nor White, neither bourgeois nor socialist, but a third colour, a "Third Way"—Jamahiriya. It is the way of Islam *and* the way of modernity; the way of a unified people with no tribal factions to divide them, and no competing ideas to distract them.

To Qaddafi, this people's democracy with no state, no government, and no bureaucracy is a living refutation of Western parliamentary government. He sees it as the remedy for all of democracy's weaknesses, but particularly for what he calls the fraud of representation—that is, the destructive self-interestedness of political parties, the domination of one class over all others, the misleading and arbitrary character of plebiscites. Most Westerners see these as minor defects, but Qaddafi appears sincere in his judgement that representative government is not democracy at all.

In Qaddafi's Libya, formal government disappears—in name if not in fact. Where Libya once had a government there are now People's Congresses; where there were parties there are revolutionary committees; where there was a president there is a leader of the revolution, although he does not head an administration; where there was the Libyan state there is now the "Socialist People's Libyan Arab Jamahiriya". Like Adam gone mad in the Garden of Eden, Qaddafi seems to believe that by renaming the organs of power he can transform them.

Qaddafi may have expected that as soon as he announced his new democracy, the people would seize upon it as a tool of their own liberation. They did not. Instead they were baffled by it—as baffled as Soviet farmers would later be when Gorbachev suggested they return to something like a free market. Incensed by their apathy and skepticism, Qaddafi created the Revolutionary Committees, not unlike China's fearsome Red Guard—young zealots closely linked to the Revolutionary Guard and the secret police, who would spread across the nation as the prophetic vanguard of the revolution, assuring that people followed "the correct way".

Whenever you hear the word "correct" you can be sure democracy is in trouble. And we were to hear it often. When revolutionary vanguards assume the task of "straightening out" dissidents, it often turns out—as it has in Libya—to be at the end of a rope—and often on live national television, before chanting mobs. Later Qaddafi announced that he was abolishing Capital Punishment.

As for the congresses themselves, it is doubtful whether they are anything more than opinion polls to let Qaddafi know what he must do to mollify public unrest. There is no discernible mechanism for the development and promotion of policy or ideas at the grassroots level, and the major initiatives come from the top down, the agenda being set by the leader himself or his increasingly influential Revolutionary Committees. For it is these committees that have really replaced the old structures of government. And the indoctrination of young—often very young—disciples in militant cadres suggests that there will be no shortage of zealots to spread the message—in Libya, or elsewhere.

Qaddafi is a stubborn man, however, and when he is confronted with hard questions he does not budge from his convictions. He consents to an interview with us, but he has been anxious and fearful since the American bombing raid on Tripoli, and has been constantly on the move. He only agrees to be seen in the desert, not far from the traditional home of the Qaddafa clan—one of the nine Berber tribes.

He begins the interview unenthusiastically, his eyes half-closed under the sun-shield of a tent, as if the words that will pass from his lips have been said a thousand times before. Moments of liveliness only occasionally punctuate his cold, aloof manner. He waves off the idea of a "system where there is give and take—a dialogue between government and people" with a dismissive "There is no need for conflict!" and goes on to insist that his revolution is "not against a given regime, but against government as such, government as 'institution' in general. This struggle will continue as long as there is somebody who is governing and somebody else who is governed. For this struggle to stop, all the people must govern."

What of his own leadership? He claims to "exercise no real power" and yet he is bound by no legal system and limited by no accountability. What is his role then? He remains serene, with only the slightest hint of impatience in his voice—as if he were explaining an obvious principle to a dull child. "I lead the revolution. Nobody appointed me to be leader of the revolution and nobody appointed me to be a revolutionary. [I am] a revolutionary by nature. If I left Libya everything would continue the same. I have no daily political or administrative work to perform. I only incite the mass of the people to rule itself by itself." We listen, but it is not easy to believe: if rhetoric were democracy, most of the world would be free.

But if we look for first-hand evidence—if we seek to follow a modern-day Phidias into the Arab bazaar of Tripoli to learn about Libyan "democracy" from the ground up—we will be sorely disappointed. For Qaddafi has declared that profit from another man's labour, and thus retail trade, are hostile to the new democracy. The once teeming souks that dot this Mediterranean port are today eerily silent. The shops are boarded up and padlocked, and the vines that once adorned the covered walkways have withered away. Where once crowds pressed their noisy advantage in rowdy bargaining sessions around rows and rows of busy stalls, the streets are today almost empty. Shopping is done at state-run supermarkets in the suburbs, leaving the city centre silent. The raucous sounds of public debate can still be heard in the well-orchestrated People's Congresses, but the squares are vacant; hotel rooms are said to be bugged; the press is definitely muzzled, and under "people's control" television has become a ludicrous medium of propaganda—the weather maps have gaping holes where Egypt and America should be, and reports about Washington talk matter-of-factly about "mad dog Reagan" and "the Black House".

Even the mosques have lost their pride of place. Many were pulled down during Qaddafi's quarrel with the Moslem clergy, after the Mufti of Tripoli was apparently murdered by members of a Revolutionary Committee. The mosque that once dominated Green Square was razed in the name of freedom, along with the conservative philosophy it stood for (Libya is not Iran!).

We hear words about freedom, but the sounds of freedom have vanished. Even Saad Mujbir concedes that he misses what he calls "the public play of imagination". Without that, he says, "without creativity, everything is sterile. Our TV is sterile and boring and everyone who runs it is afraid of making mistakes and being called counter-revolutionary. We need arts and play and entertainment, not propaganda all the time." But Qaddafi is bent on "democratizing" his nation by executing his enemies at home, assassinating his foreign foes, disrupting the outside world through terrorism, and securing the future by capturing the minds of the young. He seems to have little interest in mosques, bazaars, or arts and entertainment (although his quarters in Tripoli are full of furnishings fit for television's *Dallas*, and he is fond of Italian design and sunglasses). Revolutions may often be instruments of purification, but they are not always compatible with the results they strive to create. It would be ironic to call Libya a police state, since its state has been cancelled and its police no longer officially exist. But it is still more ironic to call it a democracy.

On the other hand, Libyans do not go hungry, and their form of one-man rule does not seem, from a domestic point of view, to be much more dangerous than Robert Mugabe's one-party state in Zimbabwe—unless you stand in opposition to it. Moreover, women have achieved a degree of liberation rare elsewhere in the Moslem world. These improvements are cause for reflection on the fate of democracy in the non-Western world. Libya is not the only country where the struggle for democracy has been preceded by a struggle for economic viability, national unity, and self-determination. These struggles are often violent and undemocratic, and all too frequently succeed only when foreign oppressors are replaced, at least for a time, by native tyrants. History will decide soon enough whether Libya's "democratic" experiment is bogus or authentic, whether oil money and visionary rhetoric can create a stable regime in which equality is not won at the price of freedom.

Democracy: White Man's Burden or Black Man's Curse?

Less than a hundred years ago, Rudyard Kipling, speaking for much of white Europe, wrote:

> Take up the White Man's burden —
> Send forth the best ye breed —
> Go bind your sons to exile
> To serve your captives' need;
> To wait in heavy harness
> On fluttered folk and wild —
> Your new-caught, sullen peoples,
> Half devil and half child.

The "burden" assumed by Kipling's noble Englishmen was nothing compared to the burden those Englishmen and their paternalistic European cousins placed on Africa. Like much of the Third World, it has laboured mightily under this tremendous burden: it has had to modernize, to industrialize, to urbanize; to incorporate itself into the global world, into its economy and its culture, its technologies, and its consumer markets; and somehow to become democratic and free and tolerant and stable at the same time. Africa has tried assiduously to import or develop political institutions that work in the face of tribal and religious conflicts. Moreover, it has had to do all of this under the long shadow of a colonialism that has not disappeared simply because an act of independence was signed or a new flag raised.

So heavy has this burden been that Africans themselves have sometimes lost faith in their capacity to rule themselves wisely. Says a character in Buchi Emecheta's Nigerian novel *Destination Biafra*, "When the Europeans ruled us, few people died. Now we rule ourselves, we butcher each other like meat-sellers slaughtering cows."

As recently as 1987, Aggrey Klaaste, editor of the black South African daily *The Sowetan*, commented on the mutual slaughter of pro- and anti-government Zulus in Natal with a despairing fury: "If this is the type of retribution that will become common when blacks rule blacks, then perhaps we need a great deal more oppression to make us humble, responsible, and dignified in our anger against oppression."

There are many ways in which the new Africa has failed democracy. Yet Klaaste and Buchi Emecheta are too hard on themselves, for democracy, and the Europe from which it came, have likewise failed the new Africa. Clearly the struggle for democracy and the struggle against the colonizers are two different struggles; and in achieving independence many nations seem to feel compelled to abjure democracy. Perhaps the greatest test of democracy will be whether they can find a way to resolve these damaging tensions and not by merely exporting one nation's constitution to another, or imposing one country's government upon another. This may mean combining ancient forms of tribal co-operation with innovative forms of government, combining the power of universal rights with the uniqueness of each nation's own traditions and customs. Such solutions will not be easy, but they need to be found if the global aspiration to democracy is ever to become a global reality.

The Tyranny of the Majority

FOR MOST PEOPLE DEMOCRACY MEANS GOVERNMENT for, by, and of the people—government by free and equal individuals. But the liberty of individuals can fall prey to the equality of individuals—for in practical terms, equality means the rule of the majority. Yet the rule of the majority can become so cruel, so wrong, so oppressive to individuals and to minorities, that it perverts democracy itself, and the rule of the people becomes the tyranny of the mob.

The achievement of majority rule has a basic fairness about it—those who are outvoted usually say, "if that's what most people want, we'll go along with it." Yet when the majority will collides with a minority's deeply held beliefs—as often happens when religion is involved—this perception of fairness can quickly evaporate. History is strewn with examples of initially judicious majorities indulging their power to the point where the rights of individuals or minority groups are violated. Some regard the trial of Socrates as the first great example of such abuse. By the end of the eighteenth century a revolutionary majority in Paris had turned the French Revolution into an instrument of terror, and the new American republic was wrestling uncomfortably with the balance between the liberties of individuals—guaranteed by the Bill of Rights—and the right of the majority to legislate its will through a democratic Congress.

It came as no surprise to many Americans, then, when Alexis de Tocqueville warned that equality was the future of the world, a tide that could not be stemmed; and that the government of the majority—man-

79

dated by this equality—had the potential for a terrible new kind of tyranny. "Absolute monarchies have dishonoured despotism," he wrote. "Let us beware lest democratic republics should reinstate despotism and render it less odious and degrading in the eyes of the many by making it still more onerous to the few."

However villainous some monarchs may have been, their oppression was easily recognized as injustice and their cruel deeds condemned as illegitimate. But a citizen majority that believes its voice is the voice of God invests the most oppressive behaviour with the illusion of democratic legitimacy. In the hundred years following de Tocqueville's American visit, anxious liberals throughout Europe and North America worried that a monumental revolt of the masses would sweep away not only absolute government and injustice but the fights and liberties of individuals as well.

In the many countries to which we travelled, we met democrats aplenty who aspired to both liberty and equality, but who found that the two have a way of obstructing and even defeating one another. A people secure in their numbers and certain of their rightness can too easily forget that democracy also requires tolerance.

Catholics have been murdering Protestants and Protestants murdering Catholics for almost as long as the two have existed. Sixteenth-century France saw the St. Bartholomew's Day Massacre, when Huguenots were slaughtered in their beds by rampaging Catholic zealots who viewed the Protestant Reformation as a blasphemous outrage waiting to be avenged. The quest for tolerance helped give birth to democracy, but that has not necessarily spelled improved relations; Catholic and Protestant majorities now find themselves armed with ballot boxes and the law as well as their ardent prejudices.

Thus, in countries with more than a single major race or religion, the story of the struggle for democracy has become the story of the struggle between equality and liberty. Our journey took us through a number of stable democracies that are deeply embattled in this struggle.

Free at Last, Free at Last. . . .

In the short span of our own lifetime, America's white majority has gone from supporting segregation and injustice to supporting integration and equal opportunity. If popular opinion took a long time to catch up to the legislators and judges who led the political struggle, if terrible costs were paid by those who waged the campaign in the field, and if the battle begun on parchment is still to be finished in deeds, none the less the story of America's black minority is one of hope—of dreams well dreamed if not yet fully realized. It is also a model for native American Indians and for women, both of whom have had to wage their own battle for full civic rights.

For the first half of America's modern history, the majority, and with it the law, were on the wrong side of liberty. Most black Americans were kept in bondage until the Civil War, when Abraham Lincoln's 1863 Emancipation Proclamation freeing the slaves, and the constitutional amendments guaranteeing their rights as legal persons and citizens, were enacted. Even then, in many places they were kept from the exercise of their rights by segregationist and racist discrimination enforced by so-called "Jim Crow" laws, and by vigilante organizations like the Ku Klux Klan. With its shotguns and hanging ropes, the Klan was a ubiquitous and deadly reminder that it takes more than proclamations to vanquish racism.

American blacks in fact remained victims of economic discrimination (poor education, all-white unions, job bias) and political discrimination (poll taxes that kept them from voting, party machines closed to them) into the middle of the present century. They acquired the genuine legal substance of equality only in 1954, with the notable Supreme Court decision *Brown* v. *Topeka Board of Education* (see Chapter Six) that finally put an end to the policy of a "separate but equal" life for blacks. This policy had been endorsed by the Supreme Court in 1896, in the notorious case of *Plessy* v. *Ferguson*, and had remained the lynch-pin of America's overtly segregationist policies. Blacks had to ride at the backs of buses, use segregated bathrooms, stay in segregated hotels, eat in segregated restaurants, and be educated in separate (and radically inferior) schools, because, the Court had ruled, there is nothing unfair or unequal about separate, segregated facilities.

Yet the real story of the struggle in America gets under way only after the legal story ends. For while the courts had set the judicial record straight, blacks still had to put their rights to the test in the everyday world of the schools, buses, public rest rooms, train stations, and luncheon counters of the American South. The historic question this test raised was: could a minority bring a reluctant majority to live by laws enforced in the majority's name?

Like so many great national stories, this one started with a solitary individual vowing to embrace an abstract legal principle as her own personal cause. Mrs. Rosa L. Parks of Montgomery, Alabama, was an ordinary black citizen of extraordinary courage and conviction. A hard-working, middle-aged woman with a stubborn disposition, she had grown tired of being chased to the back of the bus on her way to and from work in a department store tailor shop. One afternoon in 1955 she simply refused to leave her seat and "move to the back of the bus" when ordered to do so by the bus driver.

She remembers her feelings vividly: "I had had problems with bus drivers over the years, because I didn't see fit to pay my money into the front and then go around to the back. Sometimes bus drivers wouldn't permit me to get on the bus. . . . One of the things that made this get so much publicity was that the police were called in and I was placed under arrest. See, if I had just been evicted from the bus and he hadn't placed me under arrest or had any charges brought against me, it probably could have been just another incident."

But it was not just another incident, it was the first shot in a war, the beginning of a new age of civil disobedience that would change the public face of America. By persuasion, by example, by moral intimidation, by political pressure—by whatever means it took—those who followed in the path of Rosa Parks were intent on making democracy work the way it was supposed to.

To much of the black leadership that flourished in the churches of the South, where the civil rights revolution really started, to win the battle democratically meant to fight the battle non-violently. The Reverend Martin Luther King, Jr. knew—as Gandhi had known before him—that overcoming the tyranny of those who thought they acted in the name of democracy meant not only curbing their prejudiced conduct but altering their prejudiced thinking. To achieve this, King advocated a form of resistance that was non-violent but active and forceful, that aimed at embracing and thereby changing the oppressor.

At first, King's strategy seemed a recipe for martyrdom. No one who experienced those years will forget the press photographs flashed around the world showing little black girls trying to go to school under the snarling muzzles of police dogs; dazed "Freedom Riders" standing next to burning Greyhound buses from which they had been taken and beaten by white thugs; muscular young men, black and white, lying on the floor in front of luncheon counters with their arms around their knees, their heads tucked in for protection, stoically enduring blows from a policeman's billy club or the butt of a civilian vigilante's rifle.

Yet from tragedies and disappointments came progress. And of the many crucial elements of the era, none was perhaps more decisive than the white and black Freedom Riders who in the spring of 1961 rode the interstate buses all over the South, at grave risk to their safety, to test new federal regulations requiring the desegregation of interstate travel facilities. James Farmer, director of the Congress of Racial Equality (CORE) which had organized the freedom rides, notes that it was the *Brown v. Topeka Board of Education* decision that "erupted into the nationwide explosion" of the civil rights movement. "'If it's true in the field of public education,'" Farmer said in a voice still resonant with the conviction of those times, "people asked, 'why is it not true in the other fields such as public accommodation, transportation, employment?'"

The Freedom Riders won their struggle because the federal government—representing the national majority—was finally moved to enforce laws and judicial rulings that state resistance had until then rendered unenforceable. Halfway through their bold journey across the segregated South, under constant threat of injury and death, CORE's footsoldiers finally forced President Kennedy's hand. The president and his brother, the attorney general, had tried to persuade Farmer to suspend the rides; when he refused, they had to order in federal marshals, and then the National Guard as well. Once the federal government was involved—as happened when James Meredith stood up to the Governor of Mississippi to defend his right to attend university, and federal troops were brought in—the resistance of the southern states collapsed. The minority had forced the local majority to live up to the letter of its own laws. Nearly one hundred years after the South's surrender at Appomattox, the Civil War was finally over. The country stood on the brink of a new era of integration and racial justice.

On a spring day in 1963, a century after President Lincoln's Emancipation Proclamation, hundreds of thousands of Americans gathered in Washington on the great mall stretching out from the Lincoln Monument towards Capitol Hill. Before this impressive and peaceful throng came the Reverend Martin Luther King, Jr. In lilting cadences acquired at Baptist pulpits in Montgomery and Atlanta and Memphis, he addressed those who had brought their faith to the nation's capital that day. Over and over again, King appealed to an America that did not yet exist. "I have a dream," he whispered; "I *have* a dream," he thundered; "I have a *dream*," he promised. And with each ringing "dream" came a murmuring tide from the thousands who stood swaying in front of the grave, carved face of Abraham Lincoln perched high on his marble chair—"Yes, Reverend . . . a dream . . . we're with you. . . . That's right, yes, yes, yes. . . ."

"Yes, I have a dream," he proclaimed, to an audience beyond the mall, beyond Washington, to the great majority in whose hands the future of justice in America lay; "a dream that one day this nation will rise up, live up to the true meaning of its creed: 'We hold these truths to be self-evident, that all men are created equal.' I have a dream that my four little children will one day live in a nation where they will not be judged by the colour of their skin but by the content of their character. . . . I have a dream that we will be able to speed up that day when all God's children, black men and white men, Jews and Gentiles, Protestants and Catholics, will be able to join hands and sing in the words of the old Negro spiritual—'Free at last, free at last, thank God Almighty, free at last!'"

Today, King's dream still seems remote to many Americans. But progress had been real, and King was celebrating as well as dreaming in front of those hundreds of thousands. In July 1964—just eight months after Kennedy was gunned down—the new president, Lyndon B. Johnson, signed into law a Civil Rights Act outlawing segregation in public accommodation, an act that made it clear that "separate but equal" was unconstitutional in all public facilities. A year later, he signed the Voting Rights Act, giving the full force of the law to black voting rights that had been obstructed by poll taxes, registration laws, and other segregationist devices. The majority's law was now firmly and fully on the side of the minority, though the struggle was anything but over.

On a cold day in April 1968—five years after the march on Washington, four years after he received the Nobel Peace Prize—Martin Luther King, Jr. was shot to death on a motel balcony in Memphis, Tennessee. At that moment, his dream seemed further away than it had ever been. Not long after his assassination, the National Advisory Commission on Civil Disorders, reacting to the racial violence and urban breakdown besetting American cities, warned, "Our nation is moving towards two societies, one black, one white—separate and unequal." And statistics from the 1970s and 1980s suggest that things are getting still worse, with unemployment soaring to almost 60 per cent among black teenagers, pregnancy among nonwhite teens racing ahead of the rest of the population, female-headed single parent homes becoming the rule rather than the exception in the black community, and heroin and crack addiction (and the crime that attends them) becoming especially virulent among black youths. Many Americans argue that the majority has lost whatever commitment it made in the sixties to the interests of the minority and that King's dream has all but vanished. But if the opinion of the majority vacillates on how much is required in the name of racial justice, the law remains crystal clear. And if America still has a very long way to travel before arriving at the threshold of King's vision, it has also come a long way—at least in racial matters—from that tyranny that de Tocqueville feared would be its certain destiny.

But de Tocqueville's fears continue to vex democrats throughout the world. According to its constitution India is fully democratic, with fair election practices and a free press. But the ideas of participation, equal justice, and tolerance for minorities have not yet spread very widely and the majority there seems moved by the same opinionated self-righteousness found in America. We travelled to this one-time jewel in the British imperial crown to explore the problem of majority tyranny in a non-Western setting.

Democracy's Untouchables

India emerged from the British empire in both glory and chaos, with hostile populations of Moslems and Hindus colliding even as they sought a common independence. The partition of the subcontinent into a predominantly Moslem state (Pakistan) and a predominantly Hindu state (India) did not solve the problem, for independence in 1947 left a minority of Hindus in Pakistan, Moslems in India, and Sikhs in both. The rival populations turned on one another in the two countries, even as Gandhi fasted to try to restore peace (he was assassinated a year later). Refugees poured over the border in both directions, and for a time the integrity of Indian independence seemed at grave risk. The nation has survived and, as a democracy, has in many ways flourished. Yet a deadly rivalry between India's Sikhs and the Hindu majority has replaced the quarrel with the Moslems, and the two hostile sects have been at each other's throats since. They have arrived at a *modus vivendi* based on mutual slaughter; in 1984 it cost Prime Minister Indira Gandhi her life.

But in India religion is only one of the divisive issues—another is caste, a system that divides people into rigid classes and defines the lowest as "Untouchable". Originally, the Untouchables were religious outcasts relegated to impoverishment by Hindu beliefs concerning bodily purity. True Hindus were allowed no contact with excrement, death, and certain impure animals; they relegated tasks involving these taboos to the lowest caste and thereby turned them into untouchables. Members of this "unclean" caste—a full one-fifth of India's nearly 770 million people—became a cause for India's great pacifist leader and national founder, Mahatma Gandhi. He redubbed them the *harijans*, or "children of God". It was easier to change their name than their status, however. Although the Indian constitution of 1949 outlawed the caste system and gave the *harijans* full civic rights as well as special seats in Parliament, and although a few *harijans* have become prominent politicians or successful businessmen, the majority remain trapped by poverty and prejudice. As recently as 1982, a government commission declared that the caste system continued to pervade and corrupt the nation. And while the problem stems from religious and cultural bigotry, the rule of the majority seems—in keeping with de Tocqueville's fears—to have compounded it by giving persecution the aura of democratic legitimacy. No modern Indian government has been willing to move decisively to uproot caste prejudice or correct its economic effects—presumably because the prejudiced majority has had other priorities.

It may be argued, however, that in both India and America majority tyranny is more a matter of mass opinion than enlightened self-interest, of prejudice rather than purpose. The law, while it cannot perhaps change hearts in the short run, can alter mass opinion over the long haul—if citizens can be brought to examine and reconsider their prejudices. Nowhere was this more evident to us than in Australia, which we visited not long ago as it prepared, happily, to celebrate the bicentennial of its stupendously unhappy founding.

Down and Out in Australia

There are few lands on earth more blessed than Australia, a vast island tucked away from the rest of the world where the sun always seems to be shining and where the relentless pursuit of happiness actually seems to work. It has been called the lucky country, and that is certainly how most white Australians view it. Its government, based on the Westminster model, meets the criteria almost anyone would offer for a fully democratic country.

Yet few modern democracies have had more unlikely beginnings. The nation was created as a penal colony for England. A dozen years after America had been lost as a colony and a dumping-ground, shiploads of convicts, petty thieves, prostitutes, and even child "criminals" were herded onto boats and sent off on an eight-month journey halfway round the world. The first 736 of what would eventually be 148,000 forced emigrants embarked on the hellish journey in 1787; one in seven would die during the voyage. The survivors landed at Botany Bay and settled in a new town named after England's Home Secretary, Viscount Sydney, whose scheme the penal colony was. For the next eighty years, Britain shipped cargo after cargo of human refuse to Australia's sunny shores, until this unexplored continent on the edge of the world resembled a vast open-air prison. Independence was won only at the end of the nineteenth century.

The symbol of government on this fatal shore was the lash, used with consistency on men, women, and children. So noisome was the stench of Britain's authority as overseer in these early years—gunpowder and human blood were its chief ingredients—that Australians have held their noses in the face of governmental authority ever since. Men who seem too hungry for power are known as "tall poppies", in need of a sharp-edged scythe. In the words of the Sydney novelist Thomas Keneally, "I would think that anyone who tried to be a demagogue in Australia would find the going tough because Australians mistrust demagogues and mistrust grandiloquence, grand political statements, manifestos. . . . They smell rats in manifestos. . . . This is their good, rough fraternal cynicism, which is both one of the greatest limitations on the development of Australia and one of the greatest guarantees of Australian democracy."

In their common need to survive in the bushland and the great outback, Australian men turned to one another. Together they felt the potency of fraternity, what they called "mateship". It was an ethic of absolute loyalty to one's mates, and it gave a rough and ready sense of equality to Australian social relations duplicated, if anywhere, only on the American frontier. But, as in America, this powerful sense of kindredness and loyalty dealt two crucial groups right out of society: women and the indigenous people. The story of women in frontier societies is not always a story of inequality, but in Australia it was. The story of natives persecuted and exploited by colonizers is more universal, and the fate of the Aborigines is only a variation on that of the Aztecs or the North American Indians.

When the convicts arrived in Australia, they ignored the rights of the Aborigines. No treaties were ever signed with these hunters and gatherers who had walked the continent for millennia before the first whites appeared. The English simply declared it *terra nullius*—"no one's land"—and claimed it. And as Australian society developed, the Aborigines continued to be left out. In the blunt words of Keneally: "We were very paternalistic to them. We felt that the vote would mean nothing. Even at the time of the federation when the Constitution was drawn up and promulgated in 1901, it was taken for granted quite blithely that they were a dying race."

So it is not surprising that in the late 1960s the Aboriginal peoples, a minuscule 1 per cent of Australia's sparse population of sixteen million, finally grew disgusted with two centuries of non-citizenship and resolved to fight for their rights. Charlie Perkins, angry, opinionated, committed, represents the new activist Aboriginal who emerged in that era. He was born in a campground beside a dry river bed and raised on a Christian mission station outside Alice Springs in Central Australia. Unlike so many of his impoverished kinsmen, he fought his way out of Alice Springs, and became the first Aboriginal to graduate from university.

As the American struggle for civil rights ignited, Charlie Perkins and others were watching. The freedom rides, he recalls, were heady incitements to concrete action: "Well, we got in a bus in about 1964, a group of Aboriginal students at New Sydney University, and we just went from town to town in no planned sort of way, and where we saw there was discrimination or prejudice anywhere, we just got placards out and we demonstrated in the street . . . swimming pools, hotels, clubs, cinemas, restaurants, they were all barred to Aboriginal people." Charlie Perkins and his colleagues, and the Australians he provoked and embarrassed and upset, together created the climate for a referendum that in 1967 offered Aborigines the vote, equal welfare benefits, standard wages, compulsory education, and (in Australia, no small matter!) the right to drink in a bar. Supported by all parties, the referendum passed by an overwhelming majority.

So far so good. Yet the great symbol of Australia's crime against the Aborigines—the stolen land—remained a bitter issue. While the white majority was preparing to wave the flag in a boisterous, upbeat celebration of the country's 200th anniversary in January 1989, Aborigines used the opportunity to renew their demand for territorial redress. And slowly, painfully, but honestly and thoughtfully too, the white majority began to face up to this embarrassing problem. As a consequence, attitudes of exceptional conciliation and mutual recognition have begun to develop.

Marcia Langton was only a very young woman from Queensland back in the 1960s, when the Aborigines of the Gurindji tribe first tried to reacquire their ancestral lands. Their struggle turned her into an articulate advocate of Aboriginal rights. "Aboriginal people everywhere were being told that the reason why they were being moved was because they were useless and the only way they were going to be any good to anybody is if they moved into towns and assimilated. The Gurindji stood up . . . and said, 'This is our land and we're staying here.' For one group to stand up and say that meant that every Aboriginal person could stand up and say that."

And stand up they did; they erected a tent embassy in front of Parliament in Canberra. Though the "sit-in" was officiously dispatched by the police, Prime Minister Gough Whitlam's newly elected government acted swiftly to pass what would be called the most progressive land legislation in the world. Whitlam saw immediately to the heart of the matter: "The simple fact is that the identity and the integrity of the Aboriginal peoples in Australia rests upon their association with the land, so we had to devise some way of vesting land in Aborigines."

As Gandhi inspired the American civil rights movement, so the American civil rights movement inspired the Aborigines, and so the Aborigines inspired the North American Indian movement. During this same period, Maine's Passamaquoddy and Penobscot tribes brought a lawsuit laying claim to nearly two-thirds of the state's territory (inhabited by 350,000 white residents), and in 1980 they won the victory of the Maine Indian Claims Settlement Act, which provided 81 million federal dollars for Indian land purchases. In Canada during the same period, armed with tax money from (majority!) governments every bit as embarrassed before world opinion as the Australians had been, Cree and Blackfoot Indians were having some success forcing both the federal and the provincial governments belatedly to recognize treaties that were valid in international law but ignored in Canada.

In Australia there were no treaties; the Aborigines had never been legally recognized. But under Whitlam's leadership, Parliament established Aboriginal Land Claim Councils, and then encouraged Aborigines to press their claims. All this with federal money!

In 1985, in a great symbolic act of reconciliation, the most sacred Aboriginal shrine in Australia—known to whites as Ayers Rock and to Aborigines as Uluru—was legally returned to the Aborigines, and leased back to the country as a national park, so that it would be accessible to all. Aborigines call the whites who scramble up the great sacred rock formation for recreational purposes "ants", but they tolerate the ants as a small price to pay for repossessing their spiritual shrine and the symbol of their special relationship with the land.

"Repossess" is not really the right word, however, as white Australians learned when they began to listen to the Aborigines, who see their land as the creation of mythic ancestors in what they call the dream time. Since they "belong to it", it cannot belong to them—at least, not in the Western sense of ownership. They are its guardians, its healers, its conservators. In their eyes the land is traced with "dream tracks" or "song lines" invisible to whites. They have been following these paths for centuries—paths that take them to food or water or distant enclaves, sacred paths that take them to sacred places, deeply felt guidelines for life. No wonder the land commissioners sent to adjudicate the claims have been so vexed!

The court at Lilla Creek, which we visit one parching afternoon, is a model of exasperated goodwill. Government officers point to a location on a map and ask a native of the area, "Who owns this region?" His brow furrows as he tries to read the strange markings, he will respond only with a set of puzzles of his own: "I know about this place. I walked through it here [pointing to the map] when I was a child. I still walk through here today. I can tell you about this place; I can tell you what that rock means. I can tell you how important that tree is." How is one to divine from these evocative responses useful information about boundaries, acreage, or ownership?

And some questions cannot be asked at all. The Aboriginal culture can be deeply secretive; its taboos are absolute and can quite literally be matters of life and death. Anthropologists used to insist that Aboriginal law was men's law: only when female anthropologists went into the field did they discover a parallel body of law known only to women. These laws cannot be discussed across the sexual divide. When a commissioner got too close to a tribal secret at Lilla Creek and Marlene Cousens, the interpreter, was asked to pursue questions about a place sacred to men, she refused even to pose the question, saying, "Don't ask me about Wiputa. I don't want to die!"

This gentle but monumental confrontation of cultures is a slow and laboured process, and it may take ten years or more before it is over. But ceded lands already make up an area larger than New Zealand, and this is clearly a genuine attempt by the majority to redress historical injustices, even if it means redrawing the map of Australia by rules no cartographer has ever heard of. In Australia, at least—where the minority is small, and the majority relatively responsive—prejudice is giving way to law, and law has created the climate not merely for formal justice, but for a novel attempt to find a language that gives recognition not merely to Aboriginal claims, but to the strange and rich philosophy of life from which those claims have arisen. Perhaps the Aborigines of Australia have a secret to teach the children of Athens about democracy: that for individuals and groups to live together, they need new and creative languages that transcend the idea of "majority and minority". We have come to assume that the language of democracy is the language of majority rule. Yet "citizenship", "public good", and just plain "community" are all words that suggest a co-operative political relationship, where people define themselves by their common membership rather than by antagonistic special interests and private goals. Majorities and minorities divide: common citizenship can unite. From Mark Twain's Huck Finn to Eddie Murphy's Beverly Hills Cop, American popular culture has frequently managed to forge a superficial but embracing language that bridges the worlds of young whites and blacks. Popular music can do the same. If the Aborigines of Australia enlarge on this tradition of common talk, they may help us all towards genuine fraternity. In bridging a cultural divide, we may discover new forms of understanding.

On the other hand, religious differences have been less tractable—particularly in democracies where the establishment of a majority religion creates the spectre of legitimized intolerance. All too often there follows the persecution of the religious minority under the guise of the public interest. Two of the world's most troubled countries, both democracies, are beset by the seeming incompatibility of democracy and deeply held religious convictions which have been given official sanction. In Israel, where Arab and Jew face each other as irreconcilable enemies, and in Northern Ireland, where Protestant and Catholic stare across a barricade of hatred made impassable by the centuries, the quarrel of majorities and minorities still has the feel of a fatal disease: democracy's own special cancer.

Vox Populi, Vox Dei

The case of Israel (whose history we look at more carefully in Chapter Ten) is in many ways unique—the product of a set of tragic circumstances to which centuries of anti-Semitism, global power politics, the Holocaust, domestic Arab politics, and the special conditions of the settlement and birth of Palestine as a Jewish state have all contributed. Yet Israel also faces de Tocqueville's question: can a majority fairly govern a minority of a different religion? The answer appears to be an unqualified and terrifying "No!" A state devoted to the principles of Zionism—a democratic home for all Jews from around the world—can honour majority rule, but it may not be able to honour the spirit of democracy.

The Arab minority within Israel, and the one million Arabs living in Gaza and the occupied West Bank, create a dilemma for which there appears only one solution: elimination of the minority! One right-wing extremist member of the Knesset (Parliament), Rabbi Meir Kahane—an American by birth—would simply expel the Arabs from the occupied territories, while on the left there is a large constituency in favour of giving up the territories in which the Palestinians live, taken in the 1967 war—even creating an independent Palestinian state. What does not seem possible is for a Jewish majority devoted to the principle of a Jewish state to live in peace with an Arab minority on the basis of the democratic principle of one citizen, one vote—particularly when population growth may in time turn the Jews into a minority in their own country.

If Israel, which can offer a powerful model of ideal citizenship, also sends shivers of despair up the spines of aspiring democrats, its problems can be attributed at least in part to its unique circumstances: the Zionist quest for a secure Jewish homeland, and the danger that this homeland would be lost if Israel became a multinational, multireligious state. So special are Israel's problems that the democrat may well conclude there is little to learn from them but the inevitability of human suffering. Meron Benvenisti, an Israeli social scientist, has written, "I don't see an end to it. I see only more violence. . . . It has become a tribal war, the descendants of Isaac and Ishmael battling over land with stones and clubs." If Benvenisti is right, the problem is not one of democratic contradictions but of ancient quarrels that make democracy irrelevant.

Can the same be said of Northern Ireland, where all of the traditional conflicts of a Protestant England and a Catholic Ireland seem to collide with a force utterly destructive to the life of democracy? Our visit there did not inspire hope.

The Tragedy of Ireland

Overlooking the Catholic enclave of the Bogside in Derry, in the North of Ireland, a scrawled graffito reads, "Remember 1690." That was the year when the Protestant population defended its dissenting religion and defeated the Catholic army of England's King James II. The cannon that helped defeat James are still mounted on the high walls, and are pointed towards the Bogside—a symbolism not lost on the people who live below.

The history of Ireland has been one of rebellion and unrest ever since the English first invaded the island in 1171. The conflict deepened when Ireland remained Catholic despite Henry VIII's break with Rome, and again when the Catholic James II was deposed in favour of the Protestant William of Orange. But today's minority—majority conflict really began in 1607 when England, in the hope of settling the country, gave land in the northern areas to settlers, mostly Scottish, who brought their Protestant religion with them. In the southern areas too, hundreds of acres of the most fertile land were given to English gentry for services to the crown. Although many were "absentee landlords", some settled on the land and eventually became known as the Anglo-Irish; George Bernard Shaw, W.B. Yeats, Lady Gregory, and J.M. Synge are from this stock. Many were nationalist heroes: Theobald Wolfe Tone, an aristocrat, was greatly influenced by French ideas of *liberté* and *égalité* and tried to unite the mutually hostile planters and native people in the unsuccessful "Society of United Irishmen" uprising in 1798. That was the last time Protestants and Catholics were united.

On Easter Sunday, 1916, the movement for Irish independence from England—led by Sinn Fein, the Irish Republican Brotherhood, and James Connolly's Citizen Army (precursors to the Irish Republican Army, the IRA)—proclaimed the Irish Republic. The rebellion was quickly crushed. Most northern Protestants were adamantly opposed to being absorbed into a Catholic Irish Republic, and were determined to remain within the United Kingdom. (At one time they had even threatened, paradoxically, to use force against the English army to *maintain* their connection to England, if the army did not support them.) The only solution seemed to be to divide the two communities. The South became the independent Republic of Ireland, while most of the northern province of Ulster remained within the United Kingdom as an autonomous region called Northern Ireland. There the Protestants outnumbered their Catholic brethren two to one and were a clear majority, while in the South the Protestants were out-numbered three to one.

With partition, however, the majority–minority problem did not van-ish; it merely festered. To make sure they kept their majority in the North, the new Stormont government (a "Protestant parliament for a Protestant people") blatantly enacted job discrimination, unequal voting rights, and gerrymandering, all designed to keep the Catholic "Fenians" in a perma-nent underclass. The tragedy was that the Protestants were motivated by fear of a wholly independent, united Ireland in which *they* would become the persecuted minority.

In 1967 a civil rights movement took to the streets. The marchers were attacked, the demonstrations proliferated, and the fights became more vicious until they culminated in 1969 with the Battle of the Bogside: a peaceful demonstration was attacked by the Royal Ulster Constabulary, the B-Specials (a reserve military) were called in, barricades were built. The battle raged for days. From Dublin, the Irish government announced it could no longer stand "idly by". And since Stormont could not control its own police force, the British government made the fateful choice of send-ing in troops in an effort to *protect* the Catholic minority.

So less than fifty years after partition, British troops again arrived in Ireland—but this time they were welcomed and given cups of tea. The civil rights movement—begun in 1967—looked as if it might stand a chance. But within a year the British troops found themselves again in a shooting war with the IRA. Curfews were imposed, houses searched. In 1971, under pressure from Stormont, imprisonment without trial—internment—was reintroduced; torture and mass arrests were reported. And then, on a cold day in January 1972, an event occurred that seemed to put an end to any hope for the non-violent movement; it would become known as "Bloody Sunday". At a massive demonstration, the British army fired on a crowd of people singing songs and behaving generally as though they were at a festival—and this time they fired not rubber bullets but real ones. The street violence took a deadly toll: thirteen dead, scores injured, deep new wounds cutting through old scars.

Nell McCafferty was a writer in Derry, and she remembers Bloody Sunday well: "I ran up in through the front garden of a passway and knocked on the door, and asked the woman to let me in . . . and a fellow came running up the path to get into her house and I heard a shot, and he fell down in front of me outside the window . . . and another fellow came running back and he was shot. And he lay there and I could hear the two of them groaning. . . . A Red Cross worker was running across the court-yard, and so the shots started again. The soldiers made her dance, she was dancing around the bullets. And then it was all over and I opened the door and walked out, and I stepped over the bodies." A vivid anecdote that could be retold in a dozen different tongues in democracies around the world— democracies where people live in terror not of tyrants but of majorities to which they do not belong.

From its zenith of popularity following the aftermath of Bloody Sunday, the IRA has now become one of the major terrorist groups in the world. The vicious bombing of both civilian and military targets has lost them popular support. Now, however, while still continuing their "military cam-paign", which they believe they can win, they are again making belated attempts to enter the arena of electoral politics through their "political wing", Sinn Fein.

Stormont was suspended by Westminster in 1972 and now sits empty and discredited. Protestant hardliners say, "No Surrender", and their coun-terparts to the IRA, the Ulster Volunteer Force and the Ulster Defence Association, carry on the "war"; British soldiers are still there—young men facing frightening enemies they cannot see in a situation they can nei-ther fathom nor resolve; the ordinary people are worn out.

Various attempts have been made to come to some understanding; "Women Together", whose two leaders received the Nobel Peace Prize, was a beacon of hope for a while. But all these left matters no better than before. Today, meetings are held in church halls and schools to get people to talk. There have been ecumenical peace marches. Even the IRA graffiti, in addition to calling for "Troops Out", mention housing and jobs again. In this tormented part of a beautiful island, the inability to institute a demo-cratic form of government has come to mean reconciliation or death.

If Britain withdrew its support from the North (constitutionally if not economically; Britain has major investments in both North and South), if the country became united under one government, would the northern

Protestants find the kind of equality and civil rights the northern Catholics are demanding? The question is moot. Not only is the South desperately grappling with unemployment, inflation, and street crime, but its social programs are far inferior to those in the North. The Catholic Church still influences political decisions and, until 1972, in fact held a "special place" in the Constitution.

A recent referendum clearly demonstrated that a secular society is not in sight. In 1986 the government introduced a bill that would have allowed civil divorce. Although the bill was extremely modest and a five-year period of separation would have been required prior to divorce, the Catholic Church campaigned vigorously against the bill and defeated it in a nationwide referendum by a large margin. The rights of anyone who was not a Catholic (and of any Catholic who might want a divorce) were cheerfully overruled.

Clara Clark told us about her situation—"ridiculous", she calls it. She has obtained a Church annulment of her marriage, but cannot obtain a divorce from the state in order to remarry. Separated from her husband for years, she lives with another man and has a new baby. The victory of the Church means Clara will be unable to legalize her situation; she will have to go on "living in sin". One Catholic woman grimly assured us, "I do not need divorce for *my* marriage." When we asked her about the rights of minorities—of Jews and Protestants—to live as they wished in Ireland, she replied with disarming candour: "Ninety-four per cent of the people of Ireland are Christians and I don't see that we should really get overly bothered about trying to view a situation from other denominations' points of view. . . . We are a Catholic country and I think we should go from there."

Of all the prejudices afflicting majority rule, religion is perhaps the most perilous, because it suggests that the voice of the people and the voice of God are one and the same. Church and monarch once ruled Western civilizations, until the revolt of the masses put that power into the hands of the majority. Yet today, in too many countries, it is Church and majority that threaten liberty. If such countries are to find true democracy, their citizens must learn to separate their beliefs about what they require of God from their beliefs about what they demand from one another.

Democracy can be saved from its errors only by more democracy, by bringing people together to discuss and understand differing points of view, so that they may deal with each other as individuals rather than as agents of private interests or beliefs. We discovered in the civil rights movement of Martin Luther King, Jr. and the innovative discourse of Aborigines and white Australians possibilities for more co-operative and humane forms of democracy. We may never fulfil the powerful formula advanced by John Stuart Mill, the nineteenth-century English liberal, in his book *Utilitarianism*: "If all mankind minus one were of one opinion, and only one person were of the contrary opinion, mankind would no more be justified in silencing that one person, than he, if he had the power, would be justified in silencing mankind." But if we learn to reconcile individuals and communities in ways that do not require the dominion of majorities over minorities, democracy will have won a very great victory.

The Rule of Law VI

OF DEMOCRACY'S MANY PERPLEXITIES, NONE IS perhaps more confusing than those of the law. The law seems to be both on the right and on the wrong side of morals, both for and against liberty, both to increase and to diminish privacy. Sometimes we think of it as the instrument of our liberty: the way we protect our freedoms through great charters and constitutions like the American Bill of Rights or the United Nations Declaration of Human Rights. And sometimes we think of it as liberty's nemesis: an ever-rising tide of legislative gobbledegook that can drown us in restrictions and limitations. We are finally unable to decide whether law is how we tether the state and keep it in check, or how it tethers us, restraining our liberty in the name of the public good.

When a Canadian police car stops a peaceful motorist in a "random spot check" for drinking drivers—an action that in some countries would be illegal—is the law interfering with the poor chap's liberty, or protecting his neighbour's security by deterring drunk driving? When Dutch laws guarantee the rights of citizens to buy and sell pornography, does this guarantee democratic ideals? Or does it outrage the rights of all those who are offended? When a group of international judges prosecutes German officials for obeying and enforcing the laws of Nazi Germany, is this a triumph of international jurisprudence or a violation of the country's sovereign rights?

These seem to be paradoxes. But there is a useful set of words we can employ to deal with them—and the key words are *right* and *utility*. The contest is between a law that secures the *rights* of the individual to be left alone, and a law that enforces the community's *utilitarian* interest in legislating on behalf of the public good, even at the cost of individual liberty. Laws prohibiting pornography, for example, emphasize *utility*: the good of the community—in protecting the quality of its neighbourhoods. Laws guaranteeing the *right* of citizens to buy and sell pornography emphasize individual liberty: the rights of free speech and access to information that permit people to do as they please.

Caught on the horns of the dilemma that places right and utility in tension, law is something of a harlot, seeming to serve everyone whether scoundrel or saint, every cause whether noble or base. Some would say it serves neither right nor utility, but only the wealthy and powerful by (in Rousseau's words) throwing a garland of flowers over man's chains. When it reinforces rather than checks power, the law in its majestic equality—in Anatole France's bitter remark—prohibits both the rich and the poor from sleeping under bridges.

Ideally, of course, we look for the law to protect liberty *and* the public good. The policeman who stops your car to see if you have had too much to drink is trying to protect you *and* the community. The question is whether the law can do both at the same time. The answer that impressed us as we looked back through history was that law can work for a community without encroaching on the rights of individuals only when individuals participate one by one in making the laws or choosing the judges who interpret them—that law is the servant of citizens only if the two are united through a democracy. As Rousseau put it, we can remain free while we obey the law only if we obey laws we have prescribed for ourselves.

What is obvious in theory is difficult to apply in practice—especially where democracy means not active participation in law-making by all, but majority rule by elected representatives—but that became clear to us only when we first went to The Netherlands to talk with inhabitants of what many people regard as the freest society on earth under the government of the law.

Drugs, Sex, and Law in The Netherlands

The Netherlands (Holland) is an old constitutional monarchy pushed by its neighbours up against the North Sea. Much of its land has been reclaimed from those raging waters, which are held back by a chain of vigilantly maintained dikes. Even so, the country is not much larger than Haiti—and with fifteen million people crowded into it, The Netherlands is understandably sensitive to issues of liberty and privacy. Here the law—or at least the way it is enforced—is seen as still another dike, this one to wall out the encroaching state and preserve an impregnable free space for tolerance and privacy. As a consequence, the Dutch have been as free a people as any that Europe has known in the last three hundred years. Political and religious dissenters found a haven here when no other country would have them. Among them was the tiny group of Puritans who embarked in 1620 for the New World on a ship called the *Mayflower*.

Anyone who wanders down the streets of Amsterdam today can confirm that the Dutch have pushed the legal protection of liberty to its outer limits—and perhaps beyond.

Gert Hidskes would certainly not disagree. He is a former local government official, serious, well read, and articulate. He still has the demeanour of a public servant, but today he runs a sex shop in the red light district which offers customers everything from pornographic literature and videos to ingenious sexual devices whose uses the uninitiated can only guess at. Hidskes tells us matter-of-factly that "at the moment, the only [depiction] forbidden is sex with children, say under sixteen." But even before the new law made all other depictions legal, finally spelling out exactly what is and is not allowed, Holland's traditional tolerance countenanced just about anything customers might be interested in.

At the garish Bulldog Café, as well as dozens of more discreet dairybars around the city, in addition to the familiar selections of orange juice, milkshakes, and T-shirts, clients could choose from an international menu of hashish and marijuana of every price and quality—from the cheapest local grass to high-priced hashish from Afghanistan. There was even a cake containing hash, recommended for insomnia! The city did more than tolerate the Bulldog's thriving business: it collected taxes on the sales and even operated a tramway token booth on the Bulldog's premises. Shortly after we visited the Bulldog the police closed it down. But what they really wanted to stop was the rowdyism, loitering, and noise; other "grass bars" were left alone.

Like America and some other countries, Holland now offers "telephone sex". But in Holland the government runs the telephone company that collects the fee and forwards the profit to the pornographers who operate the service. Prostitution is licensed by the state, and high-class call girls feel comfortable in the knowledge that their business is legal and controlled by the police. When we are invited into a club to see for ourselves what these legally operated facilities look like, one professional, lounging in a bath, tells us as she runs a sponge over her pink shoulders, "Ours is a rather free country, especially Amsterdam. I mean you could do anything here, you know? It's very good, it's so common, so accepted by all the people." We ask about her life, but she cannot see why we are interested: "I just lead a normal life. Well, I sleep later. . . . But the rest of my life is normal. Really."

Certainly it is more normal than it was a few years ago, when houses of prostitution were illegal. But the owner of the brothel told us that, even then, he consulted with the police on how to operate his house. They not only co-operated; they sought *his* advice when the new law legalizing brothels was being drafted.

The law here is generous, flexible, and often seems to be defined by whatever agreement can be worked out between those who operate the drug, pornography, and prostitution industry, and the relevant government agencies. The system is a tolerant one, where the law means whatever it needs to mean, even at the cost of a certain confusion about what is and is not legal.

Things are equally ambiguous in the world of drug-users—a much more public (not to say more respectable) world than would be found in North America. Take the pamphlet offered to tourists visiting Amsterdam. "Amsterdam is proud of its tolerance and freedom," it boasts, even as it warns, "Foreigners often think that everything is permitted here, even hard drugs. But the whole drug trade is illegal." Having acknowledged the legal situation, however, it concludes with some friendly advice: "So watch your step; check the quality; don't use drugs near where you scored; if you shoot, first get a clean needle; never shoot up alone." The publisher of this useful and instructive pamphlet is the municipal health department of the city of Amsterdam—and that says a great deal more about the practical state of affairs on the streets of Amsterdam than can be gleaned from the law books.

If the story of Holland's open cities sounds a little too good to be true, it is. Rudi lives on the dark side of this Dutch paradise. He is one of an estimated ten thousand junkies in Amsterdam, many of whom support their habit by theft and mugging. Rudi subsists on heroin—a technically illicit substance—and says he has survived by dealing dope and relying on the Dutch welfare system for the last twenty years. The Amsterdam City Council pays for a Junkies' Union where free needles can be obtained. Rudi's conversation with us is confused, seemingly thoughtful phrases thrown together with ramblings that add up to a kind of articulate non-sense. The manager of the Junkies' Union, Pieter, is not much more coherent, but his message is clear. "I think," he tells us, "that when you should live in a decent society where people could choose to live the life they want to live, I'm for free drugs." Does he mean a decent society is one where, if people want drugs, the law makes them legal and the state provides them gratis? Chief Inspector Okke Roosjen, who runs Amsterdam's Vice Squad, is more clear-headed. He urges us to remember that "the law is made in favour of people" and suggests that "you can help people . . . by concentrating a problem in one area." What he means is that allowing open sales of soft drugs lets the police keep an eye on the traffic—to stop it when it becomes troublesome, as it did at the Bulldog—and helps them monitor the hard-drug dealers, who tend to seek customers among the tourists attracted to the "grass bars". Despite the openness of the Junkies' Union, the Chief Inspector declares that the police do *not* tolerate hard drugs, and when we tell him how often we have been approached by cocaine dealers he replies with a knowing twinkle, "I hope you *get* cocaine, if you buy it!"

Well, perhaps every democracy gets the laws it deserves—or gets the kind of laws that reflect, more or less, what the voters want, whether very free, as in Holland, or very orderly and secure, as is perhaps the case in Toronto, where the police stop cars at random. Yet law is not only about balancing the rights of the state and community with the rights of the individual. It is also about justice.

From the time the human race was young, people have looked to constitutions and systems of law not only for rules and regulations but for fairness and justice. There may well have been just and democratic social arrangements in pre-literate societies, where customs and common laws were passed along orally—or even instinctively, through the fingertips, as it were. But since the advent of literacy every democracy that we know of has been based on written law. And that law has been more than a codification of rules and customs for common living: it has been an attempt to capture certain principles of fundamental justice.

Law and Democracy: The Birth of Twins in Ancient Athens

One of the world's first great dramas—the tragedy of the Oresteia by Aeschylus, written as Athens was emerging from kingship into democracy—is the story of a quest for justice. At the start of this trilogy of plays (which retells a story from Homer), Agamemnon has just returned home from the Trojan Wars. His wife, Clytemnestra, and her lover, Aegisthus (son of Agamemnon's blood enemy), murder Agamemnon to avenge a long line of blood debts. For justice is here still defined by the savagery of the vendetta: "An eye for an eye and a tooth for a tooth." But by the end of the drama, when Agamemnon's son, Orestes, is tried for avenging his father's death by slaying his mother, the foundation of justice has shifted. Though pursued by the vengeful Furies of the underworld, who wish to avenge the grisly matricide and extend the blood quarrel forward into eternity, Orestes is saved by Pallas Athena, goddess of a new justice recently come to Athens. Athena manages to move the trial to the city's new court on the hill of the Areopagus, where Orestes is found innocent and the Furies are placated by being made household gods of Athens. The past is finally laid to rest, the tradition of personal vengeance is ended, and the idea of justice as a tolerant and objective fairness is introduced to ancient Greece and to the world.

This splendid legend of the arrival of justice in Athens coincided with the establishment of democracy. The new justice was to be meted out by citizens chosen at random to serve in large, impartial juries—and all citizens would be equal in the eyes of the law (*isonomia*). No more Furies hounding the scions of cursèd families; no more special punishment for special victims; instead, each man the equal of every other, to be treated with dispassionate fairness. The new justice and the new democracy were one and the same thing. Law and democracy have not always existed in harmony, but they were initially united in the workings of the Athenian political system. The court which began up on the Areopagus was soon brought down to the agora, where the people were, and became no less crucial to their democratic life than the Assembly. Citizens served as diligently on juries as they did in the Assembly, and the law they interpreted and enforced in the courts was the law they themselves made in the Assembly.

The Athenians understood a long time ago what the English poet Dryden wrote on the threshold of our own modern era:

Laws are vain, by which we right enjoy,
If kings unquestion'd can those laws destroy.

No man or woman, no ruler, was above their law. Sometimes, however, their application of the laws seemed to clash with justice. The most famous confrontation between the two is also one of history's most notorious trials: that of Athens' brilliant philosopher Socrates in the anarchic period following the Peloponnesian Wars (see Chapter Two). Socrates, who taught unpopular and undemocratic ideas, was brought to trial by three of his adversaries of the democratic party, charged with not believing in the gods of the city, and with corrupting the young. These two crimes were among the few that carried the death penalty.

Socrates pleaded his own version of justice against the law of Athens, which he deemed unjust; but he was condemned to death by a small majority. Athens was not looking for a martyr, however; Socrates was offered the possibility of flight from the city, with officials promising to look the other way. Yet he insisted on dying under the laws of his native city, rather than living as an outlaw exiled from it.

Since the day Socrates drank the fatal hemlock, the story of his trial has been told mainly by philosophers, beginning with Socrates' pupil Plato. Plato, despising democracy, turned the trial into a symbol of the unruliness of mass opinion and the perils of mob rule—his definition of democracy. But Socrates himself was less scathing. Explaining his refusal to escape, he declared that his respect for the law reconciled him to what he thought was the wrongness of the jury's decision. In declining his friends' offer of exile, he asked them, "Do you imagine that a city can continue to exist and not be turned upside down, if the legal judgements which are pronounced in it have no force but are nullified and destroyed by private persons?" Whether he actually said this, or whether Plato invented it as part of the canonization of his revered teacher, nobody in ancient Athens ever enunciated more clearly the role law played in the city's democratic life.

Law Survives the Eclipse of Democracy

Although democracy gradually disappeared in the ancient world after the decline of Athens, the idea of *written* law—laws accessible to all—persisted. The Roman republic was governed by a mixed constitution in which the democratic element (the tribunes) was weak, but the rule of law was strong. And even under the five centuries of empire that followed the military conquests of Julius Caesar a half-century before the birth of Christ, law was the major instrument, along with its legions, by which Rome spread its influence throughout Europe. Where the people spoke tongues as strange as Allemanic, Frankish, and Celtic, where they lived by radically different customs, they still remained bound together by a skein of edicts emanating from Rome.

Caesar is reported to have said that "arms and laws do not flourish together" and, when forced to choose, he obviously preferred arms. But in fact the greatest legacy of the Romans was law.

In the early fifth century A.D., after the fall of Rome to the Visigoths, Emperor Justinian I ordered a systematic codification of the Roman laws that had developed over the preceding centuries. The result was the Corpus Juris Civilis, which would become the inspiration and model for the civil law codes of most of Europe's nations.

What made the Corpus so significant was not its particulars but the very idea of a code of rules universally applicable, a code under which each citizen was the equal of every other citizen. Through law, and the equality it suggested, a potent egalitarian seed was allowed to germinate through what was otherwise the thousand-year sleep of democracy.

If democracy was not to reappear in Europe until well after the Renaissance, it did come to life in a new and unexpected locale as early as A.D. 930. On a frigid island in the North Atlantic, a group of Viking people who had settled what they called Iceland gathered together and agreed to live under a common law. The three dozen or so tribes, each with its own chieftain, would meet annually, deliberate, and legislate all things of common concern. Their meeting became the Icelandic Althing, the grandmother of all parliaments. Within a few centuries—and long before any other European nation had anything resembling a parliament—Iceland's open-air Althing had grown into a two-week summer festival where goods were bought and sold (slaves too, in the beginning!), sagas were told and retold, trials were held, and an official called the Lawspeaker recited aloud the whole of the law of the commonwealth of Iceland—one third of the entire body of law each summer, in three-year cycles, until it was complete. Law was thus dramatically made the centre of the common existence of the Icelanders.

One of the early laws the Althing passed required that everyone be baptized as a Christian. But the water in the Thingvellir ("The Valley of the Assembly") was always near freezing, so they marched everybody forty miles to the hot springs. And hot springs are still an important democratic institution in Iceland. Each morning, in the great natural hot baths in downtown Reykjavik, politicians and teachers and plumbers and fishermen and housewives—all manner of men and women—meet in the water, where they can talk and talk and then talk some more. In a single hour, they like to say, they can solve all the problems of the world.

But Iceland's wondrous experiment in talking problems out was an exception; in the late Middle Ages, decisions—and laws—were for the most part still made by church and royal court. The debate over whether law embodied justice or was contrary to it that had begun with Socrates continued to agitate cardinals and kings alike. Was the law something men *discovered* through reason, like the natural laws of science, a product of God's will that men incorporated into their legal codes? Or was it something they *made*, a mere product of human will, "just" only because it was said to be so? The Pope and his college of cardinals claimed not to make law but only to interpret and apply God's laws. Monarchs likewise preferred to be thought of as vessels of God's law—carrying out the mandate of the divinity who had anointed them—rather than inventors of rules they contrived to suit their own less heavenly purposes.

When William of Normandy conquered England in 1066, he inherited a kingdom with a developed notion of law—thanks in part to the earlier reforms of the Anglo-Saxon king Alfred the Great, who had insisted Latin law codes be translated into English, and who had introduced a complex court system that incorporated German tribal ideas. Law requires common standards and consistent application that guarantee subjects a predictable legal environment. William saw that both would be reinforced by administrative centralization. Hence, he built a huge new fort in London from which he could administer justice for his whole realm. He also compiled the Domesday Book, a remarkable survey and census making possible a system of national taxation.

Trial by battle, which may be the forerunner of the adversary system which dominates modern English-based trial law, was another of William's innovations. When in a modern courtroom one side wins and one loses— in a legal battle where the judge is more an umpire than a wise arbiter—it is William's trial by battle that is the model. How antagonistic this adversary approach is compared to the French system (based on Roman law) of a jury of impartial judges asking questions, directing investigations, and actively seeking the truth!

The idea of law was clearly strong enough in medieval England to compel the monarch to govern with the consent of the most powerful of his subjects, to whom he was bound by the same feudal contract that made them his vassals. In 1215 the weak King John, aspiring to despotism, was forced by his rebellious barons to put his seal on the Magna Carta. Almost eight hundred years later, this parchment remains the single most significant legal document in the history of the West, above all in England and North America. Magna Carta was hardly a fully democratic document, but it did specify limits to royal power, and in doing so illustrated the role law would play in defining the limits of government henceforward. Until Magna Carta, English monarchs made the law and were the law—above it, beside it, indistinguishable from it. After Magna Carta, they were subject to it. The twin seedlings of democracy—the access of all to law-making, and the subjugation of all, monarch and commoner alike, to the law— were thus reborn in England's medieval kingdom, centuries before full democracy was to arrive.

The ink was hardly dry on Magna Carta when the dispute over who was finally sovereign, who had the right to make the laws of England, was rekindled. Monarchs like Henry VIII felt free to set aside its conditions whenever they chose. And by the seventeenth century the fight for political and religious freedom had plunged England into its greatest crisis since the Norman invasion. The country was racked by episodic civil war, families were split by royalist or Puritan Commonwealth sympathies, Catholics and Protestants made bloody war on one another, a king was actually tried by Parliament and beheaded. So cruel were these times that the great political philosopher of the civil war period (1635–60), Thomas Hobbes, seemed to be portraying not only the "state of nature" but his own anarchic England when in his *Leviathan* he described how men lived in a state of "war of everyone against everyone", a state where force and fraud were the cardinal virtues, where life was "solitary, poor, nasty, brutish and short."

Parliament was controlled largely by the gentry (wealthy landowners), and despite the efforts of radical democrats like those early egalitarians who called themselves "Levellers" (some even argued for a degree of women's suffrage), there was never any real question of universal suffrage. But the new Protestant rulers, William and Mary—brought in from The

Netherlands after the last of the Catholic Stuarts, James II, was deposed in 1688—were to govern on terms laid down by Parliament, which became the supreme legislator of the land. The victory of the parliamentary forces was a victory for the anti-Catholics but it was above all a victory for the rule of law, if not yet for democracy.

This whole upheaval had lasted more than fifty years. The final victory is still called the Glorious Revolution, and it resolved the costly quarrel over who would act as the sovereign author of Britain's laws, but it did not resolve the more ancient quarrel between law and justice—between law as the voice of the sovereign (positive law), and law as the voice of nature and God, protecting individuals and their rights against that power (natural and divine law). For now that the English sovereign was the Parliament, it made positive law with even greater assurance than the kings. Speaking now directly for "the people", it was in a position to override both natural law and the rights of individuals protected by natural law—so that, ironically, a democratized law maker became potentially a greater threat to individual liberty than kings had been.

Like many seventeenth-century political writers, Hobbes had grown tired of the tyranny of monarchs rooting their authority in natural or divine sanction, and had argued that law was something made exclusively by men: there could be no justice, no morals, no propriety, but that which was willed by the sovereign—whether that sovereign was a king or a parliament. John Locke, Hobbes' great philosophical successor, who had written on behalf of the reforms of the Glorious Revolution, worried that Hobbes' idea of pure positive law—justice made by men alone, unconstrained by reason, nature, or God—could endanger liberty and property. Hobbes, he said, employed a sovereign lion to keep the polecats and foxes from destroying one another; but who was to protect them from the lion? Locke preferred to think of Parliament as a *trustee* of the rights and liberties of individuals—such rights as "life, liberty, and estate"—and insisted it did not possess the right to legislate these rights away, even in the name of the common good or the common law. In sum, Hobbes argued for a powerful sovereign whose legitimacy derived entirely from popular consent (the Social Contract), while Locke argued for a government that was itself constrained by the rights of individuals. But they both shared in the new idea that the legitimacy of any government depended on consent.

In the meantime the gentry and the common people alike continued to be told, and for the most part to believe, that God's law demanded allegiance to the monarch, and that everyone's place in life had been deter-mined from on high. They were told this by the Anglican clergy, who con-tinued to play a powerful role in British political life, and indeed do so today. (The bishops are still appointed on the advice of the government.)

But despite this—slowly, agonizingly—man-made law and democracy were beginning to make some headway in this class-ridden and still defer-ential society.

In the victory of Parliament over the king, law had served democracy by placing the law-making function in the hands of the people's represen-tatives. The next requirement was to give all men and women the vote, something that would happen over the next two and a half centuries.

Yet at the same time law continued to mean the laws of nature which protected the rights of individuals to liberty and property against every encroachment—whether from other individuals or from the state, even the democratic state. So the tension between law as a protector of indi-viduals *against* the state and law as a vehicle *through which* the state estab-lishes community justice remains. And while this tension between positive law (as the will of the people through their elected Parliament) and natural law (as the rights of the people by nature) may seem a meta-physical matter in the quarrels of theorists like Hobbes and Locke, in America, where the sealing of Magna Carta is depicted on the bronze doors of the Supreme Court, the conflict became a practical matter of revolutionary significance.

Law As Right versus Law As Popular Will: The American Story

From the outset in 1775, when dairy farmers from Lexington, Massachusetts and plantation owners from Williamsburg, Virginia, and commercial bankers from New York declared themselves fed up with George III's long train of abuses and together seized their independence, America's founders were driven by two conflicting needs: to free them-selves from the grip of tyranny, colonial or domestic, and so preserve their property and their private liberties; *and* to govern themselves through common laws that expressed their common needs. "Give me lib-erty or give me death!" cried politician Patrick Henry, voicing the American impulse towards law understood as the protector of private lib-erty. "No taxation without representation!" cried the citizens of Boston, voicing the American impulse towards law understood as the vehicle of collective self-government.

To achieve both private liberty and collective self-government, the Americans had to make a number of compromises. To govern themselves autonomously and lawfully, they eventually fashioned a federal constitution that delegated powers to a powerful central government. But to protect themselves from abuse by every tyranny, including the potential tyranny of the government they had just created, they devised a set of lawful constraints on government—dividing its power into three co-equal branches (executive, legislative, and judicial) and erecting a towering legal wall around it which they called the Bill of Rights.

The Bill of Rights was passed in the wake of the Constitution's ratification (1789–91), and prohibited the government from abridging freedom of speech, religion, and assembly; from establishing a state religion; and from imposing excessive fines or cruel and unusual punishments. Perhaps most important of all, it specified that the new federal government had only those powers specifically delegated to it, and that all others were reserved to the states and the people.

Here law was divided against itself: the people's right as a body to make law, confronting the people's rights as individuals to be protected from abuse by the laws. The story of American politics since 1789 has been the story of the tensions between these two functions of the law. Fortunately, the conflict has had an arbiter—to some extent self-appointed, but useful all the same: the Supreme Court. It has become the final interpreter of the Constitution—the judge in clashes between the law as embodied in Congress and the presidency, and the law as embodied in the Bill of Rights.

Constitutional law may seem a dry subject, but in the dusty pages of its history can be found some of the bloodiest episodes in America's struggle to become democratic—through the law, and against it. In the previous chapter we traced the great struggle for civil rights that began in 1954, when the Supreme Court overturned the 1896 decision that had permitted "separate but equal" educational facilities in the South. The court's decision in *Brown* v. *Topeka Board of Education* opened the doors of an all-white school to a little black girl named Linda Brown, but it also set off a twenty-year civil rights struggle that would eventually transfigure the face of America. Jack Greenberg, the young Columbia Law School lawyer who argued Linda's case in court, recalls, "Well, we thought we'd win the case. . . . But we had no sense that [it] would precipitate the civil rights revolution that resulted in integration of virtually all of the institutions in the United States—that *Brown* itself would not only be a legal decision but a great moral catalyst."

Here was the Supreme Court speaking the language of higher law, holding Linda Brown's natural rights as a human being above a set of segregationist laws that had been duly made by elected representatives of the American people in several states. Here was higher law saying that the people's law was defective. Here was the liberty of one little girl being valued more highly than the legitimate legal voice of her community's large white majority.

What makes America's dual law system exceptional is that it often elicits the reluctant respect of the majority, whose will it thwarts. Bobby Garroway, the white ex-mayor of Poplarville, Mississippi, where the last classic lynching (with the connivance of the jailer and the tacit approval of many of the townspeople) of a black man in America took place in 1959, remembers how he changed in this violent era. "I think most Southerners did. I was originally a segregationist. As events started unfolding, I started thinking. Number one, I was an American. I had gone to Korea in the Korean conflict. And then the rightness of things that are involved: I didn't like to see people taking law into their own hands. . . . We had to be ruled by law, and I believe in the system, I believe in democracy. So I had to come around, change my views."

What this thoughtful American was saying was that taking the law into your own hands—as good a definition of democracy as we have!—must be curtailed if we are to live under the rule of law. That for him democracy does not mean people doing whatever they want, using the law to legislate their prejudices, but doing what is lawful. Doing what comports with the Bill of Rights and the Constitution. Yet if Americans can be judicious in permitting the courts to restrain democracy, they also insist on being democratic about their judges, who in a number of American states are elected to office and must engage in electoral politics. Thus democracy is subjected to the law, but the law is also subjected to democracy. A delicate balance, but one which can protect people from the tyranny of the majority without paralysing their capacity to enact common laws.

If this tension runs deep in America's history, it runs even deeper in the history of international law—where individuals are exposed to the whims of sovereign nations with all of their collective powers and are left to defend their freedom abetted only by abstract universal justice and the rhetoric of human rights. Occasionally it has been otherwise, usually when the power of a conqueror in war is put in the scales on the side of international justice. Then, for a moment, the scales balance.

Nuremberg: National Law versus International Justice

If law in a democracy is merely the codification of the will of the majority, then there is nothing the law cannot be made to do. Anything that is possible can be made legal by the legislative enactments of an elected parliament: the confiscation of property, the abrogation of freedom, the sterilization of paupers, discrimination, expropriation, and even genocide.

The National Socialists (Nazis) came to power—quite democratically—in 1933. In 1935 they passed the infamous Nuremberg Laws—legalized by Parliament and the courts, and approved by the Catholic hierarchy—for "the protection of German blood and honour". The laws—aimed at "impure races", above all the Jews—stripped innocent civilians of the right to education and property, then to citizenship, and eventually became a legalistic smokescreen behind which a campaign of genocide could be launched.

Arno Hamburger was a teenager living in Germany when the laws were passed. He remembers the increasing vulnerability of the Jewish community as the law systematically took away their rights. In November 1938, just before he fled Germany, he witnessed the mob violence of *Kristallnacht*, that nightmarish orgy of hatred in which black-shirted thugs smashed and burned Jewish property throughout the country, beyond the compass of any laws. "Of course I remember Crystal Night. I was fifteen at the time. I had a cousin born [two months before]. They had to carry the baby from room to room while the SS smashed everything in the flat. There wasn't a cup or a spoon or a plate left in the morning." In the years before Crystal Night, however, the thugs wore judicial robes emblazoned with swastikas (Hitler had required they be worn by all judges) and injustice found sanctuary in the law itself. Without justice, the law can be more monstrous than no law at all. By legally excluding Jews and other unwanted people, Germans had persuaded themselves that these fellow Germans were, in strictly legal terms, a race of outlaws—fair game for plunder, violation, and, in time, slaughter.

The Nazi legislation that paved the way for the Holocaust was an unprecedented example of law-making run amok, with no respect for per-

Germans from East and West stand on the Berlin Wall in front of the Brandenburg Gate in November 1989, one day after the wall opened. The euphoria of the unlikely peaceful revolution of 1989 has long ago given way to the culture shock of 16 million Germans trying to create a new identity in a nation where every sphere of influence, the media, politics and the economy, is controlled by westerners. A half-century of isolation and authoritarianism had produced several generations with no experience of the kinds of personal responsibility and tolerance that a free society requires if it is to function peaceably.

(AP Photo/Visar Kryeziu)

Chief U.N. war crimes prosector Louise Arbour, on a two-day trip to Kosovo inspects sites of suspected war crimes. Once the totalitarian powers were lifted in the former Yugoslavia and the former Soviet Union, ancient Eastern European tribal enmities flared up. They had been suppressed for decades by dictatorship. These people had not lived the long, patience-demanding deliberation and discussion that democracies require if tribal exclusiveness is to be replaced by the inclusive civility of the greater community.

(CP Photo/Ryan Remiorz)

Ethnic Albanians look for friends and family across the barbed wire at the NATO refugee camp in Brazda, Macedonia, April 1999. Where centuries of ethnic and tribal dispute have been held in check by despotic governments, it is to be expected that they will ignite when the despotism is lifted, unless there is a long and careful period of deliberation and public education to help people learn the difficult lessons of living civilly with tribal differences.

(AP Photo)

In a sign of the persistence of ethnic nationalism in some of the world's largest democracies, the Hindu nationalist Bharatiya Janata Party has developed the Congress Party, now India's governing party. In this photo, women protest against the BJP outside their office in New Delhi on September 2, 1999. The women were enraged at a comment from a BJP leader who said, while referring to Congress party leader Sonia Gandhi, that widows amongst Hindus are often termed as a bad omen and voting for her would ruin the country. After the comment, India's Chief Election Commissioner appealed for an end to unseemly smear campaigns against candidates in elections.

(AP Photo / Zia Mazar)

Even as most of the world opts for more democracy, some nations continue to opt out using old "People's Republic"-style propoganda to justify their cynicism. Here, not long after the military coup in Pakistan led by Musharraf (October 17, 1999), children in Karachi hold a poem honoring him.

The Internet links everyone, supporters of modernity and their opponents alike. The new technology can serve old customs and ancient religions. Here, two women staffers at AwalNet for Ladies, Saudi Arabia's only women-only Internet Service Provider, search the Internet in Riyadh, July 24, 1999.

Ten years after the Gulf War, Kuwait is still not truly democratic. Here, Kuwaiti women gather in the gallery of the National Assembly in Kuwait City, November 30, 1999, where delegates rejected by 32 votes to 30, a new law granting them political rights.

Burundi Tutsi children (above) who survived the massacre on July 20, 1998 at Bugendana camp, 45 miles northeast of the capital, Bujumbura, walk alongside the layered bodies. Their mother was among 300 people, mainly women and children, killed during the attack by alleged Hutu rebels. Ethnic violence has wracked the tiny central Africa nation since October 1993, when the country's first democratically elected Hutu president was killed by Tutsi paratroopers. Skulls (below) lie on display at the Ntarama Genocide Memorial. The memorial occupies a former Catholic Church which lies 28 km (17 miles) south of Kigali, Rwanda. About 5,500 people were killed here during the April 1994 genocide after seeking refuge in the church. The rapid achievement of democratic electoral structures, before the culture has had time to experiment with and develop its own forms of civil interaction, respect for individuals, tolerance, and the legitimation of deliberation as a tool of conflict resolution (instead of force) is not a promising scenario.

(CP Photo/Moe Doiron)

Child activist Craig Kielburger (left) speaks to Ottawa Citizen reporter during an interview at his home. Kielburger had recently returned from a fact-finding mission to bring light to the problem of child labor in Asia. On the other side of the world, young people—when not victims of death squads—may be enlisted as unwitting warriors. On the right, 12-year-old twin brothers Johnny and Luther Htoo (with cigar) during a meeting with The Associated Press at their jungle base, Ka Mar Pa Law, in Myanmar, 95 kilometers (59 miles) west of Bangkok. Fighters in the area have rallied behind the brothers because they believe the young boys offer divine protection. The brothers are leaders of a jungle children's crusade that blends elements of the Old Testament with the "Lord of the Flies."

(AP Photo/Brennan Linsley)

A young Congolese rebel shares a cigarette with a fellow "soldier" in Goma, in the eastern Democratic Republic of Congo, near Rwanda and Uganda. A long way from democracy, these ongoing tribal and military conflicts are often fuelled by an arms trade that enriches functioning democracies and are often fought by and against children.

Despite the promising democratic dawn of May 30, 1989, when the Goddess of Democracy (left) was paraded through the streets of Beijing, the demonstration ended in violence and the end of the democratic movement. The bodies of dead civilians (right) lie among mangled bicycles near Beijing's Tiananmen Square early on June 4, 1989. Tanks and soldiers stormed the area overnight, bringing a violent end to student demonstrations for democratic reform. Irrespective of how they viewed the protests' calls for democracy, many Chinese in Beijing resented the military attack on unarmed students. But the vast majority of Chinese, pleased with their new prosperity, are more interested in stability than in reform and would never have supported the students.

A Chinese man looks at Internet links on a computer at a café in Beijing in February 1996. Since the government started allowing commercial Internet accounts in the spring of 1995, the number of Internet users in China has grown from a few thousand in the universities to 100,000. This kind of contact with the rest of the world, and its concomitant liberty of investigation and communication, will more radically change the political and social face of China than any traditional group of reformers could hope to do.

The new world of emerging democracy is still afflicted with the ethnic and nationalistic rivalries of the last century. Russia's new President Vladimir Putin rode to power on a wave of Russian nationalism kindled by the war against seccessionist Chechnya. Chechan capital Grozny lies in ruins today, but the war continues.

Despite eloquent popular expression from the people of Northern Ireland who declare in growing numbers that the old tribal divisions are obsolete, the entrenched power of the opposing Republican and Unionist forces continue to hold peace and democracy hostage. In this photo, Sinn Fein leader Gerry Adams, right, addresses the media at the Parliament Buildings in Stormont Castle in Belfast, Northern Ireland, in February 2000 after British Secretary for Northern Ireland Peter Mandelson suspended the province's Protestant-Catholic government. Britain stripped the provisional government of its powers in a bid to prevent its collapse over the Irish Republican Army's refusal to disarm.

Here, two world leaders apparently playing a role dictated not by their electorate, but by an emerging technology. President Clinton (left) watches his computer screen for questions posed to him over the Internet during a town-hall chat held on the campus of the George Washington University, on November 8, 1999. Only a few months earlier, Russian President (right), Boris Yeltsin (since suceeded by Vladamir Putin) also made his Internet debut, answering questions from around the world from his Kremlin office on May 12, 1998. Yeltsin spoke about a variety of issues from nuclear arms, to which foreign leaders he likes and what he thinks about smoking.

A sick man sits on the floor of a room he shares in Democracy City in Port-au-Prince, Haiti. The return of a modicum of democracy to Haiti has not improved life and it has left many Haitians feeling hopeless. Once again, the world learns the tough lesson that democratic electoral instruments do not work well in a culture not prepared for them.

In the 1980s, Africa was a promising home for democratic development. But, globalization, AIDS, and tribal war stalled many of those efforts and left much of the continent on the margins. In the recent election held in Nigeria, a former General, Olusegun Obasanjo, was elected in a long-awaited transition from military rule. Promising that "we shall not fail," Obasanjo became Nigeria's first civilian president in 15 years, ending a string of disastrous military regimes that crippled this African giant. Nigeria's deeply entrenched traditions of corruption as a normal way of life for government officials, combined with profound tribal differences, have been a powerful obstacle to a democratic civil society.

Anti-foreign sentiment in the most "advanced" democracies has slowed the pace of globalization and created new worries about European democracy. Here, demonstrators march past the natural history museum on the way to the Heldenplatz in front of Vienna's Hofburg Palace, February 19, 2000. An estimated 150,000 people gathered on the historic plaza to protest the new Austrian coalition government between Joerg Haider's right-wing Freedom Party and the conservative People's Party.

Supporters of Ayatollah Ali Khamenei, Iran's supreme leader, carry the Iranian flag and pictures of Khamenei during a rally in Tehran on July 14, 1999. Hard-line Iranian clerics mobilized tens of thousands of supporters at the rally to counter six days of pro-democracy demonstrations and unrest on a scale unseen in Iran in two decades. But the growing popular support for democratic reforms seems to be making headway against the fundamentalist resistance of the orthodox leadership.

In a sign of an emerging global public opinion, Chilean dictator Augusto Pinochet was detained in England on a Spanish indictment of his alleged crimes. Returning to Chile (too ill to be tried) he was met by thousands of well-wishers, but also huge crowds who wanted an end to the violence he used to bring prosperity.

Political parties across the democratic world routinely campaign on the Internet, often raising significant funds, as John McCain did. Here, U.S. democratic presidential candidate Vice President Al Gore responds to a question received via the Internet during a debate with opponent Bill Bradley at the Los Angeles Times in Los Angeles, March 1, 2000.

Despite the rapid commercialization of the Internet, electronic democrats continue to fight for the dream of a global civic space in which a virtual community is realized. Robert Johnston is using the Internet to form a Constitutional Action Network. Johnston says "It's about all of us—who we are, where we are going and what kind of nation we are going to be."

Native loggers from Big Cove take a break after logging near Minto, N.B., in October 1999. The natives cut logs on Crown land in defiance of provincial law as they exercise their treaty rights. The old myths of aboriginal "harmony with nature" can seem a little doubtful when economic issues and tribal rights are at stake. How should environmentalists and democrats act to reconcile the conflicting—and probably legitimate—rights and interests?

sonal liberties or social justice. But, in one of history's more astounding ironies, this law without justice was finally righted by justice without law—in the very city where the Nazis had first legalized the campaign of genocide: Nuremberg. Following the defeat of Nazi Germany, a few survivors among the vanquished were put on trial there by the victors. Germans found themselves being tried for complying with the very laws that their government had made in Nuremberg a decade earlier. But there was no legal precedent for trying the law of the land, however evil that law might be, and the Allied prosecutors had to rely on the idea of a higher law, of the natural right of women and men not to be abused by their government. The trials proceeded, and resulted in a number of death sentences.

Lord Elwyn Jones, former Lord Chancellor of Britain, was a junior prosecutor on the British team at Nuremberg. He reflects on the momentous change this created: "Before Nuremberg, the doctrine and approach of international law was that the way in which a government treated its own people was entirely a matter for the sovereign decisions of that sovereign state. After the war and the creation of an international code of human rights [in 1948], the position of the individual human being was transformed as a matter of law from being a mere object of compassion to being a subject of *rights*."

The new post-war United Nations enacted a Declaration of Human Rights and under Article 92 of its charter established an International Court of Justice. Much as the American Supreme Court has policed the American people in the name of liberty and justice, so the new international court was to police the states of the world, arbitrating disputes among them, but also protecting individuals against them.

The limits of justice are still, however, the limits of power. The punishment meted out to the Nazis at Nuremberg was as much a product of the military power of the victorious Allies as of their spirit of justice; and the International Court has no army, no police, no executive to fall back on for enforcement of its decisions. When Stalin was warned in the 1930s about provoking the moral censure of the Vatican, he is said to have responded, "And how many divisions does His Holiness have?" The International Court cannot raise even a brigade, and in fact the record of compliance to its decisions has not been good. A number of nations have thwarted its will, and many have questioned its jurisdiction: among these recalcitrant parties are France, Iceland, and the United States—three of our chief examples of democratic political life.

Citizens VII

AN EASY WAY TO DISTINGUISH DEMOCRACY FROM other forms of government is to look for *citizens*. The citizen is not a mere subject—nothing more than an obedient servant of a monarch—nor the passive client of government bureaucracies that service the people, although we often take the citizen to be little more than this. The true citizen is an active participant in politics, someone engaged in self-government.

We had an opportunity to confront the differing experiences of citizenship people can have when we attended a Hindu wedding in Toronto. It offered a provocative start for this part of our story.

An Indian Wedding—a Canadian Contract

The groom, Dipek, is a young Canadian citizen of Indian descent; the bride, Rainu, has come from India for the ceremony. She brings to him a sum of cash, a dowry that in India would have been a crucial condition of the marriage (although both in Canada and, since 1961, in India dowries are not legal). He brings to her the possibility of Canadian citizenship, and perhaps an identity as a wife more consistent with modern ideas of what it means to be a free person. For this is a traditional Indian wedding but it is also a modern Canadian civil contract. And while Canadian women are still fighting to make good on formal rights won some time ago, they are much better off politically than their counterparts in India.

The two people about to be joined in this ritual ceremony bridge two worlds. Each is a "citizen" of a large democracy, but for each citizenship has a radically different meaning. For Dipek, to be a citizen of the world's largest democracy (by landmass) is to enjoy all of the formal political and civil rights of one of the Western world's freest governments. For Rainu, to be a citizen of the world's most populous democracy still means being subject to traditional Hindu customs that define women as property to be owned and negotiated—and leave them vulnerable to terrible revenge if their husbands are not content with the bargain. We watch as Rainu—a shining presence in her glittering wedding sari—makes a gesture of treading on an imaginary millstone symbolizing fidelity; she is urged to be no less faithful to her new husband. As the complex rituals are completed, man and woman become one; but how they will reconcile their two worlds of citizenship remains to be seen.

Democracy means citizens governing themselves. But citizens are not simply private persons wearing political coats. One elementary measure of democracy is whether a people have a lively sense of themselves as citizens: as members of a body politic rather than just as self-interested individuals—as men and women capable of expressing public judgement rather than just voicing private needs and wants.

There is a tendency in many democracies to measure citizenship by how many people vote, and how often, as if a citizen and a voter were the same thing. From the experience of Athens and perhaps from America in its earlier days we have learned that voting may represent only one facet of citizenship, and not necessarily the most significant facet. The mere voter votes and then goes home and leaves the elected governors to govern. The active citizen, on the other hand, actually governs—or participates in governing. In small countries like Iceland and Switzerland, a great deal of participation may be possible. In larger countries like India and Canada, this is very difficult, although not perhaps impossible (see Chapter Ten). But without participation democracy may become corrupt, and deteriorate into a kind of elected oligarchy.

Yet one crucial struggle for democracy has been to extend the franchise, to include as citizens more and more of the total population first an elite group of men, usually propertied, drawn from a specific ethnic or religious group; then all men of that race or religion; then all men, regardless of race and religion; and in time all men and women of the territory:

universal suffrage. The great victories of democracy are often associated with crucial extensions of the franchise: England's notable Reform Bill of 1832 extending suffrage to a large group of qualified property holders, or America's Fourteenth and Fifteenth Amendments, bestowing citizenship and voting rights on blacks.

Yet, though the franchise bestows voting rights, it does not necessarily create full citizens, and so it is not a reliable yardstick for democracy. Few of Athens' many inhabitants were citizens, but those who were citizens engaged in a great many public activities. Indeed, for them citizenship was nearly a full-time occupation. But history suggests that as more and more people became citizens, citizenship came to mean less and less. The Romans made citizens of *all* their adult male subjects, but the citizen had few rights to distinguish him from the subject. Today, in many democracies, suffrage is pretty much universal among adults, but the vote is only a small component of citizenship—a necessary protection, but not a very productive tool. Women in these societies are thus in a peculiar position: last in through the door of the polling booth, they seize on the prize only to find that it has been depreciated and retains little of the worth that once attached to it.

These contradictions were on our minds as we travelled to India, to Switzerland, to Iceland, and finally back to Canada in search of the true meaning of citizenship in a democracy: we were careful to keep asking ourselves not only *who* the citizens were, but what it *meant* to be a citizen. Frequently we discovered that women were not only at the forefront of the struggle to extend the franchise, but also striving to improve the quality of citizenship, by increasing the participation of citizens in public decision-making. And so our exploration of citizenship turned out also to be an exploration of the special and poignant civic problems of women—half the human species, but citizens only in the last hundred years.

We began our investigation in Rainu's homeland, India.

There are 770 million people in what the Indians like to call the world's largest democracy. But is this the same thing as 770 million citizens? India has had the formal institutions of democracy—universal suffrage, political parties, elections, courts of law, rights, and a great many enthusiastic voters—ever since it gained independence from the British empire in 1947. But is there a civic culture of engaged citizens who know how to use and benefit from the formal apparatus of democracy? Do these hundreds of millions of men and women really govern themselves in any significant sense?

As they move towards a more democratic society, Indians are held back by the traditions and customs of their past. Centuries of royal rule and separation by caste and class have kept them divided and antagonistic, and made the idea of Indian citizenship even more elusive than the idea of Indian nationality. Modern India was born in partition—the hostile Moslem and Hindu populations that had been combined in Britain's Indian empire were divided into the warring states of Pakistan and India under the provisions of the Indian Independence Act. Even so, India has remained fractured along religious and ethnic lines. Eleven per cent of the country is still Moslem, and there are over 1,500 different languages and dialects. These divisions, along with the deference born of a long tutelage to traditional princely rule and to British colonial overlords, as well as the legacy of ritual and custom that has defied modernity's equalizing thrust, all work against the practice of true democracy. Moreover, the caste system is fundamentally anti-democratic, and the Hindu idea of acceptance can translate in the political domain as resignation and complacency in the face of injustice. The traditional subordination of women to men and the male-dominated family create particular difficulties.

Many of these contradictions are apparent in Gayatri Devi, the Maharanee of Jaipur, an aristocratic oddity in a culture striving for democracy, a princess turned politician who talked with us on a parched Indian day as she showed us through her late husband's palace—which she and her family now run as a luxury hotel, complete with elephants and snake charmers. Devi is a member of one of the richest of the old royal families through whom the British once ruled India, and by most accounts remains a benevolent figure among "her people". She made the transition from traditional to democratic rule with disarming ease, as did, initially, hundreds of millions of Indians. The Maharanee herself actually ran for office in 1962 as a member of the opposition Swatantra Party, and, with huge electoral margins, served a total of thirteen years. Following the internal crises of the mid-seventies, when India's democratic politics veered towards self-destruction and Indira Gandhi attacked her politically, Devi lost her post and ended up in jail for five months.

Here, then, is an aristocrat who ran for democratic office, won often, served her people well, and endured political imprisonment. Is she to be counted as a committed democrat? A good citizen? Some of those who elected her still regard her as their princely ruler rather than their elected representative; while she cheerfully mixed with the crowds in the streets of Jaipur to question people on our behalf, it took only the merest gesture of authority to keep them from crushing her sari. Nor do her constituents act much like real citizens—other than during elections. Pressure groups, local party organizations, and voluntary associations of the kind once celebrated by de Tocqueville as the foundation of a vigorous democratic culture are not a large component here. It is hard to tell how deep the Maharanee's democratic instincts go. "I don't believe in dictatorship," she tells us carefully, "but on the other hand, there is no sense of discipline left in the citizens of India. Just look at the streets, look at Jaipur . . . the sweepers go on strike, they're not happy, and then people don't care where they park their cars, and every little thing's litigation. . . ."

It would not be surprising to learn that a great many Indians admit they "don't believe in dictatorship, *but*. . . ." There is in this vast and fractious state an overwhelming sense of the need for order and discipline. Although the economy is mixed, it shows little tolerance for the anarchic freedom of real market relations, and it leans towards socialist paternalism—with aviation, railroads, armaments, and atomic energy exclusively in public hands, and with the state dominating oil, iron, and steel production as well as shipping, mining, banking, and foreign trade. There is a tension between the need to modernize the country, which takes discipline and strong, centralized leadership, and the need to create an active citizenry, which would mean a less efficient, more decentralized administration of the kind that Mahatma Gandhi sought. There is a tension between the need to overcome the traditions and rituals that tie women to subordinate roles and the need to use tradition and ritual to hold together an otherwise unruly, perhaps even ungovernable, society. India has not yet discovered how it can govern itself both efficiently and democratically.

Not every Indian tradition obstructs democracy, however. In the countryside there are very old village institutions that help to nourish India's young civic life. Like villagers in old Russia and new Botswana and traditional Norway and nineteenth-century New England, hundreds of millions of Indians have long first-hand acquaintance with small-scale direct democracy at the village level. The panchayat or traditional village council—the word means "five men"—permits direct participation in decision-making, and holds the promise of giving national citizenship a significant local base.

Gandhi believed these village institutions might be schools of democracy for all of India.

In Tikri Brahim village in north-central India, we watch a panchayat informally try the case of a man whose pigs had rooted their way through a neighbour's land, doing both the land and the neighbour's patience considerable damage. The neighbour is asking for 500 rupees. The elders do most of the talking, while the men of the village seated around them listen intently, occasionally remonstrating with the protagonists or throwing out a pithy piece of advice. The mood is more consensual than adversarial, with the accused being asked if he agrees to the procedure. The good of the whole village seems to be the common stake, and the point is to do what is just rather than to arbitrate grievances or to divide up a pie.

"Our panchayat is going to think about how it can do justice," announces an elder, prominent in his green waistcoat. "We must go to the fields to see how much damage there was!" shouts someone seated well behind the circle of squatting villagers. "If the victim tells the truth we can do justice here and now," says another. And when a fine is announced, a sympathetic voice suggests, "It's not fair on that poor man to fine him so much!" Someone else agrees: "Four pigs can't do that much damage, so don't blame him so much." There is participation and there is deference; there is difference of opinion; but at the end there is consensus. The elders ultimately issue the ruling—the pigs' owner must post a hundred-rupee bond—but everyone has been consulted, not least of all the plaintiff and the accused.

This age-old village system is an example of the seemingly irrepressible tendency of the democratic urge to burst out in small communities all over the world and throughout history. It has given Indian villagers a tradition of self-government, and many see the panchayat as an underpinning of the steady growth of effective citizen-involved democracy. But the all-male panchayat could be an appropriate target for Indian women as they continue their collective assault on cultural barriers to full citizenship.

Historically women have often been regarded as chattels, and in many countries traces of this attitude still exist. But it persists in India in a particularly horrific form: a man's family expects to be paid for accepting a bride; if the groom and his family later decide that they have received a bad bargain, they sometimes burn the woman alive. In 1975—International Women's Year—350 women were burned to death in Delhi alone. Usually such cases are treated as "accidents", and if they do provoke police investigations there is rarely a successful prosecution. It is as if Salem-style witch burnings still took place twice a week in the pleasant suburbs of Washington, D.C.

There is today a militant anti-dowry movement that testifies to the cynicism many Indian women must feel at having secured the right to vote, while their husbands can still get away with burning them alive. For India has acquired the rewards of the franchise. But until full citizenship becomes a reality for Indians of both sexes and of every caste, democracy, though written into the Constitution, will remain some distance from the street.

The Citizen-Soldier: Democrat or Misogynist?

Halfway round the world, the mountainous little nation of Switzerland lies at the crossroads of Europe. A hundred times less populous than India, it is remarkably heterogeneous in its religious and national make-up, with four national language groups (German, French, Italian, and Romansh) that are in turn divided into Protestants and Catholics. It too is a federal state, divided into twenty cantons and six half-cantons that are remarkably autonomous in their identity and political prerogatives. Yet it is weighed down with democratic customs which, while they once enriched participation, now create inefficiencies incompatible with modern life. The central fact of Switzerland's democratic history is the concept of the citizen as a soldier and a patriot—the voter as a warrior signalling his political assent with a spear or a sword. Yet this idealized tradition is an embarrassment to Switzerland's democratic present. For the vivid image that once gave Swiss citizens a powerful sense of fraternity and patriotism has come in this century to obstruct the campaign of women to acquire full citizenship—a campaign that bore fruit only in 1972, long after women everywhere else in the West had won the vote.

Yet though full citizenship came to women very late in Swiss history, its significance is greater and its responsibilities are more demanding than in many of the surrounding nations. We noticed that, in India, citizens are often little more than voting subjects of an elective oligarchy over which they have little real influence, while in the West, individuals generally face their governments more as clients or customers of services than as engaged participants in collective self-government. To vote for the governors every few years is not the same as self-government, any more than hiring professional soldiers to defend a nation constitutes national self-defence. But the Swiss have been both governing themselves directly and defending themselves directly for nearly seven hundred years.

Although much of Switzerland is flat, and the majority of Swiss live in large towns and cities like Zurich, Geneva, Basel, Lausanne, and the capital, Bern, this sturdy nation of six million has been defined by its mountains: the villages that dot them, the customs they nurture, and their traditions of direct democracy, which could teach the world a good deal about democracy—if the world would look beyond the clichés of perforated cheese, bucolic bird clocks, and rustic watchmakers.

Nothing better captures the ideal of Swiss citizenship than the mountain-bred citizen-soldier. From earliest times, Switzerland's long, hard winters left Alpine herdsmen with little to do six months a year other than soldier for pay in countries more dedicated to war. Selling their services to neighbours like France, Austria, and Italy (where the Pope was in need of legions his clerics could not provide), Swiss men became Europe's surrogate soldiers, tough mercenaries on whom new nations struggling for survival depended for their security and expansion. It was a good bargain for both sides, but ultimately a costly one for the Swiss. "The road from Basel to Paris is paved with gold!" the kings on the Ile de France liked to boast; "The road from Paris to Basel is washed in blood," replied the realistic Swiss.

Yet even as they fought Europe's wars, the Swiss saw how ruinous war could be. As early as 1291 Uri, Schwyz, and Unterwalden, the three cantons at Switzerland's Alpine heart, had sworn eternal allegiance, and in the fourteenth century—in a revolt set off by the defiance of William Tell—they expelled their Austrian overlords.

Though they continued to be involved as mercenary soldiers in Europe's bloody power politics over the next 350 years, the Swiss longed for peace and freedom from the regular incursions visited upon them by the enemies of those they served. After the Thirty Years War—those three fatal decades of episodic war interrupted by plague and insurrection that resulted in the death of roughly a quarter of Europe's population—the Swiss signed the Peace of Westphalia (1648) and withdrew into a powerfully armed neutrality. Thereafter they were content to sit within their Alpine fortress and focus on developing civic institutions that would turn the engaged citizen-soldier into an engaged citizen-civilian. While Napoleon's ambitions temporarily suspended their independence, and the two world wars of this century put heavy pressure on their neutrality and their unity (there were strong pressures for the German Swiss to side with Germany and the French Swiss with France), Switzerland made a convincing success of its neutrality and its democracy. Indeed, so successful has Switzerland been that it has become a butt of the sorts of jokes reserved for the very lucky, the very successful, the very virtuous, and the very boring.

With the exception of a few ceremonial guards in the Vatican, the mercenaries are gone. The democracy of citizen-soldiers lives on, however. In the ancient canton of Appenzell, bordering on Austria, voters still meet annually in a large town square for the *Landsgemeinde*, where they debate and vote directly on common business. Appenzell is one of the last of the cantons to fiercely defend its right to govern itself directly, with citizens doing the active work of legislation, rather than their representatives. Hans Graff is a farmer in Appenzell, and every spring he prepares to participate in these assembly debates and elections by strapping on the ceremonial sword that symbolizes the soldierly basis of his citizenship. Then he and his fellow men gather for a day of deliberation little less uproarious and engaging than those the Athenians once enjoyed on the Pnyx. Democracy at its best—except that, as in ancient Athens, the participants were all male until 1990. In this "most democratic" of cantons, women had no vote in local affairs until the end of the twentieth century.

Elsewhere in the country, weapons remain crucial symbols of citizenship: but nowadays the symbol is not the sword, but the powerful semiautomatic rifle that is standard issue to adult males. After their annual three weeks of compulsory manoeuvres, they take their rifles and ammunition home, where the gun may be stored in the nursery closet or over the mantelpiece. And several afternoons each year, these men find their way to the rifle range, to sharpen their skills and expend their mandatory practice rounds. This is still a nation of citizen-soldiers capable of mobilizing an army of 650,000 men in forty-eight hours. It takes a certain imagination to find the spirit of William Tell among modern hotel-keepers and accountants and ditch-diggers and musicians, but scratch a cosmopolitan kid dancing to a Zurich disco band and you will find a dutiful soldier; call an ageing farmer to attention, and a home guardsman will appear almost by magic, ready to report to his unit within a few hours.

But there is a great deal more to Swiss citizenship than soldiering. The vitality and commitment of the soldier is in fact due in large part to the extended responsibilities citizens have in this decentralized and busy polity. No federal democracy has a greater sense of cantonal and village autonomy. The Swiss call it *Kantönligeist*, or "canton-spirit", in celebration of a parochialism that elsewhere would be disdained. A Swiss is first of all a Berner or a Zuricher or a Churer, a loyal citizen of the locality, and only then a Swiss national. Few outsiders are allowed in—local citizenship must be won before national citizenship can even be petitioned for! For a citizen of town and canton, there may be six or eight referendum votes a year to attend to, business at village and town assemblies, initiative and petition meetings aimed at getting new legislation on the regional or national agenda. The Swiss can make ancient Athenians look politically lethargic.

To be a Swiss citizen has been an extraordinary burden—and an extraordinary right. Yet until ten years ago some women were still disenfranchised. One reason is the old belief that the traditional male citizen-soldier represents both himself and his entire family. A nation of cantons; a canton of villages; a village of families; a family of parents and children—a family in which the man and woman have different roles to play. In other words, the exclusion of women is, in a peculiar way, an extension of Switzerland's concept of the ideal democratic citizen.

Dr. Lillian Uchtenhagen, an MP and a professor of political science who helped achieve suffrage for women in 1972, is at once understanding of and unforgiving about this ambiguous legacy. She perceives in Appenzell a historical oddity which may not be worth fighting against. She smiles indulgently at mention of the traditional notion that women there "vote in bed"—are powerful within the families that their men represent in the public domain—and recognizes that for many decades women's suffrage was opposed by a majority of women. But her tolerance of the situation in Appenzell is obviously conditioned by the fact that she and other Swiss women have fought for and won, not only the franchise, but a 1981 equal-rights amendment to the Constitution, and what she regards as the most judicious matrimonial law in the world.

Still, Swiss women are not soldiers, and to the degree that soldiering remains the heart of the Swiss spirit of citizenship neither Dr. Uchtenhagen nor Switzerland's three million other women are likely to experience fully what it once meant to be a citizen in this land where citizenship is so rich.

And there is the rub. Like the Athenians and Spartans before them, the Swiss once combined a remarkably expansive idea of citizenship with a remarkably narrow conception of who the citizen could be. Now that the compass of citizenship has been extended to double the size of the citizen body, citizenship has begun to lose its lustre. Participation in elections is down (less than elsewhere in the West, but down none the less); the *Landsgemeinde* cantons (those still holding open assemblies, like Appenzell) have dwindled to just a few; people complain about too many referenda; and among the young there is a growing tendency to defer to elected representatives and bureaucrats. There is even a referendum being planned questioning the once-sacred institution of mandatory military service. Every adult is now a citizen, but fewer and fewer care much about citizenship. As with a depreciating currency, the more citizens you mint, the less they seem to be worth.

Little Switzerland throws up one of modern democracy's biggest questions: how to maintain the value of citizenship as more and more people become politically enfranchised in democracies that engage citizens less and less. Switzerland poses the question, and in another tiny democracy, halfway between Europe and America, an exciting answer is being tentatively formulated. It is appropriate that the answer is being sought not by the men, who have been citizens for centuries, but by the newest citizens, the women.

New Citizens in an Old Democracy

Iceland is tiny even by Swiss standards; a scant quarter of a million people spread across a glaciated island just below the Arctic Circle. Its ancient parliament, the Althing, is the world's oldest, much older even than the Swiss Confederation, dating back to at least A.D. 930—when the sons of Charlemagne were still reigning in medieval Europe. But the world's oldest parliament has been until recently one of the world's most masculine parliaments; even after women were formally accorded the vote, it remained largely a male club in a nation where women, although vigorous, independent, and well respected, played little or no political role. How then, in a country that in the 1970s had only five women lawyers, did—just a few years later—a woman win a national presidential election, a new women's party (the Women's Alliance) form and go on to win three parliamentary seats in the first election it contested, and another woman get herself appointed to Iceland's supreme court? Well, starting back in 1975, when the nation's women went on a national strike during International Women's

Year, it was clear that Iceland's newest citizens wanted not a bigger share of the old political pie as made by men, but a new recipe altogether.

Their initial struggle for political power was hard, but it was made easier by Iceland's special circumstances: its small size, which makes the whole nation a kind of family; its racial, linguistic (old Norse, the language of the Vikings), and religious unity (evangelical Lutheranism is the national religion); and its responsiveness to those who are willing to wage a political battle. As a consequence, when women broke into the ranks of Iceland's male-dominated politics they moved almost immediately beyond power-sharing to an effort to rewrite the rules by which power was used.

Vigdis Finnbogadóttir, who in 1980 became the world's first elected female head of state (she has since been twice re-elected), is a figurehead rather than a chief executive with full power. Nevertheless, she is one of Iceland's political women who, as they are politicized, are feminizing politics. Embracing women's traditional values, they are working to inculcate them in the political marketplace. Such homespun ideals as household economy, a devotion to harmony, and a conciliatory and consensual approach to conflict reappear as practical guidelines urging fiscal responsibility, international disarmament, and a willingness to seek common ground with political adversaries.

We had to follow President Vigdis on a blustery, chill Saturday into Iceland's rocky interior to conduct our first extended conversation with her. On a typical North Atlantic day alternately splashed with sunshine and lashed with rain, we chatted with her as she crawled about on her knees amid a field of seedlings she was helping to plant. Images of nurture abounded as she spoke of the need to make Iceland verdant again: "We know that woods were growing here in the Middle Ages and we believe we can make this country greener," she says. She reveals an almost motherly attitude towards the small family that is the Icelandic nation. Women in other countries who have struggled to emancipate themselves from the domination of men might bridle at the aura of maternalism, but many Icelandic women in the politically effective alliance are not bothered by it at all, and might even be pleased if President Vigdis were thought of—in that pungent phrase used to capture the spirit of America's great nineteenth-century feminist leader, Susan B. Anthony—as the "mother of us all".

Perhaps it is not so surprising that in a nation of fishermen where the men are at sea many months of the year, women should be particularly self-reliant and resourceful. Up to 80 per cent work outside the home today, although generally in less-well-paid jobs, at wages far below those paid to men in comparable positions. As President Vigdis told us, from the beginning of Iceland's rough history women have shown themselves capable of not only "running the house while the men are away . . . but taking care of the banks and everything."

In commenting on the women's strike that initiated Iceland's women's movement, one participant we spoke with emphasized that for her the issue was the identity of women as citizens, not just their political clout. In her words: "What we were saying was 'Look how indispensable I am!' Not 'I want to be president!' but 'I am a housewife and I'm valuable!'" In this spirit, the official platform of the Women's Alliance, formed to contest the 1983 elections, speaks in an unfamiliar but striking voice. It calls not for control over centralized power but for decentralization; it asks that the many—women and men alike—at the local level be empowered, not simply that women gain access to the national government in the capital. The platform favours "smaller, independent units, where each individual has an opportunity to have direct influence", above all in the areas of education, health, and social affairs. In economic policy the platform offers as an ideal basis for the nation's economy "the policy of the practical housewife, a policy which suggests that the Icelandic people should live off their own production as much as possible and adjust their expenditure to their income".

By 1988 the Women's Alliance held the balance of power in the sixty-three-seat parliament. One of its first successful candidates was Sigridur Duna Kristmundsdóttir. She explained to us the Alliance's innovative approach to running a party. They have no leader, and they do not take votes on policy; instead they work out a consensus so that, in the end, no one feels left out, and every decision has a strong base. Furthermore, members elected to the Althing regularly yield their places to non-elected members—voluntarily—so that more women can gain parliamentary experience. (They are able to do this because of a regulation originally intended to release fishing and farming members to the demands of sea and harvest.)

The consensus technique is enormously time-consuming, but Sigridur Duna is impatient with impatience. "Democracy," she says, "takes time." Yes, to work by consensus is less efficient than to govern by command. "Of course there may be the temptation to do it the old hierarchical way," she tells us. "But we are very well aware of that temptation . . . and we resist it at every turning of the road." She denies that leadership of the kind prized by men is important for the Women's Alliance. If the party actually won majority power and had to appoint a prime minister, the prime minister would delegate authority: "He would be a she. And she would be very different, and she would be governing in a different way."

Although Icelandic women are well represented in the folklore of the Nordic sagas as beings of strength and independence, they have arrived very late on the political scene. But their new contribution has been to show how women can transform the nature of the political marketplace even as they establish their place in it. After all, it seems natural that the politics of women should move humankind towards a women's politics. Happily, in altering how we think about political life, the Women's Alliance is actually reviving the ancient idea of democracy as a participatory workplace governed by a public will, where citizens work to represent not merely themselves but the good of the commonwealth. Women have come to citizenship during a period where its meaning has grown uncertain. By giving it back some of its early lustre, they have shown how it might be revitalized.

But Iceland has the special advantage of being a little nation with a single linguistic, cultural, and religious heritage. And although Switzerland has a diversity of languages and religions, the people identify strongly with their cantons, and are held together by their awareness of more powerful neighbours on all sides. Larger countries torn by ethnic and religious antagonism are diverted from the politics of citizenship by the politics of national survival, their very unity being constantly under threat. India remains on the brink of fractiousness and anarchy; it does not seem likely that women there will attain the rights of Iceland's women without enormous effort. In Canada, where we began our story with a Hindu wedding, a number of women have been prominent on the political scene this past quarter-century. But it was a scene preoccupied not with sexual equality, but with national unity and the conflict between the French- and English-speaking populations, both uncertain how or whether to share this huge, free, and prosperous nation. So here too, women see themselves as engaged in an endless campaign.

Advancing Women in an Advanced Democracy

Canada is a vast land, and sparsely populated. Larger geographically than any nation other than the old Soviet Union, it has a population smaller than California's. A peaceable, orderly democracy with a calm rather than fierce pride in its almost unmatched level of individual liberty and social justice, it is still struggling patiently with a large catalogue of mass-society conflicts: French against English; east against west, and both against the industrial centre; provincial governments against the national capital; Catholics against Protestants; sad and unresolved injustices against the native peoples—Indian, Inuit, and Métis; a big, pushy neighbour that encroaches on Canada's economic, territorial, and cultural independence; and an uncertain national identity summed up in a *Maclean's* magazine contest in which readers were asked to complete the sentence "As Canadian as …?" and the winning entry read, "As Canadian as possible, under the circumstances."

But these tensions and uncertainties have been handled, except for rare excursions into violence, with a degree of civility and care and success that Canadians would be deeply proud of if they thought about it more.

For example, few Canadians realize that their country invented one of the great advances in parliamentary democracy. Canada's politics stem from Britain's, and it has Britain's two-party parliamentary system (with a third party vying to become one of the two dominant parties). But it was the Canadian leaders Louis-Hippolyte Lafontaine and Robert Baldwin, who—just before the nation emerged into independence—pioneered the idea that cabinet ministers should be responsible to and have the confidence of the House of Commons, instead of the monarch. This great democratic idea of "Responsible Government" is now followed in every parliament—*including* Britain's. And it led the way to independence not just for Canada, but for Australia, New Zealand, South Africa, and India, as the British empire became the Commonwealth.

Perhaps the most stunning thing about the country is its landscape, which ranges from the Atlantic to the Pacific, across more than 5,000 kilometres of forestland, seemingly endless prairies, and prodigious mountain ranges, and spreads from the latitude of Northern California in the south to the polar seas. These various regions, with their different problems and priorities, were lured into Confederation only by a commitment of considerable provincial autonomy, which is maintained under Canada's federal system. The national policy of multiculturalism applies not only to those of French and British descent, but also to the full range of ethnic cultures that are deliberately preserved in a "mosaic", rather than being stewed together in a "melting-pot" as in the United States. All these elements result in a political structure that sometimes seems designed to frustrate the national government's attempts to act on behalf of all Canadians.

Canada includes ten provinces, and hence ten provincial capitals, and ten powerful provincial premiers (never a woman among them yet!). Each premier fiercely guards his provincial powers—authority over education, resources, intraprovincial transportation, health and welfare, some aspects of trade and employment, the administration of law and order. And each is determined not to let the "Damn Federal Government" use its foot in the door to push its way in any farther!

It is upon this chessboard of competing regional authorities that those who battle for the rights of the individual must fight, against divisive forces that are sometimes almost tribal. This is the battlefield that Canadian women stepped onto—not very well armed—at the beginning of the 1980s.

For all its many democratic virtues, Canada has been slow in granting citizens' rights to women. In July 1982, the Queen of England, who is still the Queen of Canada, signed the nation's first home-grown constitution. It had taken 115 years—Canada first became an independent country in 1867—and as the day approached, Canadian women began to worry that the new constitution with its proud charter of rights might not guarantee women full equality of rights with men.

They had reason to worry: it was 1918 before all women acquired the right to vote federally. And as recently as 1981, the chairman of the parliamentary committee established to ask Canadians what they hoped for in a charter of rights seemed to mock the women activists who had come looking for an intelligent hearing. Senator Harry Hays closed their session with these remarks, which are part of the formal record: "We want to thank the National Action Committee on the Status of Women for being present today. We appreciate your coming. As a matter of fact, we're honoured. However, your time is up, and I was just wondering why we don't have a section in here for babies, and children. All you girls are going to be working and we're not going to have anybody to look after them [laughter]."

Government ministers argued that there was no need for a specific sexual-equality clause because other clauses would cover the issue. But when the women asked lawyers about this promise, they were warned not to rely on it; as one activist put it, the draft of the charter had so many loopholes regarding equality that you could drive a Mack truck through it.

Within a few days of intense work, phoning, organizing, meeting in cafés and living-rooms, they set up a national conference with expert constitutional legal advisers of their own choosing, bringing women together across the miles, and resolving their internal differences. It was a prodigious achievement. By the end of it they had a draft Equal Rights Amendment for the draft Charter of Rights and Freedoms, which was simple and clear and seemed to say to them, "You've done your work, you can go home now."

However, they were warned that they still had to persuade the legislators, who might otherwise ignore this seemingly obvious and useful amendment. So instead of going home they stayed in Ottawa. They prowled the corridors outside the offices of Members of Parliament, gaining access even to the sacrosanct caucus rooms, and getting away with their unorthodox methods because officials mistook them for secretaries. The activists were helped by a subversive corps of real secretaries, assistants, and women MPs who knew the parliamentary ropes and had access to photocopiers and telephones. Together, these women quickly learned first-hand what citizens have to do to get action from elected representatives—transforming themselves into a genuine citizens' lobby along the way. When it was finally put to a vote in Parliament, their proposal, now famous under its neutral-sounding designation "Clause 28", was approved unanimously and written into the draft charter.

Now it really looked like victory, so they did go home. But the battle was not over.

In any other nation with a central government, April 23, 1981, would have been a day of final victory. But in this federation of semi-autonomous provinces, victory in Ottawa is not yet victory in Quebec or Alberta or the Maritime provinces—which is to say, it is not yet victory in Canada. The same obstacle that had kept Canada without a constitution of its own for 115 years—the apparent impossibility of getting all those provinces to agree on anything—reappeared. The national government, sensing the people behind it, was prepared to act on its own and simply declare the new constitution and the charter official; Britain would not oppose them. But the Supreme Court of Canada—designed as the last court of appeal, to rule in matters of law—now ruled on a matter of tradition, saying that while it might not be *technically* necessary to get agreement from the provinces, there might be trouble if the government did not.

The government began consultations—and soon found that the premiers they consulted wanted to hold onto some rights. The government acquiesced, agreeing that the provinces could override Clause 28 at their own discretion. When the women and native peoples found out about it, the battle began all over again—from British Columbia on the Pacific coast to Newfoundland on the Atlantic.

"We turned around premier after premier," remembers Marilou McPhedran, who played a major role in the battle to give the federal victory a provincial basis. "We were being lied to and it took a while to realize that, but we were," says another woman. "It really was very difficult to believe that all the premiers across Canada could actually do that . . . but of course it was true. We were all left out of the constitution."

This time they staged vigils outside premiers' offices, and raised money to send delegates halfway across the country to other provincial capitals. The national parliament encouraged them, but it was the direct fight of the women themselves that carried the day. In the end all the provincial premiers declared that Clause 28 would be exempt from provincial override. Along the way, in another battle equally important, the native peoples' rights were spelled out as well. It was the end of a glorious, exhilarating, exhausting battle.

Battles are more easily won than wars, however, and the Canadian struggle for democracy continues. Only 6 per cent of the federal cabinet in Ottawa is female—5 per cent of the provincial cabinets, 4.9 per cent of the House of Commons, and less than 3 per cent of the provincial legislatures. Women still earn only 62 per cent of what men earn for comparable jobs, and two-thirds of those earning minimum wage are still women.

Still, while their American sisters had failed to win the ERA (an Equal Rights Amendment to the U.S. Constitution), the Canadian women had made it to another plateau. Or had they? By 1988 it began to look doubtful once more, as the ten male provincial premiers and the national government tried to change the Constitution once again. Said Gerry Rogers, one of the Newfoundland activists—in a phrase that applies to so much of the work of democracy—"It's sort of like doing dishes—they're never done. There's *always* another dirty dish."

But vigilance remains the price of liberty, and Canadian women know well how much time and energy vigilant citizenship consumes. One of the leaders, Linda Ryan Nye, describes to us how she felt during the campaign for Clause 28: "I don't think at any point in my life that I ever have been or wish to be again as exhausted, mentally, physically, and emotionally. . . . I don't think unless you work trying to get your government to be democratic and to work with you . . . that you discover the kind of pain you feel when you find out you're invisible. . . ."

Invisibility is a form of impotence, for which the cure is more democracy, more citizenship, more engagement. But citizenship is exhausting—which may be a greater barrier to participation than the resistance of entrenched elites. As Phidias learned thousands of years ago, democracy does take up a great many free evenings—and free days and weeks and months. That is perhaps why advanced democracies have preferred the representative system, where political professionals—we might call them professional citizens—do almost all of the actual work of governing, while the rest of us try to hold them accountable by voting once in a while.

But passive vigilance is a contradiction in terms. What the women of Canada, Iceland, Switzerland, and India have learned is that unless citizens engage directly and permanently in politics, at the cost of their own blood and their own tears, the winning of the franchise can have little meaning and democracy will remain provisional.

Nor does that lesson apply only to women. Their struggle, in "free" countries all over the world, suggests that citizenship can be—must be—something more than a tired hand thrusting a ballot into a wooden box, or pulling the lever on a voting machine.

The First Freedom

IN THE SUMMER OF 1987, IN FRONT OF A PACKED senate caucus room and a national television audience, Lieutenant-Colonel Oliver North was lecturing the United States Congress on duty and political morality. The former National Security Council officer from the White House and sometime cloak-and-dagger operative for its private spy network confronted his congressional interlocutors with an engaging self-effacement: it was his country, not the colonel himself, his demeanour seemed to say, that stood in need of his advocacy. To some his humility was a kind of naivety. To others it was pure arrogance, as he admitted that he had lied over and over again, insisting all the while that he had been fully justified.

Oliver North's testimony in what was dubbed the "Irangate" scandal revealed that in 1986 President Ronald Reagan and his administration had, in a secret and ultimately futile attempt to free hostages in Lebanon, used profits from the sale of weapons to Iran to provide aid to the administration-backed Contras fighting against the Nicaraguan Sandinista regime. But the more startling revelation was that in the course of this illegal operation, Congress had been systematically lied to by the president's staff.

The deceit exposed certain deep flaws in the American system, which vests separate and equal power in a Congress of elected legislators and a directly elected president, both of which derive their power from the people. In parliamentary governments like England's, the prime minister is responsible to Parliament and, through it, to the people, so there can be little conflict between the legislators and the prime minister and his or her cabinet. In America, Congress and president vie for control of foreign policy, each making their appeal directly to the people. In this struggle, the president is often tempted to use noninformation and disinformation as critical tools in getting his way with a Congress that, in his view, has no right to meddle in foreign policy to begin with. Yet if Irangate revealed embarrassing flaws in the system—a government at odds with itself, an executive branch tempted to deceive the public—the way in which the country dealt with those flaws points to one of its greatest virtues, what is perhaps the single most extraordinary achievement of Western democracy: its deep devotion to freedom of information, freedom of inquiry, and freedom of the press—the right of all to speak and to know. Only a nation committed to a public airing of its problems, only a legislature willing to expose deceit, corruption, and conspiracy—whoever might be embarrassed—could have put Colonel North before a national television audience and let the public decide who was telling the truth and who was lying.

As co-chairman Lee Hamilton said in summing up the hearings, "Honesty can be hard in the conduct of government. But I am impressed that policy [in Irangate] was driven by a series of lies: lies to the Iranians, lies to the Central Intelligence Agency, lies to the attorney-general, lies to our friends and allies, lies to Congress, and lies to the American people. So often during these hearings . . . I have been reminded of President Thomas Jefferson's statement: 'The whole art of government consists in the art of being honest.'" History teaches that the only way to guarantee an honest government is to guarantee freedom of information—freedom of expression by citizens, freedom of access to information by all. Democracy is communication: people talking to one another about their common problems and forging a common destiny. Before people can govern themselves, they must be free to express themselves. Without free expression there is no communication, without communication no citizenship, without citizenship no democracy. Freedom of expression is the lifeblood of democracy, a fundamental right that encompasses other related rights such as freedom of assembly, of worship, and of conscience. If there is a single right upon which all others depend, a single freedom on which democracy is founded, it is the right of self-expression, the freedom to communicate and exchange information—to speak the truth freely as one sees it, to have free access to the truth even when it is embarrassing to the government. This is why, in our pursuit of democracy, we take a trip back in time, to

England and Europe in the fifteenth century and at the beginning of the sixteenth century.

Democracy's dependence on freedom of expression was not learned overnight. But by the sixteenth century it was emerging with distinctive force as a consequence of two momentous and mutually reinforcing events: the discovery of movable type, which made possible revolutionary changes in literacy and in the distribution of power; and the reform of the Catholic Church, known as the Protestant Reformation, in turn made possible by the printing of the Bible for "Everyman".

Sources of Freedom: Print and Protest

If democracy involves common self-government by citizens who are equal one to another, and if self-government depends on self-expression which in turn depends on free communication, then there was no more important innovation in the early history of technology than movable type. In 1440 Laurens Koster of Holland accidentally dropped a carved letter A into the sand; when he noticed the imprint it left, it occurred to him that pouring molten lead into such an impression could create individual letters from which words, paragraphs, whole books might be printed and reprinted. In Germany Johann Gutenberg refined a similar idea into a truly workable technology, so while his Bible did not appear until after Koster's invention, Gutenberg is usually given credit for first discovery.

The discovery revolutionized the world. In 1620 Shakespeare's contemporary the humanist philosopher Francis Bacon wrote in his *Novum Organum* that gunpowder, the compass, and movable type were the three great new inventions. "For these three," he wrote, "have changed the appearance and state of the whole world." Gunpowder had equalized power by permitting the weak and unskilled to kill the strong and the aristocratically trained, while the compass had facilitated exploration and had opened the world to traders, travellers, and adventurers. This opening would in time lead to new ideas and a new epoch of commerce, capitalism, and overseas colonies. But movable type offered to the common people the key to all worldly power: information. Freedom without access to information is meaningless. Self-expression without knowledge is only opinion. The printing press brought books to everyone; and with books came information, knowledge, and power.

A great humanist scholar of the fourteenth century like Petrarch, living in a world without type, had but a few hundred volumes in his library. Each of these would have been meticulously copied, word by painful word, over years and even decades, by scores of scribes leaning over their slow-moving quills. By the beginning of the sixteenth century, print runs of a thousand books at a time were common, and the literate who were also wealthy were acquiring collections of fifteen thousand titles—or more. Books began to appear in French and English as well as the scholastic Latin that only a few could read, and by 1600 as much as half the adult population of England had achieved a minimal literacy. Books increasingly became passports to a better life and social position. The printing press was to change people's lives—and religion—beyond imagining.

Although Christianity had begun with a revolutionary sect preaching the brotherhood and the equality of all mankind, by the late Middle Ages it had become a religion of the powerful and a career for the well off—a mammoth, power-hungry institution. With the Pope at the top, and bishops and priests acting as paternalistic guides to their illiterate parishioners, it had come to rival the worldly empires of medieval Europe.

The medieval world was deeply superstitious, and the Catholic Church wielded immense power over both bodies and souls. Conservative, anti-scientific (it was to condemn Galileo for arguing that the earth revolved around the sun), and profoundly corrupt, it robbed Christianity of its initial democratic zeal. The powerful word of the Christian God, once spoken directly to the prophets, was now mediated through the rituals of priests. Masses were conducted in a strange tongue, and "God's Word" in book form existed only in rare, hand-written Greek and Latin Bibles available only to the priesthood and aristocracy. The feudal world was governed, controlled, and ordered by the universal Catholic Church—so much so that the great empire of the Middle Ages came to call itself the Holy Roman Empire of the German Nation. Christianity had begun as a spiritual revolution; by the fifteenth century it had become a worldly hellhole. When the German priest Martin Luther travelled to the Vatican in 1510, what he found was "the most licentious den of thieves, the most shameless of all brothels, the kingdom of sin, death, and hell. . . . a completely depraved, hopeless, and notorious godlessness." Rebelling against the corruptions of Rome, the passionate priest soon found himself in revolt against Catholicism as an institution. Both Luther and his counterpart in Geneva, Jean Calvin, preached that the individual could commune directly with God and did not need "the mediation of any merely human institution." The Protestant Reformation had begun.

The idea of personal citizens' rights first gained a place in English history in 1215, when King John was forced by his barons to sign the Magna Carta, the first great charter of rights, which placed some limits on the king's hitherto absolute power. But in practical terms the story of self-expression began over two centuries later, with the printing press, which in time gave both bibles and secular books to everyone, and gave a new strength and independence to the power of conscience against established authority. Yet even bibles printed by the thousands could not free Christians from the sovereignty of the priesthood—unless they were able to understand them. This meant that genuine religious and political liberty had to await the translation of the Bible (and other books) from the dead Latin of the Church elite into the living languages of the parishioners.

Enter William Tyndale. Only a few years after Martin Luther had made a German translation of the Bible, Tyndale gave England a Bible that could be read in English. To do so, he had to give up first his country and ultimately his life.

William Tyndale was working as chaplain and tutor to a landed family in south-west England. He grew deeply offended at the ignorant arrogance and arbitrary power of the local clergy, and it is reported that he shouted at one of these rednecked local clergymen, "If God lets me live I will see to it that the lad who follows the plough shall know more scripture than thou dost!" A century and a half earlier, John Wyclif and his followers had created an English Bible from relatively recent Latin versions (the "Vulgate"); it had been suppressed by outraged papal and royal authorities, and the few copies had been destroyed. Now Tyndale began to work from earlier Greek and Hebrew texts. And he was determined not only to translate but to print and publish.

However spiritual Tyndale's work may have been, the king and the bishops knew very well that this upstart pamphleteer was now a serious political risk. Give ordinary people the chance to disagree with the establishment about the word of God? The idea was outrageous—and subversive. Tyndale had to flee England. And he soon discovered that there was no sanctuary on the Continent beyond the long arm of Henry VIII. He was harassed wherever he went, and a first printing of his translated New Testament was seized and destroyed. But in 1526, in Worms, he managed to print his English edition, and by wrapping the books in bales of cloth, to smuggle bound copies into England. Many of these were seized and burned, and today only two survive.

Within a few years a secret agent named Phillips, despatched by Henry VIII, was tracking the translator down. When Phillips caught up to him, Tyndale was working in lonely seclusion on the Old Testament, and was easy prey. He was arrested and imprisoned in Vilvoorde, near Brussels, where a few months later he was dragged from his cell, strangled until nearly dead, hauled to a nearby Catholic church, and burned to death before its portals—crying out, as he perished, for God to "open the eyes" of the King of England.

The English king's eyes were wide open, however, and what he saw was that English Bibles in the eager hands of English subjects were a prompt to private conscience and a spur to individual thinking, perhaps in time to revolution. Tyndale's Bibles survived his death, and King Henry learned that to keep a people in servitude it is not their bodies but their books that must be burned. For the flames did not die down with the cooling of Tyndale's ashes; from them were to spring fires that would consume monarchs and tyrants across Europe down through the following centuries. Just as Henry had feared, rebels who learned to throw off the dominion of a tyrannical Church in the name of liberty of conscience soon became rebels against the tyrannical state: if popes were superfluous, then monarchs too might be superfluous! Although the Stuarts claimed to rule by Divine Right, the English Puritans, practised rebels against Rome, found it easy to defy them. Little more than a century after Tyndale's martyrdom, the tables had turned; Charles I was executed in 1649, after years of fighting Parliament for power, and a Puritan Commonwealth was declared.

The power of the written word proved to be a weapon for democracy more potent than the sword. By the 1650s, Puritan preachers were successfully creating new and zealous converts to their egalitarian religion simply by putting books into the hands of scullery maids and manservants. At the same time, freedom of speech was becoming the single most important measure of success in the new struggle for political freedom. And though the Puritan Commonwealth collapsed in 1660 and the Stuarts returned to the throne, the lesson of liberty had been learned. The great Puritan poet John Milton's *Areopagitica* was only the most lofty of the many tracts and pamphlets written in defence of free expression in this era that turned protest and revolution into foundations for England's future democracy.

John Locke provided further argument for liberty of expression in his celebrated *Letter on Toleration*, and the idea itself was included in Britain's Bill of Rights of 1689. One hundred years later, the precious right of free expression was codified in the American Bill of Rights, where it found its simplest and finest expression. The First Amendment commands with unmistakable clarity that "Congress shall make no law . . . abridging the freedom of speech, or of the press", and to be sure self-expression is protected it guarantees the right of religious expression and free assembly as well.

From the inventions of Gutenberg and the Dutch printers and the passion of Luther and Tyndale has come the boldest achievement of Western democracy. But the liberty thus created has never been secure. It soon found itself in conflict with other aspirations—to security and order, for example—and it has had to grapple with conformity in America and a penchant for official secrecy in England that have often undermined it.

Free Information or Official Secrets?

Freedom is no sooner won than we must struggle for its survival. Thomas Jefferson, drafter of the Declaration of Independence in 1776 and later president of the United States, believed its preservation required something akin to permanent revolution: "The tree of liberty must be refreshed from time to time with the blood of patriots and tyrants. It is its natural manure."

Translating the Bible into English cost Tyndale his life, and there have been few champions of liberty since who have not run afoul of the state. In the Virginia colonies, emigrants from England's persecutions found a New World censoriousness already in place. Sir William Berkeley, who was governor of the Virginia colony in the 1660s and 1670s, was hardly a hospitable host to the idea of free expression: "I thank God there are no free schools nor printing . . . learning has brought disobedience, heresy and sects into the world and printing has divulged them. . . ."

Nor did the transformation of the state into a democracy necessarily enhance the reception of liberty. Democratic majorities filled with the sense of their own legitimacy could often be more abusive of free expression than monarchs, who at least had to elicit a certain consent from their subjects. Enlightened despots of eighteenth-century Europe like Frederick the Great were often more tolerant of philosophy and literature than the unenlightened majorities of more recent eras. In times of war (see Chapter Ten) most democratic societies stifle dissent as energetically as any dictatorship—and are often more self-righteous about it. For all their celebration of free expression, the Puritans had their own rigid censorship. And both England's war in the Falklands and America's invasion of Grenada were conducted under official wraps, to exclude the probing eyes of the free press—a model more recently imitated by Israel in its struggle against insurrection in its occupied territories.

And did their 1689 Bill of Rights give the English the right to speak their minds, from that time on? Ask John Wilkes, a magnificently irksome journalist and politician who began his own periodical, *The North Briton*, in 1762. Wilkes' tough, critical articles gave George III something to worry about in addition to his rebellious American subjects. The king labelled the paper "seditious and treasonable"; to him, its aim could only be "to excite traitorous insurrections against the government." But it was members of the Parliament in which Wilkes himself served who gave him the most trouble. The Commons hated Wilkes' forthrightness as much as did the king—though it is hard to say what outraged them more, his free-thinking publication or his free-wheeling sex life. He belonged to the libertine society The Order of the Knights of Saint Francis of Wyckham, notorious for its spirited free thinking and its still more spirited orgies, held in an abbey on the banks of the river Thames.

Wilkes was in time expelled from the Commons, imprisoned in the Tower, wounded in a duel, and driven from England. But the voters loved him all the more. Four years later, still under indictment, he won re-election by a huge majority. Convict and outlaw, barred from taking his seat by a scandalized Parliament, he was none the less re-elected over and over again, until he became a symbol of free speech on both sides of the Atlantic. Pennsylvania named a town after him, and the slogan "Wilkes and liberty!" became a rallying cry for freedom-lovers everywhere. Eventually Parliament was compelled to shift its gaze to the New World, where rebels were finishing with guns what had been begun with printing presses by the likes of Wilkes and the American revolutionary and radical democrat Tom Paine.

The greatest achievement of Wilkes and his formidable followers was the fact that, after a long battle, they won the right to report to the people on what happened in Parliament. All over the world, British-style parliaments still issue full reports on their proceedings, naming the transcripts "Hansard" after the Hansard family, the London printers who signalled Wilkes' final victory when in 1803 they began to print reports of Parliament. (In the United States, the equivalent is the Congressional Record.)

Yet though Parliament's proceedings are published today—in fact, Parliament has its own stenographers to take down every word—things are not so very different than they were in Wilkes' time. For though it was initially the king to whom Wilkes gave offence, it was Parliament that prosecuted and banned him. And it still sometimes seems as though parliamentary government and freedom of expression have become adversaries in the land of liberty's birth. Unlike Canada and the United States—whose ideas of freedom were born mainly in Britain—Britain itself has no Freedom of Information act. British politician Roy Jenkins has called his country's government "the most secretive in the Western world". We did not believe that when we began our investigation. It was a reporter who did his best to change our minds.

Duncan Campbell, a very angry hornet in modern Britain's secrecy bonnet, is a prime modern example of how the good intentions of a democratic Parliament can be undermined by an obsession with security. Campbell got involved in his campaign in order to expose the dangers of England's 1911 amendments to the Official Secrets Act, which had been passed precisely in order to enhance "security", only because the government stirred up his nest. It was back in 1972, when Campbell—a young, aggressive, eccentric, freelance reporter—was doing a piece for *Time Out* magazine on security scandals in British intelligence operations in Cyprus, that he first ran afoul of the government. Though his story was assembled mostly from public information, Scotland Yard impounded his entire home library, including files, press cuttings, telephone directories, personal letters, and such dangerous novels as Ernest Hemingway's *For Whom the Bell Tolls*. Campbell and his co-authors were eventually discharged, but not before he acquired a taste for holding the British obsession with official secrecy up to ridicule.

In 1987 Campbell again got into trouble, this time for his BBC television series on government secrecy. In one episode, he revealed how the British government had financed a spy satellite called Zircon without informing Parliament. Campbell was attacked for exposing secrets to the Russians, and indicted under the Official Secrets Act. In a now familiar process, his library was raided and personal materials impounded, and his program was banned (although parts were aired in the United States and

Canada). Campbell had little patience with what he calls the government's "Nanny knows best" position, and he offered a trophy and a thousand-pound reward to anyone who could demonstrate that he has in fact endangered national security. Noting the lack of takers, he observed that "in Whitehall's upside-down rule-book, it often seems to be a greater sin for a civil servant to leak information to Parliament than to the Russians."

England's Official Secrets Act was amended to its modern form in the pre-war espionage hysteria of 1911, and then further strengthened in the post-war espionage hysteria of 1920. Its provisions make *government* information and *secret* information almost synonymous. In the concise words of Sir Martin Furnival Jones, head of M.I.5, "it is an official secret if it is in an official file." Under this generic definition, *no* government document can be reproduced in a newspaper or a book like the one you hold in your hands without violating the act. Moreover, anyone who reads such secret information—*this means you!*—is as liable to prosecution under the act as we who write and print it.

This might be amusing if it were not for the fact that the Official Secrets Act not only is invoked over and over again by the British government, but is often used to intimidate, silence, and even imprison critics in and out of the government. In 1984, for example, an employee of the Foreign Office named Sarah Tisdale was fired and prosecuted as a criminal for leaking information which the court itself acknowledged was no threat to national security. And Clive Ponting, a senior civil servant in the Naval Affairs office after the Falklands War, was charged in 1984 under the same provisions for leaking information to a Labour Member of Parliament. Ponting's bosses at the Defence ministry had been systematically lying to the parliamentary committee investigating the sinking of the cruiser *General Belgrano*. Ponting believed that when Prime Minister Thatcher ordered the attack on the Argentine cruiser, it was already leaving the war zone. There were 368 Argentine lives lost in the sinking, and many Britons were killed in reprisal. Feeling that, two years later, a cover-up was still in effect, Ponting decided he owed a higher allegiance to truth and to Parliament than to his bureaucratic superiors. Arrested and tried by the government, Ponting was eventually acquitted in a much-publicized trial at the Old Bailey, by a jury of twelve ordinary men and women who, like their fellow citizens, saw no harm in a civil servant insisting on honesty in government. But his case did little to encourage honesty among higher civil servants or would-be whistleblowers.

In the United States conformism and economic pressure from the private sector can also put a chill on broadcast programming, but freedom of expression has been enshrined in the Bill of Rights, and freedom of information has been protected both by government and against government, by the Supreme Court. England, however, has displayed more concern for the sovereignty of Parliament than for the freedom of the press.

Censorship has been a powerful weapon of tyranny from the beginning. Fifty years after Gutenberg, there was an official censor in nearly every major city in Europe, and princes and popes alike had taken to telling their subjects what they could and could not read. Today secrecy is so well entrenched in Britain that government censorship is often undertaken without recourse to the Official Secrets Act. And where the stick fails, there is always the carrot.

The carrot is called the parliamentary lobby system. Through it, reporters, who seem to think they are getting special access to government officials are actually being co-opted. Every morning, four days a week, parliamentary reporters gather at No. 10 Downing Street (or, as in the past, in the Commons lobby) for unofficial background briefings, where officials of the prime minister's office can speak off the record to journalists in search of scoops. Their unwritten agreement is that statements made "on lobby terms" cannot be attributed. Officially, no meeting has taken place! When the phrase "it is understood" appears in a newspaper about a government proposal, the unnamed source is usually a civil servant close to a minister. The manipulative possibilities of the lobby system are endless, while ministers are relieved of responsibility for their statements. While some newspapers such as *The Guardian* and *The Independent* have recently refused to participate in the lobby system, most continue to regard it as a journalistic necessity.

What a remarkable and vigorous contrast the Canadian press "scrum" presents to the British lobby system! Where the lobby system is private, confidential, secretive, and manipulative, the Canadian scrum is public, open, and conversational. Where British ministers try to manipulate the public by anonymously ingratiating themselves with the press, Canadian ministers and Members of Parliament face a veritable rugby scrum of aggressive reporters who pressure and test and argue with them, using camera, microphone, and pen and pad to grill them on behalf of the public. Where in England the government tries to use the press to lead the public, in Canada the press forces the government to be accountable to the public.

The scrum is a Canadian invention, and may be Canada's most important contribution to democratic freedom of information. By contrast, the presidential press conference so central to American public information is called at the pleasure of the president, and leaves little room for the combative style of the Ottawa scrum—a unique celebration of the fact that freedom of the press and the right of the people to know are one and the same.

Television has become the preferred medium of political information and electioneering. The new art of "video politics", geared to images rather than to ideas, to pictures rather than to words, is having a disturbing effect on the way people respond politically (see Chapter Eleven). Television can purvey quick, cheap, misleading images, and can turn politics into a game of ratings. Yet television can also bring information to a larger number of people. The televised hearings on Senator Joseph McCarthy's investigation of the American army in the fifties, on the Watergate break-in in the seventies, on Irangate and the Clinton testimony in the Lewinsky case in the nineties, all began as spectacles that many feared would undermine the public's capacity for deliberation. Yet each of those hearings became an extraordinary instrument of civic education watched by tens of millions of Americans—letting the public participate in an invaluable political learning process.

But it is the records initiated by the Hansard family that have above all helped to guarantee that no Parliament or Congress operates in secret. The proceedings available from Hansard and the Congressional Record make democracy's embrace of "open government" a reality rather than a mocking boast, and prevent free legislatures from operating behind closed doors.

However, freedom of information is seldom interpreted to mean total freedom, total lack of constraint. Even Duncan Campbell, with all his journalistic aggressiveness, referred to genuine security issues as "real secrets" which he will not disclose. Even the First Amendment to the American Constitution conveys something less than an absolute right to speak and to know. Would the citizens of the United States feel safer if their government disarmament negotiators revealed their plans in advance? Should jurors read lurid tabloid accounts of a murder case they are trying? Many democratic aims are at times incompatible with freedom. Security, the integrity of intelligence operations in war and peace, and fairness injury trials are only a few of the many wholly legitimate concerns a democracy may have in curtailing press freedom. The distinguished Canadian civil rights champion Alan Borovoy recently wrote a valuable book, *Where Freedoms Collide*. It shows how we have to balance equally cherished ideals that may conflict with one another, and one measure of the maturity of a democracy is how well it manages this balancing act.

If the balance between freedom and security often seems uncertain in those parts of the world that have had the longest experience of democracy, then it is not really surprising that we find it tottering precariously in developing democracies such as Mexico. The story of the spirited newspaper *El Popular* takes place in a media environment that by British or Canadian or Australian or West German standards is profoundly corrupt. There is, to be sure, an abundance of comment and debate—Mexico is not Chile or North Korea—but there is also bribery, menace, and occasionally death in the pursuit of freedom of expression.

Press Freedom in a One-Party Democracy: Mexico

In much of the world, the journalist is less a bearer of democratic responsibilities than a martyr to democratic aspirations. To speak or write or publish in the name of freedom means to be threatened rather than co-opted, imprisoned rather than indicted, tortured rather than badgered—to be not intimidated but murdered. Yet in many developing countries the struggle is not simply that of democratic idealists against established dictatorships, but of fledgeling democracies trying to survive freely, without forfeiting security and order.

Nowhere is the dilemma more evident than in Mexico. The country has known a greater degree of peace and stability in the last fifty years than most of its Latin American neighbours, but it has had a difficult time nourishing open debate, multi-party pluralism, and genuine freedom of information. Mexico has many newspapers but also a great deal of fear. There is courage but enough intimidation to unnerve even the most courageous. Mexico—like other countries struggling with internal poverty, external neo-colonialism, and debt—is encumbered by democratic ideals it often finds painful and costly to live up to. Its mighty neighbour to the north, self-righteous in its democratic success, seductive in its economic prosperity, does not make things easier.

Amelia Gil de Flores is a survivor. In 1986 her husband Ernesto, an influential Mexican journalist, was assassinated in a crime that still has not been solved, and that may or may not have been an attempt at intimidation of his independent newspaper *El Popular*, based in the northern town of Matamoros, across the border from Brownsville, Texas. Yet she continues to operate the paper, one of Mexico's few relatively uncorrupted dailies— no easy job in a nation where press freedom has always been a hostage to a single ruling party.

Since Mexico's revolution, which began in 1910 with the overthrow of the dictator Porfirio Díaz and culminated in the constitution of 1917, Mexico has developed a political style remarkably free of military coups or overt repression. But much of this is due to the unity brought about by one-party politics. For the last sixty years a single party, the Institutional Revolutionary Party (PRI), has won every state and local election and ruled the country successfully, in what can at best be called a quasi-democratic reign. There is a powerful minority party on the right (the National Action Party) and a coalition party of the left (the United Socialist Party), and the PRI's predominance was severely tested in the 1988 presidential elections, but Mexico remains fundamentally a one-party state—in no small part due to the cosy relationship the PRI maintains with the media.

This relationship is not openly repressive. There are no official censors. That is not Mexico's style. Even in politics, there has been only sporadic official violence. But when soldiers fired on a protesting crowd prior to the 1968 Olympic Games, killing up to five hundred citizens and detaining over five thousand, the official count was only fifty dead, a report faithfully reproduced in most of the country's "independent" papers. A few years later, in 1971, police brigades as well as unofficial thug brigades over-responded to student violence in another operation that was played down by the press. Journalists have themselves been victims—estimates range from thirty to forty killed in the last two decades—but this too has gone relatively uncommented on by much of the press. In a developed democracy, even one such killing would dominate the nation's media for days or weeks. How does Mexico's government, representing a single party and operating without censors, control newspapers and television in a nation of over eighty million people living in thirty-one federated states? How does a nation in possession of a nominally free press get so little independent information and end up reading the news the government's way? Is this a price of Mexico's independence? A soft form of dictatorship?

The government does not officially censor but it does maintain a monopoly over newsprint and ink, and it can cut off supplies to papers that displease it. Also, it is responsible for up to 70 per cent of "advertising" revenues for most newspapers. In this case "advertising" usually means government-written stories and photos that are run, without identification, alongside "hard news" stories. The PRI need not force reporters to tell its story, it simply buys the space to tell its own story—anonymously. It fortifies this system with official bribes ("bonuses" to otherwise under-paid journalists) that deter investigators from looking too far into stories that might embarrass the government. Sometimes an industrious reporter will not wait for a bribe (called an *embute*, slang for the envelope in which the cash is actually handed over), but will go out and extort it, reversing the flow of corruption. No wonder that John Carlin, an English correspondent in Mexico, says "Journalism in Mexico is prostitution."

When necessary, Mexico's ruling party can act more directly. *Excelsior* was perhaps the most interesting paper in Latin America, with quality reporting, and a balanced and thoughtful editorial viewpoint. It was run by a co-operative and was thus not in debt to the wealthy families who own most of Mexico's media outlets. President Echeverría saw the need for a national "safety valve" and apparently believed a more independent press might provide it. He lacked the patience of the true democrat for criticism of his administration, however, and eventually engineered the removal of *Excelsior*'s outspoken editors. (When *Excelsior* went under in 1976, it took its distinguished literary monthly, edited by the great Mexican novelist Octavio Paz, with it.) Since its demise, only two independent national periodicals remain: *Proceso*, a left-of-centre weekly, and *Vuelva*, both of which are products of *Excelsior*'s ousted editors, but still have too small a circulation to be threatening to the government. One daily newspaper, *La Jornada*, is making efforts at serious journalism, but still plays the game according to the government's rules.

In light of this unhappy history, Amelia de Flores' stewardship of *El Popular* seems all the more extraordinary. Faced with the possibility of a displeased government withholding newsprint, she stockpiles her own. Uncertain of distribution on the streets and stands, she goes out into the streets to supervise sales herself. Wary of corruption, she balances her books carefully, assuring that she will not become a candidate for bribery. She accepts government "advertising" but does not disguise it as news. She does not claim to be a gifted editor, and has had no previous managerial experience——she is carrying on for a husband she loved and admired. She says in the most matter-of-fact way, "They will have to burn the paper, take it away, close it down, put me away." Is she not afraid for her life? "No," she declares. "Do you think it helps me to be afraid? . . . I am fighting for justice. If my blood helps to clean up this town, here it is, take it."

Watching this courageous widow maintain *El Popular* as one of Mexico's few relatively independent voices, one cannot help feeling that the flames of William Tyndale's pyre are still burning. And that Amelia de Flores is in fact herself a William Tyndale of Matamoros, a modest Martin Luther, using the printed word to bring information to her people and to nourish the vigorous self-expression that is democracy's most cherished possession——and which, along with hallowed constitutions and great revolutions, gives lasting meaning to the struggle for self-government.

The Price of Democracy

EDWARD HEATH TOLD US THAT WHEN HE WAS BRITISH
prime minister, the prime minister of then-democratic Ghana came to him
in the early 1970s with a request for funds to provide fresh water to
Ghana's villages, saying that such a measure might help him win Ghana's
upcoming election and stave off the anti-democratic forces stalking the
nation. The British ultimately decided not to supply the funds. A coup followed and, said Mr. Heath sadly, "that was the end of democracy in Ghana."
Africa is a complex continent and there were presumably other reasons for
the loss of democracy in Ghana; but it is still disturbing to wonder
whether modest assistance might have made a crucial difference.

Like all good things, democracy has a price. How rich must a country
be to afford that price? Most poor countries are not democracies, while
most of the democracies are prosperous.

Behind every struggle for democracy there is an issue of money: of too
little capital to ensure economic stability and support political freedom—
as in such embattled countries as Haiti; or too much wealth too unevenly
divided to support political equality—as in Argentina. Indeed, although
the absence of wealth can hamper democracy, prosperity does not necessarily guarantee it. Saudi Arabia has a stratospheric per capita income, but
as an almost feudal monarchy it is hardly a populist or egalitarian nation.
And while the overthrow of Ferdinand Marcos' dictatorial regime in the
Philippines was sparked by an increasingly prosperous middle class, the

divisions of wealth and class continue to cause problems for President Corazon Aquino's democratic reforms.

All the same, nations that have not yet acquired a minimal level of prosperity make poor candidates for free institutions. And as countries become economic powers their peoples' democratic aspirations are unleashed. There is no better evidence for this than the democratic noises coming out of China and the Soviet Union. While these noises hardly augur full Western-style democracy, they do seem linked to both growing wealth and the desire to overcome economic sluggishness, to compete in international markets.

Yet prosperity also creates problems for democracy. In Plato's *Republic*, the tough and canny Thrasymachus tells Socrates that justice is never anything else than the "interest of the stronger". Ever since, people have worried that terms like justice, political equality, and even democracy itself may be just so much camouflage for the real power of interest and money. Realists and cynics argue that no legal code, no political institution, no bill of rights can conceal the fact that behind every political system is an economic system where the power of money and class can distort the paper provisions of a constitution.

In both Europe and North America, civic virtue and commerce have been strange and uneasy bedfellows at least since the seventeenth century. Back then, many believed that with the coming of capitalism citizens would turn away from public affairs to pursue personal gain. How could busy industrialists find the leisure for politics? What stake could labouring proletarians have in a public order? To the critics of the new commercial age, commerce and a lively sense of public spirit were simply not compatible. Against these prophets of doom, advocates of the new industrial society argued that commerce had virtues all its own—like frugality, hard work, and a willingness to defer gratification—and that the economic order of capitalism was a powerful motor that would provide the thrust for great civic empires of the future.

This debate carried on into the eighteenth century, in London coffee-houses, Paris philosophical salons, and the streets of revolutionary Boston and New York. It was not just a political debate, but an economic debate, introducing a whole new economic vocabulary. Nowadays we talk about politics in terms of economics without a second thought, but thinking that what is political is economic—that politics is also about money, and production, and systems of distribution and exchange—is itself a product of the coming of capitalism. So accustomed are we to this revolution that we routinely classify nations in economic rather than strictly political categories. The "East–West" split used to be defined less by the political constitutions of the Soviet bloc and Western countries than by the Marxist-socialist and entrepreneurial-capitalist philosophies that allegedly direct their economies. Moreover, both sides agreed that the virtues and defects of their respective political systems grew out of these economic differences. By the same token, the "North–South" split is based on the distinction between developed and developing nations—the rich versus the poor, the haves against the have-nots.

Even in prosperous nations like England and America, wealth can skew political institutions. The costs of campaigning in the United States have increasingly limited the pursuit of office to individuals from the highest income brackets. Where influence can be purchased both directly (television advertising, for example) and indirectly (the influence of corporations over public decision-making), millionaires make the best candidates. In the late 1980s a campaign for the U.S. Senate cost up to $10,000,000, and to pay for even a modest $3,000,000 re-election campaign a senator in effect had to raise $10,000 a week for every week of his six-year term of office! Joseph P. Kennedy III "lent" his own 1986 campaign for the House of Representatives a quarter of a million dollars. In 2000, consumer advocate Ralph Nader's presidential bid was based on a promise to change all this. There is a lot to change.

Well over one-third of the winning candidates for Congress in 1986 raised more than half of their campaign funds from so-called Political Action Committees (PACs), and 82 per cent raised at least 30 per cent from PACs. As Senator Russell B. Long has said, "The difference between a large campaign contribution and a bribe is almost a hairline's difference."

The lesson is that money counts. In exploring the price of democracy, we confront the dilemmas created by class and cash. There are a multitude of questions and no clear-cut answers, so we looked at a number of examples: small developing nations like Jamaica, caught in the web of international finance; old class systems like England's, where things are not quite what they seem; free-enterprise economies like the one in the United States; and socialist economies like East Germany's and the Soviet Union's.

In each of these countries, behind the complexities of political constitutions and institutions we discovered some telling truths: that as poverty obstructs the struggle for democracy, so does wealth—at least in some of its manifestations; that political equality cannot be severed from economic equality; that slavery comes in many forms, some old, some new.

Slaves of Men, Slaves of Debt

The world's first democracy and the nation with the world's first written constitution were both founded around, if not on, slavery. The Athenians used slaves to work their mines, fuel their economy, facilitate their empire, and provide them with leisure to engage in politics. The Americans used slaves to open the land, sustain their agrarian economy, and reach for their own transcontinental empire. Both established governments rooted in equality, which, paradoxically, tolerated and even encouraged slavery.

No modern democracy countenances slavery, yet there are forms of economic dependence hard to distinguish from it. In the world's most populous democracy, India, there are quarries at Faridabad, near Delhi, where men, women, and children work under conditions which appear very like slavery. Despite the efforts of a swami named Agnivesh—formerly a legislator and a minister of education in the state of Haryana—to guide these indentured bondsmen towards organization and resistance, most of the thousands of workers here might as well be working the ancient Athenian mines at Laurium. They are in debt to the quarry owners, must pay for their tools as well as for protection against the owners' goons, and end up pocketing less than a dollar a day for their back-breaking labour. They must subsist to work and must borrow constantly to subsist, so the more they work, the greater their servitude. This is all in violation of the Indian Constitution, but that only seems to prove that economic reality often outweighs legal codes.

Swami Agnivesh, a holy man, escorts us through this feudal enclave. A worker named Haru, his eyes glazed over by defeat, says that he is a virtual prisoner of the owners. "I have fallen into the trap of debt bondage. We are not allowed to leave this place unless and until we have cleared the debt. Since we are not earning enough, there is no way of getting out of debt . . . so we are more or less bonded for life."

The mines are unsafe, children often work alongside adults, and the conditions are wretched. Water must be hauled from unconscionable distances—but when a court ordered that drinking water be made available, the quarry owners simply erected sheds over empty wells, posted signs announcing "Drinking Water", and produced pictures in court as evidence of compliance. When we asked an owner about the dreadful conditions that produced his wonderful profits, he smiled. Standing a few feet from his late-model car, he explained that he could "scarcely make ends meet" and observed that he would probably be better off if he changed places with his workers.

Swami Agnivesh has made some small difference, and perhaps if he succeeds in organizing the quarry workers into a union he will one day make a larger difference. But the underlying cause of this scandalous bondage is less tractable, for it is a bondage dependent on an economic system that, in the name of the free market, permits vast inequalities of wealth and a kind of wage slavery that the poor cannot fight. The freedom of the marketplace is protected but at the cost of radical social inequality. Yet this tragic situation goes on in a country that is politically devoted to egalitarianism and is governed by a ruling party that talks a lot about socialism. Which domain can be said to govern reality? The aspirations of a democratic government? Or the circumstances of the marketplace?

To an impoverished quarry bondsman, a vote in a free democratic India (the workers at Faridabad have votes worth no less than the votes of the owners) may not seem worth much. To an impoverished nation, an independent voice in the free global economy may also not seem to be worth much. The island democracy of Jamaica elects its own government, fields its own army, and has a vote in the United Nations General Assembly worth the same as the vote of the United States or the Soviet Union. It is among the world's largest bauxite producers, and in normal times can do a good business in sugar and tourism. Since the 1970s, however, it has carried an increasingly overwhelming international debt that has devastated its naturally prosperous economy and compromised its nominal independence in the family of nations. This former English colony in the Caribbean boasts a tiny population of about two million but carries a staggering debt of over three billion dollars U.S.—in other words, each Jamaican owes the world—its lender banks, its lender nations, its lender organizations like the U.N.-created International Monetary Fund—$1,400, well above the country's per capita annual income. Jamaica's debt may seem modest compared to Yugoslavia's or the Philippines' ($20 billion each), Argentina's (over $50 billion), or that of the world debt leaders, Brazil and Mexico (each over $100 billion!), but for an island nation the debt has been crushing—the dominant force in its domestic politics and its international policy for fifteen years.

Michael Norman Manley, the son of the founder of Jamaica's People's National Party, came to power in 1972 and for eight years tried to govern Jamaica by principles a good deal more socialistic than those of his predecessors from the Labour Party. But his tenure in the early 1970s was marked by the oil crisis and a disastrous decline in world demand for bauxite. The ensuing social unrest frightened off the tourists and further damaged the domestic economy.

As the nation's debt increased, and the weight of its unaccustomed poverty fell more and more on the island's poor, Manley was forced into the arms of the world's lenders—including the International Monetary Fund, a bank of last resort for countries that need not only long-term development aid but immediate financial credibility. The IMF understandably drives a hard bargain, insisting on measures of fiscal discipline it believes necessary to the borrower's stability in return for its assistance. Social programs may be drastically curtailed, currency devalued, and other constraints imposed. However well intended, its measures are often regarded by borrowers as repressive and insensitive to local needs. Like the quarry workers, the debtor nations have little choice but to play the game the way the lenders call it—but this fans local resentment and may even compromise national independence.

Faced by one problem after another, Manley blamed the IMF—it had become Jamaica's favourite scapegoat and has more recently come under attack from larger debtor nations such as Argentina. But the opposition Labour Party blamed Manley and his leftist policies, and managed to sweep him from office in 1980. Manley's defeat has not changed his mind: "What the IMF does is to impose an ideology. It imposes a [free-market] theory of economic management and organization. But there are many ways to develop an economy. We had believed very strongly in a mixed economy where the state plays a role and the private sector plays a role. They put enormous pressure on us to dismantle state participation." Labour Party leader Edward Seaga, who became prime minister in 1980, declared that the problem was Manley's ideological radicalism. "They behave like Communists, they associate with Communists, they work like Communists, they think like Communists, and they do the things that Communists do." To Seaga, the IMF was not looking to intervene in domestic politics but to put Jamaica on a sound economic footing, something that, Seaga said, Manley's politics prevented. Yet for Manley, the IMF's fiscal constraints amounted to capitalism imposed from the outside, benefiting the island's wealthier classes but devastating its poor and the social programs that served them, "stripping from the bone into the marrow, not just taking flesh off the bone."

Seaga's victory, which was punctuated by class violence and the death of hundreds of Jamaicans during the bloody election campaign, did not vanquish Jamaica's suspicions about the IMF, and in time even Seaga lost his enthusiasm for it. Today, when Manley's party is again on the rise, calypso singers playing in the streets of Kingston sing not only of too little love and too much rum but of too little independence and too much borrowing—the initials of the IMF appearing in their lyrics like the name of an unfaithful mistress:

> The graffiti on the streets say I'm heavy, for true I'm a burden.
> I will raise my hand and the seas will part
> And my people will walk in the promised land.
> But they won't walk very far. They will drive motorcar.
> Ten dollars a gallon! ...
> Food in the store, for tomorrow we'll borrow some more.
> Food galore, for tomorrow we'll borrow some more from Arabia.
> Arab is the best, so let go IMF.
> Arab is the best, so let go IMF.

"Neither a borrower nor a lender be," said Polonius to Laertes. But survival in the modern international economy makes such prudence impossible. And so nations large and small fall into forms of bondage no less compromising to their independence than the debt bondage of India's quarry slaves. And however good-willed international lending institutions may be, they cannot help interfering in the economies of those they assist.

Crippling as they are, wage-labour bondage and national debt are only two of the forms that the power of wealth over equality can take. In older, more stable democracies free from the direct effects of wage slavery of international debt, the forces of money are still visible. Nowhere is this more evident than in England, long a prosperous nation, one of the world's most stable democracies, yet still working to reduce its once-impenetrable divisions of class and wealth.

Lords and Commoners: Class in English Democracy

Class is the disguise money wears to legitimize itself; it comprises the social arrangements that turn brute economic privilege into gentle historical precedent. Those with money may want power, but those with class have a right to and a responsibility for it.

The Right Honourable Charles Edward Stourton, Lord Mowbray, is the twenty-fifth generation to inherit the title of Baron Mowbray. He is a hereditary peer who sits in the House of Lords and exercises an influence over English politics that is not in any obvious way connected to democracy. Yet the early battles for sovereignty in England (see Chapter Six) were fought not between the crown and the common people, but between the king and his noblemen. Magna Carta was a document promulgating the rights of these lords against the king—indeed, one of its signatories was the first Baron Mowbray. Until the 1911 Parliament Act that finally curtailed the lords' power by eliminating their veto, the House of Lords had long reigned alongside the Commons in a bicameral Parliament.

The long struggle between the two houses is today a matter of history. Since 1949, the Lords has been able to do no more than delay a Commons bill, though it continues to exercise this right liberally—in the nine years Margaret Thatcher has been in power it has voted "no" over 110 times. For many centuries, however, the House of Lords was a non-democratic body engaged in a democratic enterprise: checking majority rule and balancing power by dividing legislative authority from within Parliament.

The current Lord Mowbray has no illusions about the modern House of Lords, as peculiar an institution as any democracy is likely to see. "I know," he tells us, "in a pure democracy the House of Lords doesn't appear to have any sensible reason for being there." Nowadays it includes in its membership not only a preponderance of hereditary members but also hundreds of "life peers" appointed by prime ministers, including many from the Labour Party. It acts as a useful check on the more politically motivated Commons, and the quality of its debates is often quite high—particularly when led by life peers with previous political experience such as former Conservative prime minister Alec Douglas-Home (who renounced his hereditary peerage to sit in the Commons, and later re-entered the Lords as a life peer) and former Labour prime minister Harold Wilson.

Whatever its traditional virtues and its role in the balance of power, however, the House of Lords is something of a fossil in a modern democracy. Founded on the power of the old nobility, it today represents no particular constituency; each peer represents only himself or herself. They are not paid (other than travel expenses), and many never attend at all.

Lord Mowbray says of the House of Lords, "We are, believe you me, better than nothing." The House of Lords is a reminder of how deeply traditional British political culture is. After more than a century of suffrage (for men), people still defer to those they take to be—if not their "betters" overall—at least their betters at governing. This deferential attitude has served to preserve class institutions and to allow the dominance of Conservative (Tory) governments in this century, in a nation where labourers outnumber the wealthier classes at least two to one.

Even the House of Commons has had its history as a sometime creature of class and wealth. Up until the Reform Bill of 1832, certain members of the supposedly representative Commons were anything but democratically chosen. In the many so-called rotten boroughs that dotted the English landscape before the Reform Bill, landowners controlled parliamentary seats in districts that might have no population whatsoever—the town of Old Sarum, for example, which was long abandoned by the eighteenth century but none the less sent two members to Parliament to represent the interests of the rich family that owned it. Meanwhile, new industrial cities like Manchester and Birmingham, populated by hundreds of thousands of workers in the new manufacturing industries, found themselves wholly unrepresented. Nor was it just the labourers who were deprived of representation. The rich manufacturers of Birmingham and Liverpool were as powerless in Parliament as the men, women, and children who sweated in their mills and shops.

The English may have been deferential, but they have also engaged in a ceaseless struggle for a fully democratic franchise from the time of the Reform Bill of 1832 into the present. Tony Benn, a Labour Party leader who renounced his hereditary peerage in order to take a seat in the Commons, is adamant in resisting the suggestion that the privileged classes have led the way to reform. "How do you think trade unions got rights in Britain?" he asks. "Was it because the House of Lords woke up one day and said, 'You know, old boy, we've been a bit unfair to the working class'? . . . Do you think that the Chartists won because [the elite] said, 'Oh, we forgot to give the common people the vote'? There were struggles, there were demonstrations, there was a risk of revolution, and they capitulated."

Many socialists regard the disabling effects of wealth on democracy as inevitable products of the underlying capitalist economy. In this view, the only long-term cure for economic inequality is the political transformation of the economic realm. Here we run straight into the question lurking behind all the debates we have been listening to in Jamaica and England and the United States: is democracy finally compatible with capitalism? Is it nourished or undermined by socialism?

Capitalism, Socialism, and Democracy

At least since Karl Marx published his *Communist Manifesto* not quite one hundred and fifty years ago, democrats have been asking themselves which form of economic organization best supports their political aspirations. Democrats in the ancient and early modern worlds said commerce corrupted civic virtue, but its English and American practitioners—the new commercial and capitalist classes—forged new theories of capitalist democracy which insisted that the best citizens were men of property. Political economists like the great Scotsman Adam Smith and statesmen like the American founder Alexander Hamilton argued that the energy and frugality of what would later be called the "Protestant work ethic" were good for democracy, and that in a free society a relatively limited state that left the capitalist market alone (so-called *laissez-faire*) was the surest guarantor of political liberty.

Nowadays, free-market critics of socialism, Marxism, welfare-statism, and government planning continue to argue that a powerful state that intervenes in the economy encroaches on the freedom and privacy of individualism, interferes with bargaining and exchange as well as supply and demand, and turns the private labour of workers into a means for realizing abstract social ends—a classic case of the abuse of individuals being justified on the grounds of collective utility.

Social democrats insist, on the contrary, that pure capitalism brings in its train powerful social inequities that are then reproduced politically; that it leaves the weak, the powerless, and the poor to fend for themselves in a dog-eat-dog environment that guarantees their destruction. For them, they say, the unregulated market economy is never really free at all, since it advantages those who already possess wealth and power and disadvantages those who are without.

To put it simply, capitalism would seem to serve private freedom, particularly for the well off, but at the expense of equality; socialism would seem to serve equality, but at the expense of freedom, privacy, and property. Capitalism demands a limited state whose primary job is to guarantee that the market works well; socialism demands an interventionist state that regulates, plans, and controls in the name of social justice; and Marxist socialism requires a powerfully interventionist (some would say totalitarian) state to promote what it calls economic justice. Capitalism argues that there can be no political freedom without economic freedom. Socialism argues that there can be no political equality without economic equality. If democracy is defined by its freedoms, capitalism wins the argument; if it is defined by its equality, socialism wins the argument; if it is defined by both—and, as we have seen, it is in fact defined by both!—then we are lost in paradox and contradiction. And that is why the argument goes on unabated among Tories and socialists, market liberals and social planners, advocates of *laissez-faire* and advocates of the welfare state. Is the American Securities and Exchange Commission a democratic instrument of the people to control the bankers and brokers, or is it Wall Street's lobby group in Washington? Does the Canadian Broadcasting Corporation give the Canadian people a public voice, or does it create a cosy inner circle in the broadcast market at public expense? Is Royal Dutch Shell a private or a public body? Whom does it represent? As we explored the international banks, the cartels, the multinational corporations, the state regulatory agencies, the capitalist experiments in socialist countries, and the socialist experiments in capitalist countries, we became convinced that the battle between capitalists and socialists was irrelevant—because neither capitalism as the unregulated competition of small businesses, nor socialism as the total ownership by a democratic state of all property and productive wealth, exists today.

At the dawn of the industrial age capitalism meant the competition of small family firms to produce the goods demanded by a growing society. Its crucial virtues were technological invention, deferred spending (saving), investment, and a constant battle to increase productivity. But capitalism has come to mean consumer capitalism, the capitalism of the takeover-minded, monopolistic, multinational corporation, and this is far less competitive, less inventive, less productive, less enterprising. It focuses on consumption more than production, on spending more than saving or investment, on short-term profitability rather than long-term productivity. It may even welcome government intervention in the form of protection from international competition, price and tariff supports, emergency financing, and social insurance against investment catastrophes.

In the United States, the federal government is formally loyal to capitalism. But it has been anything but *laissez-faire*: it has intervened constantly in the private sector, not in the name of socialism or welfare but in order to support big business. It has taken over a major part of the bankrupt national railway system, bailed out the failing Chrysler automobile corporation, supported foreign trade through Import-Export Bank subsidies to selected companies, provided price supports for the agricultural industry, and imposed quotas and tariffs to regulate foreign competition. This may all be prudent, even humane economic policy, but it is hardly free-market capitalism. Political scientist Ted Lowi has suggested that what America has done is to introduce a new form of socialism: it leaves profit to the private market but it socializes risk, which is in effect assumed by government, which then spreads the cost across the backs of taxpayers. Adam Smith's *laissez-faire* capitalism has all but vanished.

Nineteenth-century socialism has undergone parallel changes. It once meant state control of all major industries, guaranteed jobs for all, ongoing regulation of every part of the economy, and long-term national economic planning which, under early Leninist and Stalinist models, meant inflexible five- or ten-year plans. Socialism today is a Swiss cheese, full of small capitalist holes. The Soviet-bloc nations are toying with incentives, decentralized control, and schemes that leave room for forms of worker participation and spontaneity that would have been unthinkable in classical socialist economics. And the democracies of Scandinavia have experienced decades of social democratic government without giving up their free economies, forging interesting new forms of the "mixed economy" that combine some of the security of socialism with some of the freedom of capitalism.

Indeed, some of the most interesting democratic experiments involve policies or institutions that cannot be clearly identified as capitalist or socialist, but point towards a convergence of ideologies that may in time support democracy better than either of the pure forms.

England's Capitalist Revolution

British Prime Minister Thatcher's experiments with selling subsidized housing to residents, with helping citizens to buy stock in great national corporations such as British Airways, and with Employee Stock Ownership

Plans (ESOPs) defy easy economic classification. Naturally, Thatcher's Conservative government likes to think of them as experiments in property-owning democracy, a new twist on old capitalist ideas. But an egalitarian capitalism in which everyone becomes an owner can also begin to produce something like a classless society. In Reagan's America, capitalism has been socialized; in Thatcher's England, socialism is in effect being privatized and individualized so that equality is achieved through the market itself rather than directly through government intervention. Critics say that in her campaign to privatize as many state functions as possible she is selling off the national heritage as well as England's precious public goods, but Thatcher regards what she is doing as a "capitalist revolution" in the spirit of democracy. Supporters like Joyce Sargent agree.

Joyce Sargent is a washroom attendant at a Birmingham financial institution, and was a long-time Labour Party supporter. Her husband, Ron, used to be a union shop steward. But the Thatcher revolution has made Joyce Sargent a capitalist. When shares in British Gas were offered at an attractive discount, Sargent bought some; she also bought into the company she works for. She tells us, "If you've got shares in the company, you don't want to see it go down, do you? So naturally you work hard to keep it going, because it's actually your company as well." Under Thatcher's Employee Stock Ownership Plan, an idea which is now gaining strength in the United States, employee ownership of corporate shares has increased 550 per cent.

When the government offered the council houses on her street for sale to their tenants, Sargent jumped. As a proud home-owner, she has painted and polished her new treasure and made it the jewel of the neighbourhood. "Forty years ago," she says, "I wouldn't have dreamed about shares in a company and owning my own house, but when the government gave us the opportunity. . . ." Sargent has abandoned the Labour Party, as has her husband, the former shop steward.

Whether this dream can be realized for everyone, however, is not clear. There is a growing divide between people like Joyce, who had sufficient means and motivation to take advantage of the government's plan, and those who have nothing: no house, no shares, no job—not enough to parlay into ownership of any kind, even under the government's generous terms. The price of Thatcher's revolution may in fact be the growth of an impoverished underclass that is unemployed, dependent on the welfare bureaucracy, passive and powerless now (and often homeless and hungry as well) but possibly dangerous down the road. Some individuals try to work—collecting scrap from noisome rubbish dumps, combing through garbage cans for deposit bottles, all for a few pennies. But no one can make a living off a bit of copper here, a few empty bottles there.

The reality is that up to one-fifth of the British population seems to be falling into this underclass, and there is little prospect that they will benefit from the democratization of capitalism. The figures in the prosperous United States are similar, and although a great majority of the American population calls itself "middle class", one out of five still lives near or under the poverty line. In New York alone there are three hundred thousand on welfare, tens of thousands who are homeless and—among young blacks and Hispanics—50 per cent or more unemployed. It is not clear that either classical or revolutionary capitalism will be able to incorporate these potentially violent masses into their versions of capitalist democracy.

Russia's Socialist Revolution

As capitalist democracies became more socialized in their struggle with inequality and injustice, socialist countries became more tolerant of capitalistic experimentation in their search for productivity and competitiveness. And where Margaret Thatcher spoke of a capitalist "revolution" to justify her departures from the classical market doctrines of Adam Smith, Soviet leader Mikhail Gorbachev, spoke of a socialist "revolution" to justify his departures from the classical doctrines of Marxism-Leninism.

A visit to the conservative "people's democracy" of East Germany does not immediately reflect these radical changes. For the German Democratic Republic was perhaps the most traditional of the Communist nations. With seventeen million people, it was dominated since its inception in 1949 by the Soviet Union—the victorious occupier of the eastern portion of Germany after the Second World War. Its constitution, most recently revised in 1968, was still patterned after the Weimar Constitution, which governed Germany after the First World War, before the Nazis, and provided for the usual panoply of parties, freedoms, and parliamentary institutions. But the reality was total control by the Socialist Unity Party (the Communist Party) that made constitutional provisions meaningless.

In all of the so-called peoples' democracies, the Communist Party was regarded as the sole legitimate organ of the working classes and, as such, the organ which must control the state, the army, the media, the bureaucracy, and every other political institution. Total party control allowed the state to guarantee jobs, public order, and security. There were unions in East Germany, but they are all dominated by the party. There were several parliamentary parties with names that sound like West Germany's, but each one is dominated by the party. There was a Youth Movement, and dozens of newspapers, but they are all run by the party. An uprising by workers in 1953 aimed at real democratization was put down violently in the name of the party's socialist values. Liberty may get short shrift, but security and social and economic order are the result.

Many East Germans found the system so constraining to their liberty that they fled to West Germany or elsewhere—often taking their lives in their hands in trying to cross the heavily fortified border between East and West Germany, or scaling the infamous Wall dividing the old capital city of Berlin.

But others actually seemed to prefer the safety of a one-party state, and argue that that security is essential to their concept of democracy. Some even tried out life in the West and then returned to the East, disappointed with the unruly freedoms they have found there. We met a man named Reinhart Oehme, born in Dresden five years before that terrible day in 1945 when the Allies sent wave after wave of bombers over the city in a mass raid that set off a firestorm the likes of which the world had never seen. Curious about life in the "free" part of Germany, like so many East Germans (many of whom watch West German television), he took his wife and son to the West in search of a new life. But they quickly found they were unprepared for the "cold wind of freedom". A lifetime spent in a total welfare state had not prepared them for the pressures and risks of life under capitalism. And so the Oehmes returned to Dresden, bringing with them a load of electrical appliances and memories of a life they could not cope with. Oehme is frank about his disappointment: "The first impression was one of many young people who were milling around in the employment offices, which is something that was completely unthinkable in East Germany. That was a shock for us." He recognizes they are less free back in Dresden—they cannot travel as they want, change jobs as they wish, do as they please. Yet Frau Oehme insists, "We live far more tranquilly and we don't have any worries about our place of employment, and that is the most important thing."

Western critics might say the Oehmes sold their freedom for economic security, but Reinhart Oehme said that "democracy does not necessarily mean for everybody to be able to do what each person wants to do . . . it means what is better for the masses." To many people around the world, being guaranteed the dignity of a job, being treated as a social equal of everyone else, is as important a part of "democracy" as having a choice of political parties or being able to travel to any point on the globe.

But this suggests that the peoples of the world still face the old nineteenth-century choice between a free but insecure and perhaps unjust capitalist democracy and a secure and egalitarian but perhaps unfree socialist democracy. In truth, this choice itself has been outrun by events, and of all the "peoples' democracies", East Germany—among the least changed and most dogmatic—may have been the least appropriate example of the modern socialist state. The archetype of the European socialist state was the Soviet Union, and in the years leading up to its collapse in 1990, the Soviet Union underwent a "revolution" no less startling than England's under Thatcher or China's under Mao's successors.

Starting with the hesitant reforms of Brezhnev and Andropov, and escalating under the leadership of General Secretary Gorbachev, the Soviet Union embarked on an astonishing campaign of economic and political reform. *Perestroika* was, in Gorbachev's own words, the "policy of accelerating the country's social and economic progress and renewing all spheres of life" in an atmosphere of openness and pluralism called *glasnost*.

Gorbachev was naturally quick to say that all of the changes being urged under the banner of *perestroika* mean not less but more socialism, and that "more socialism means more democracy, openness and collectivism in everyday life." Yet the actual reforms fostered greater incentives for individuals, greater competition, greater pluralism, and greater freedom; not less socialism, perhaps, but less direct regulation and control. Gorbachev himself used the language of revolution, suggesting that the old socialism has "lost momentum. Economic failures became more frequent. Difficulties began to accumulate and deteriorate. . . . Elements of what we call stagnation and other phenomena alien to socialism began to appear." This revolution featured newspaper letters from readers criticizing the Communist Party, a meeting of Moscow dissidents demanding to establish a non-Communist political party, major concessions on disarmament treaties with the West, withdrawal from Afghanistan, the President of the United States strolling through Red Square during the 1988 Summit meeting to chat with Soviet citizens, and an extraordinary five-part Soviet television series on American life complete with Russian-language advertising spots by Sony, Pepsi-Cola, and Visa Card.

The revolution that has taken hold of ageing capitalism and transformed free-market economies into mixed economies and *laissez-faire* states into welfare states, and the revolution that before long killed the Soviet Union, are still in their infancies in other parts of the world. But these revolutions do teach a common lesson: that words like capitalist and socialist are no longer useful labels for the realities of the modern world, that nations in the West and the East alike are finding that they must accommodate themselves to a new economic world if they are to preserve—let alone improve—their political systems. The old debates about capitalism, socialism, and democracy are using a new vocabulary that includes terms like structural unemployment, homelessness, the multinational corporation, property-owning democracy, international cartel, incentive socialism, employee stock ownership plan, and a host of other novelties—terms that capture the new economic realities that face those who still struggle for democracy. The question is no longer "How compatible is commerce with civic virtue?" or "How democratic is socialism?" but "How compatible is the multinational corporation with civic virtue?" or "How democratic can a world be in which the decisions of OPEC are final?"

In a sense we are all capitalists now: whether in the socialist or capitalist world, we are players in a global market where no one nation can find its way alone to total security. And in a sense we are all socialists now: we all depend to a lesser or greater degree on the safety nets, welfare schemes, social security, medical insurance, regulatory agencies, and economic planning of the state, which has not really "left things alone" in Adam Smith's sense for at least a hundred years. The free-market capitalism celebrated by economists like Milton Friedman (who served as a consultant to the Reagan administration, the Pinochet regime in Chile, and other governments) is as obsolete as Marxist socialism. How are we to classify Hong Kong, now restored to "communist" China but with its free-market economy still fundraising? Indeed, how to classify China itself, with its burgeoning businesses, free economic zones, and growing commitment to the values of personal wealth.

This is not to say that the question of the price of democracy has disappeared. For all the changes, what was true in Athens remains true today: money still buys power, even in a "property-owning democracy". Property still counts, long after the unpropertied are given the right to vote. Wealth can still affect political power, even where a rich man's vote counts no more than a poor man's.

A democratic society will always require more than just a democratic government: it will require a degree of social justice no free market has ever produced by itself. But it will also require a degree of private freedom no socialist regime has ever been able to allow. It will require institutions that deal with the new international markets and the new international corporations. The struggle for democracy will require more than just annual elections or the multiplication of political parties or a free press. It will require that politics be attuned to economics, that the freedom afforded by privacy and economic pluralism be reconciled to the equality demanded by justice—more freedom than pure socialists envision, more equality than pure capitalists seek. And so that struggle remains, and will perhaps always remain, not a pleasant voyage to freedom or an inevitable march to equality but a protracted and painful struggle between freedom and equality that has to be waged over and over again.

Under Fire

Democracy's War with War

IN 1941, JUST A FEW DAYS AFTER THE JAPANESE BOMBED Pearl Harbor, one of the world's most democratic governments, under fire from a coalition of aggressive Fascist nations committed to the destruction of democracy, began its fight for survival by compromising one of the basic principles for which it fought. Made fearful by rumours of Japanese plots to invade the west coast, the United States passed hastily conceived and ill-considered legislation that gave the government the right to round up any-one of Japanese ancestry. In Canada (which as a British Commonwealth nation had been at war for two years and already had a War Measures Act ready for use) and the United States alone more than one hundred thou-sand people were detained. Although nearly three-quarters of them were Canadian or American citizens, and most had been born in North America, they were stripped of their civil rights and incarcerated in "internment centres" that were in fact concentration camps. "The war to save democracy", as it was often called, had yielded as its first victim a small but precious limb of democracy itself.

At Hart Mountain camp outside of Cody, Wyoming (a town named for that great symbol of Old West liberties, Buffalo Bill Cody), eleven thousand Japanese Americans were herded together and interned. With their property confiscated, their rights suspended, their loyalty under suspicion, they sat out the war—a war many of them said they would have gladly fought, to help preserve the liberty of those who were imprisoning them.

Democracies must often make war, and war has sometimes made democracy. History records that the world's first democracy, Athens, first appeared out of the duststorm of war with Persia; and the independent and newly united states of America rose up from the fire of battle at Bunker Hill and Yorktown. Citizens often acquire their first sense of political obligation as soldiers, and soldiering has been a responsibility of citizenship in every nation that has aspired to call itself a democracy since the time of Pericles.

But war may also unmake democracy—and war and the military institutions on which it depends are themselves at odds with the openness, tolerance, and liberty on which democracy is founded.

If Athens' most glorious democratic chapter opened with the Persian wars that liberated the Greeks from the Persian empire, it also closed with the Peloponnesian War that set Athenian Greek against Spartan Greek in a bitter and destructive rivalry. Switzerland's democratic confederation was forged by the power of its citizen armies in the fifteenth century, but these same armies, drawn into Europe's power politics as mercenaries, compromised its independence for two centuries, until it established its neutrality. Just eighty years after it emerged from the revolution, America nearly destroyed itself in a civil conflict bloodier than any war the nation has known since. And Abraham Lincoln, remembered as a prophet of moral rejuvenation and democratic union, was of necessity something of a tyrant—his quest for military victory over the secessionist South compelled him to suspend such fundamental civil rights as habeas corpus.

The damage done to democracy by the conflict of nations has become even more palpable in this century: both world wars were followed in North America by Red scares and political witch hunts in which patriotism came to be measured by conformity and free thinking was construed as treason. In democracies like Israel or Northern Ireland that are subjected to continuous war or threat of war over long periods, free states can become garrison states in which liberty itself is finally at risk.

War seems to bring out the worst and the best in democracy—inspiring it at birth, but sometimes pushing it to a premature death; turning private persons into selfless public citizens, yet at the same time often making democratic dissenters look like cavilling traitors. The relationship of war and democracy reveals how unexpected and contradictory the struggle for democracy can be.

There is a scarcely a democracy in the world that has not been at war, and only a few have avoided the costs of maintaining a military establishment inside the fragile structure of free government. We went to three continents in search of war's effect on democracy: to Europe, where the French army has never been at peace with the revolutionary democratic principles established in 1789, and where a Swiss citizen army has spent three hundred years assuring that no wars would be fought; to Latin America, where younger democracies face the paradox of trying to live in freedom in the shadow of powerful military establishments; and to the Middle East, where, in Israel, a citizen army has lived under constant threat of war for forty years, and where democracy is imperilled not only by hostile neighbours but by the military occupation of captured territory. We were astonished and perplexed by the variety of experiences we encountered: in Argentina, a country struggling to free itself from military rule; in Haiti, a military struggling to maintain its hold over a would-be democracy; in Costa Rica, a country that has dared to abolish its army altogether. What we learned was that the military—whatever its form—creates problems for democracy; and that whether war is sought out or imposed from the outside, it exacts high costs in freedom, even in nations that go into battle to preserve their liberty.

The French Army against French Democracy

The Bourbon monarchs in the seventeenth and eighteenth centuries deployed large national armies to create a powerful state at home and an impressive empire abroad. Unlike the standing professional armies and small private forces of men-at-arms that had existed until then, these new armies were made up of men conscripted from the general population, as and when needed. Yet though the armies were conscripted from the civilian population they were anything but democratic. During the French Revolution, ambitious armies drawn together by the cry "Liberté, Egalité, Fraternité!" panicked England and Europe, but it was not until the democratic revolution had self-destructed and the newly crowned emperor, Napoleon, was on the march to forge a new empire that France became a genuine threat. Napoleon's successes were shortlived, however. His defeat by the bitter Russian winter following the pyrrhic occupation of Moscow was the first in a century of military débâcles that the French army would come to blame on democracy. The army, anti-democratic by tradition and bitter, drifted towards a confrontation with its own government. The situation came to a head in the notorious "Dreyfus Affair". In 1894—just a few decades after the disaster of the Franco-Prussian War, in which France lost some of its territory and a good deal more of its pride to Germany—a young Jewish staff officer named Alfred Dreyfus was convicted of selling secrets to the Germans and sentenced to life imprisonment on Devil's Island. Although it quickly became apparent that the captain was not guilty, the army would not abandon its case, leaving the public with the impression that Dreyfus' real crime was his Jewishness—and the support given him by liberal democratic politicians.

Captain Dreyfus was ultimately retried and found innocent, and finally, in 1906, fully pardoned. The affair left the army estranged from politics, and the politicians and the democratic nation more mistrustful than ever of the army. The catastrophes that the twentieth century held in store for France were not to reconcile the two, or restore the army's morale.

Though it ended in victory for France and its allies, the First World War decimated an entire generation. Moreover, it left France with a false sense of security, and by the 1930s the nation had retreated behind the infamous "Maginot Line"—the well-trenched warren of pillboxes and bunkers on the German frontier that was supposed to render France invincible. Under assault from Nazi Panzer divisions in 1940, the line collapsed—abruptly, ignominiously, completely. France fell in just three weeks, signing an armistice with Germany and Italy, and the aged symbol of France's tattered military honour, Marshal Pétain, became a Nazi collaborator.

But there was one young tank officer who would keep French honour alive. With a few thousand sailors and airmen, Charles de Gaulle fled into exile in Britain. There, as leader of the Free French forces and the government in exile, he became a symbol of liberation and the embodiment of France itself. Home again, in the aftermath of the Allied victory over the Nazis in 1945, de Gaulle's Free French forces became the heart of a resuscitated French army. But the primary lesson the army had learned from de Gaulle's wartime resistance was that it was acceptable, even laudable, for soldiers to defy civilian rulers. This attitude of defiance, echoing the army's longstanding distrust of politicians, was to become crucial in the crises occasioned by the breakup of France's empire in North Africa and, above all, in Vietnam (French Indo-China).

France had maintained the far-flung colonies that were vital to its domestic economy and its global power for a long time. Though it was the army itself that was defeated by Ho Chi Minh's forces of nationalist revolution at the fatal battle of Dienbienphu in 1954, the officer corps laid the blame at the wide-open door of the scurrying politicians. So when the Algerian revolution broke out in the middle fifties—leaving a million stubborn French settlers ("pieds noirs") bent on full union with the France they regarded as their own, facing nine million Arabs seeking national liberation from France—the army leapt in, in defiance of the French government's decision to grant Algeria independence. With some half-million troops in the field in Algeria, the army was able to precipitate a constitutional crisis more severe than anything the French had known since Napoleon.

Once again *le grand général*, the army's darling, rode to the rescue. The military had never trusted the politicians, and no military leader had been more cynical about party politics than de Gaulle, since the time he headed into exile in 1940 blaming parliamentary politics for the collapse of the Third Republic. When in 1958, in the storm of the Algerian crisis, he exploded from his long post-war silence at his retreat at Colombey-les-Deux-Eglises, the army had every right to believe he had come to save French Algeria and their honour.

For the French at home and in Algeria, these were angry, frightening years, filled with demonstrations and fighting. We got a taste of the times from talking with former *commandant* Hélie Denoix de Saint-Marc, a Resistance hero who had survived combat with the Nazis as well as incarceration in Buchenwald, and had also fought courageously in Indo-China. In the late 1950s he found himself stationed in Algeria, torn between his sense of duty to French democracy—which meant obeying the orders of civilians he regarded as traitors to France—and his sense of duty to the honour of France—which meant preserving a French Algeria by any means, including military resistance to the civilian government at home. When the civilians seemed to be selling Algeria down the Arab river, Saint-Marc rebelled. Not, he insists, "out of a desire for some pro-Fascist adventure or some such thing, but really out of moral necessity." It was not a matter of opposing France, but of representing its higher interests against civilians who no longer represented them; "In times of crisis, the soldier may be the embodiment of the nation," he says today. But democracy rarely fares well when individuals or institutions decide they represent a nation's true interests and place themselves above the elected government, and French democracy did not fare well under fire from its self-righteous army.

In its first manifestation in 1958, the military revolt quickly spread from the capital, Algiers, to the island of Corsica, where army contingents planned the occupation of France under the telling code name "Operation Resurrection". The frightened civilian government in Paris toyed with the idea of resistance; a plan by the leftist unions to close down the railways was entertained until someone observed that paratroopers were unlikely to invade the capital by train. But with the government in disarray, and President Coty threatening to resign, General de Gaulle was invited to become prime minister with enhanced and extraordinary powers.

The army and the colonists in Algeria were initially ecstatic. The great general travelled to Algeria, and with the famous words "Je vous ai compris!" ("I have understood you!") seemed to embrace his military brethren and their campaign for a French Algeria. But de Gaulle turned out to be more concerned with restructuring France than with preserving a French Algeria—in fact, with an all too French irony, this former enemy of the politicians held off the military in Algeria long enough to reconstruct the French constitution and thereby save the politicians from the army. In place of a government dominated and often paralysed by a great many weak political parties, de Gaulle established a strong presidency on the American model. The parties and their national assembly survived, but now it was the president who would give moral leadership and political direction to France. And by December 1958, the president was de Gaulle himself. The great military hero had become the constitutional keystone of the new Fifth Republic.

By 1961, Saint-Marc and his colleagues in Algeria realized their hopes had been betrayed. When asked to join the colonels' renewed insurrection, Saint-Marc did not hesitate: "Je marche avec vous!" he declared. And march they did, quite literally; for this time they tried a straightforward military putsch that they hoped would bring de Gaulle to his senses. Back in Paris, the government pulled some old Sherman tanks out of mothballs—but there was no need: although the crack professional paratroopers—men like Saint-Marc—enthusiastically followed the colonels, the conscript army commanded by the rebels, made up of youths from France who cared little about Algeria, empire, or "honour", refused the colonels' orders. With de Gaulle against them, and only the "paras" and the Foreign

Legion willing to fight, the colonels' rebellion was over before it began—
it collapsed in four days. Saint-Marc and the others were sentenced to long
prison terms. The French army had once again run headlong into French
democracy; and once again, as in the case of Alfred Dreyfus, both had
come away weakened by the collision.

Like so many practitioners of democracy, the French yearn for liberty
but lean towards security. Freedom can breed rebellion but rebellion can
breed anarchy; in their fear of anarchy, the French have turned to forceful
leaders like Napoleon and de Gaulle. Such rescuers, while restoring security, soon steal liberty, and so the people begin again to yearn for less
restraint. From 1947 to 1957 there were twenty-seven governments
under the weak parliamentary system of the Fourth Republic; from 1958
to 1969 there was de Gaulle. Under the chaos of the Fourth Republic
there was much freedom, little security, no order at all; under the strong
hand of de Gaulle in the Fifth there was much security, but less liberty.

Who then could be surprised at still another turning of the wheel
when, in 1968, the international student movement brought spontaneity
and rebellion to the streets of Paris to reclaim France and revive the raucous voice of dissent? A noisier democracy was restored, less dependent
on heroic leadership. But the underlying conflict of order and liberty, of
honour and democracy, of the army and the politicians, survives, and even
now, as President Mitterrand begins his second seven-year term, France is
still trying to decide just how much politics, how much anarchy, is compatible with order. And while there seem to be no generals waiting in the
wings this time, the fear of chaos that has in the past brought them centre-
stage persists—and with that fear, a risk to the future of democracy.

Stability—through the Military?

The suspicion with which the French military regard democratic parties and
politicians has been widely shared. At the time of the American founding
James Madison railed against parties, and Thomas Jefferson told his followers in the 1780s that if the only way to go to heaven was with a party he'd as
soon not go at all. But Madison and Jefferson changed their tune when, as
presidents, they came to understand how well parties functioned as con-
duits between a people and their representatives. De Gaulle never grasped
this, even when France's young took to the streets of Paris in 1968—he was

defeated on a reform referendum a year later. Nevertheless, his years of success are a reminder that when democracy is under fire, the public looks for rescue not to faceless bureaucrats or loyal party men but to national heroes. And for heroes, there is no better place to look than the army.

Civilian rule is a paramount constitutional principle in the United States, yet Americans have frequently elected military heroes as their leaders: from the War of Independence came General George Washington, from the Civil War, General Ulysses S. Grant, from the Second World War (and the reaction to the Korean War), General Dwight D. Eisenhower. If war heroes and the discipline of the military appeal to stable old democracies like France and the United States, they are downright seductive to newer Third World countries, where the army often represents the sturdiest, the best-educated, the most coherent force the nation possesses. It may be a non-democratic, even an anti-democratic force, but the alternative to it can be chaos and national disintegration.

In much of the world, the army is regarded as a counterweight to the anarchy of party politics and as the most effective instrument of national unity and order. But the army can also be a faction unto itself—divisive, destabilizing, and deadly to democracy. Perhaps nowhere in the world are these contradictions more evident than in Latin America. Almost every Latin American country has had its military "saviour"—its Perón (Argentina), or Batista (Cuba), or Duvalier (Haiti), or Pinochet (Chile), or Ortega (Nicaragua), or Stroessner (Paraguay)—and for every country that has gone from military dictatorship to democracy in the 1980s (Ecuador, Peru, Bolivia, Brazil, Argentina) there is a democracy that has fallen to or remained under the sway of a military junta (Chile, Grenada, Paraguay, Panama, Haiti). Too often, in countries that have recently emerged into the open air of free government, democracy seems a fragile sapling too weak to stand against the storms of class conflict and party politics that are natural to the climate of new nations.

Argentina—Bullets to Ballots?

In 1983—for the eighth or tenth or twelfth time in this century (depending on how you count the coups and putsches)—democracy returned to Argentina. An army that had just fought its only foreign war in a century, and had lost, was obliged to yield power to a civilian government. To the cheers of crowds chanting, "The People, United, Will Never Be Defeated!" the new president, Raúl Alfonsín, announced, "We are at the beginning of one hundred years of freedom, peace, and democracy."

Yet if Argentina's history was any indication, this was more a wish than a prophecy. The great Argentinian writer Jorge Luis Borges has written that "there are no citizens in Argentina, there are only inhabitants of a territory to be exploited." From 1810, when a fledgeling army created the independent Argentine state, until that day in 1983 when Alfonsín put an end to seven catastrophic years of military rule, the predator was the army itself. By 1982 it boasted 100,000 men, yet it could claim no credible external enemies. It was humiliated in its attempt to win the nearby Malvinas (the Falkland Islands) from the British. It apparently existed only to control the civilian population: during the late seventies and early eighties, it managed to torture and murder up to 30,000 Argentine citizens, and to intimidate hundreds of thousands more. In its domestic war against "subversives"—known to the generals as the "Third World War against Subversion" and to the natives upon whom it was practised as the "Dirty War"—the army created a new language of fear punctuated by strange terms like "the disappeared". But this unholy campaign against "subversion" was only the latest instalment in a long history of anti-democratic activity by a military establishment that had overthrown seven civilian governments between 1930 and 1976, and had never been far from the seat of power even during periods of civilian rule. Raúl Alfonsín was genuine democrat, but he knew what the army knew: though weakened, it was still an influential factor with a potential veto over policy. Restive officers tried a barracks revolt at Córdoba in the spring of 1987, and though it failed, they offered proof of what Admiral Massera, a leading member of the pre-Alfonsín junta, said as he was being sentenced to life in prison: "The enemy is afraid because it knows that the armed forces today can return to defeat them."

It is a peculiar irony of Argentina that its politicians have managed to hold the army in check only once in its modern history, and that was during the reign of that remarkable civilian tyrant, Juan Domingo Perón. Although Perón began as a military officer, his power rested not on the army but on Argentina's poor working class. From their burning class resentments he ignited a fire that, in the early 1940s, nearly consumed Argentina's elites—wealthy urban bourgeoisie, Church, and army alike. His success was due in part to his second wife, Evita, who became a national icon. Her death in

1952 drew almost three-quarters of a million mourners (who managed to trample to death seven of their own number) and later inspired Andrew Lloyd Webber—the English composer who writes mega-hit shows for the West End and Broadway and political ditties for Margaret Thatcher—to compose a musical based on the story of her life.

No less brutal and intolerant than the army itself, Perón was for a while its true match—the only civilian Argentinian president in the century to be re-elected (in 1951) to a second term; the only to return from exile, where he spent eighteen long years following his ouster in 1955; and the only to be re-elected following exile. His third wife, Isabel, continued in office after his death in 1974, until she fell to the generals in 1976.

Perón dealt with the army in part by out-terrorizing it. Sounding like some bent civilian echo of a mad military terrorist, he proclaimed "Violence in the hands of the people isn't violence, it is justice!" Even today, Perónism without Perón remains a potent force in class-torn Argentinian politics. In the late 1987 elections, Alfonsín's traditional Radical Party, the party that had been trying since 1930 to create a democratic Argentina, found itself on the defensive against still another Perónist revival. And in the shadows, ever present, lurked the army.

Too many Argentinians remain provisional democrats, demanding the safeguards of a military regime while protesting military excesses. Even as the "Mothers of the Plaza de Mayo" called on the new democracy to help uncover the truth about their children—"disappeared" under the military terror—the middle class of Buenos Aires was complaining about the absence of "law and order" under that same democracy. Not even the impoverished have much good to say about the new freedom. We talked to several disgruntled workers in a shantytown on the outskirts of Buenos Aires. As he bitterly answered our questions about the new regime, Hector Leyes seemed to have forgotten the Dirty War and the army's abuses of rights: "Since democracy there hasn't been life here . . . because there has been a lot of disorder . . . peace was lost, now people do what they like, they do anything, here in the shantytown all sorts of things happen. . . . When the military were in power there were no shootouts or anything. . . . Since democracy the way of life here has gone rotten; we have no rights. When the military were in power, we worked untroubled, we ate well, there was work for all and we could do as we pleased, there was no tension, there were no thieves. . . . The definition of democracy is that it doesn't help us."

While the army and the politicians have been jousting for power, the rich and the poor have been locked in class conflict. The spirit of Perónism lives on in the Perónist rallies that are held regularly outside urban Buenos Aires. These rallies have the feel of a political meeting and the smell of a lynching party. *Bombas* beat out insistent rhythms, half-naked dancers gyrate on the hustings next to overheated politicians who pummel the sweating crowds with slogans. At times they speak in an almost religious chant. "*Perón viva!*" they cry. Or "*Evita vuelve!*" as if they might bring back the revered Evita. But at other times the Perónist orators come on among the twirling dancers as simple-minded Fascists, calling for the blood of traitors. Buenos Aires is a city of money and plutocrats, of treasonous soldiers and scabrous bankers, they cry; and then they start screaming for the blood of Jews—specifically, literally, name by name. A Radical Party congressman running for re-election is branded a "Jew son of a whore"; Jews, the crowd-pleasing bigots shout, are destroying the nation.

In this steaming new agora, talk often sounds like gibberish, while action is the movement of knives and bullets. Argentinian news commentator Hermann Schiller explains that "Argentina is the only country where the Second World War is still going on." And V. S. Naipaul writes, "Perónism was never a program. It was an insurrection." Under these circumstances, how can democracy survive? President Alfonsín himself said "We are still not living in a state of complete democracy. It is not enough to have democratic institutions; for democracy to work we have to destroy the demonic messianic vision of their role—[the vision that] identified the military with the state. They treated politics and politicians with contempt. . . . The dominant pattern has been authoritarian."

Argentina is still plagued by violence, and the Mothers of the Plaza de Mayo who have been searching for their children for over a decade still seek justice in vain. In the words of one of them, Renée Epelbaum, "Maybe I need to weep . . . maybe I didn't do it enough because perhaps I'm afraid if I begin I won't finish, ever."

And once again the army is waiting in the wings, insisting that it has never stepped onto the political stage uninvited, biding its time until the people again grow frustrated with the politicians, or frightened of the seething Perónists, or unwilling to tolerate the new dependency on foreigners created by the $50 billion national debt. Whether in or out of power, the army obviously has not lost faith in the rhetoric of its mission, outlined in a recent publicity pamphlet issued by the National Military

Academy: "Armies that left Buenos Aires [in the early nineteenth century] towards what is today Chile, Bolivia, Peru, or Paraguay did not march upon them merely to oust their Spanish rulers. They brought with them an ideal of self-government, of political independence. Liberating armies therefore helped to carry out a sort of ideological revolution. They helped to make a nation. . . . The country was a vast emptiness to be filled."

What is true for Argentina is true for a great many Latin American nations that, free of the threat of war, are none the less under the gun of their own armies. For example, Brazil has a distinctive history—but when we look at its military, it's the same old story.

The Same Old Story—with an Exception

Brazil thinks of itself as a world power, and aspires to global influence by the year 2000. It is one of the world's largest nations (fifth in territory, sixth in population), a land of great rivers and coasts, jungles and rain-forests, sweltering tropical regions and temperate uplands. It was originally a Portuguese rather than a Spanish colony, and its history seems at first to be very different from Argentina's. For when in 1930 the patriot Getulio Vargas overthrew the old republic, Brazil took on a corporatist character similar to Mussolini's Italy, where individuals were subordinated to the state. Yet despite this flirtation with Fascism, from 1945 until 1964 Brazil wedded itself quite successfully to democracy. It succumbed to the familiar and fatal attraction of military coups in the seventies, but in 1985, under the watchful eyes of the military, elections were again held and a civilian government returned to power.

Here, as elsewhere in Latin America, there is an impatience with democracy, its messy politics, its potential corruption, its uncertainties, its lack of orderliness. Civilian rule has excited as much bitterness as jubilation in Brazil—and some people still long for the return of the military and the reimposition of order. Some polls suggest that more than two-thirds of Brazil's middle class dream of living abroad, and Antonio José de Andrade, a businessman, said to us recently, "This is a country with no rules, no responsibility, no shame. We're living the end of an illusion."

While civilian leaders in Argentina and Brazil are trying to coax reluctant populations into the heady air of freedom, in Haiti the military is trying to coerce a resisting population into military despotism. In 1986 Haiti emerged from decades of "government" by a family of thieves and cut-throats, the Duvaliers ("Papa Doc" and son "Baby Doc"), who with the help of secret police thugs—the feared Tontons Macoute—had terrorized and exploited this island people into abject servitude. Dreadful dictator that he was, Papa Doc had at least come to power by electoral means, in 1957—but on his death in 1971, his son simply took control.

Fed up with terror, if not dictatorship, the Haitian people finally drove the young Duvalier into exile in 1986 (today he lives in heavily guarded opulence on the French Riviera). A military government under General Henri Namphy was created to fill the vacuum, and ease the way to what were to be free elections. Given Latin American history, however, asking the military to bring an end to tyranny is asking a pyromaniac to put out a campfire. The situation in Haiti was made worse by the survival of the Tontons Macoute, most of whom eluded the lynchings that accompanied Duvalier's ouster. These chameleons melted back into the army or faded into the criminal fringes of society—to wait. The new provisional military government dedicated itself to democracy—but did everything it could to sabotage the elections. A civilian electoral council appointed to oversee them was powerless, and watched as two presidential candidates were assassinated prior to the vote. Then, on election day, November 21, 1987, polling stations were turned into execution chambers for citizens who braved the climate of fear to exercise their democratic rights. Gunfire and machete attacks from Tontons Macoute made a carnage of the elections, and martyrs of the voters. While the military stood idly by, dozens of people were mowed down at the Port-au-Prince schools and churches that served as polling places.

The military government has since promoted another electoral round in which its own hand-picked candidate was voted into power, in an election in which none of the legitimate politicians ran and few citizens went to the polls. The charade was labelled the restoration of democracy.

Getting Rid of the Army—or Making It Democratic

No matter where we look in Latin America, the pattern is the same: whether it is actually in power, or a shadow government that permits civilian politicians to front for it, or a potent observer watching from its sentry posts with guns cocked, the army is an inescapable presence. Chile remains in the hands of generals who in the seventies exiled civilians who had dared experiment with socialism, Haiti and Panama are military dictatorships in everything but name, Paraguay remains under the lifetime military dictator General Stroessner, who was "re-elected" to still another term in 1988, Nicaragua—used by the United States and the Soviet Union as a battleground for ideological politics—has civilian rulers who appear mostly in military uniform, and Brazil and Argentina hang on to their new-found freedoms only by a combination of courage, good luck, and military tolerance. In fact, there is only one exception to this daunting pattern: the remarkable little nation of Costa Rica, whose democratically elected president, Oscar Arias, won a 1987 Nobel Prize for his efforts in seeking a Central American peace plan. Once again, it is one of the *little* democracies that has achieved a large victory. Democracy flourishes in Costa Rica, not as a consequence of the army's forbearance, but because there is no army. Back in 1949, in a stunning twist on Latin America's usual politics, the Costa Rican people "disappeared" their army. They wrote a quite astonishing constitution (with a 93 per cent literacy rate, they are among the world's most capable citizens) in which the national army was disbanded and prohibited for all time.

Independent since 1821, Costa Rica has governed itself peacefully, as a social democracy, through much of this century. Its 1949 constitution gave the vote to women, and then, confronting the perils of military government that faced all of Latin America, simply liquidated the problem—quite literally. Today Costa Rica has a Civil Guard of seven thousand, a tiny navy of under a hundred men, and a few transports, choppers, and light planes. Today, though it has neighbours who are engaged in revolution or counter-revolution, it is involved in no wars, faces no insurrection, confronts no terrorists, and alone in Central America retains a genuine democracy. Remarkable! Its internal stability and its security in the face of aggressors seem to be better assured by its forceful democratic politics than they would be by the military force of arms it has chosen to forgo. What would happen to it if its borders were violated is unclear, but the fact remains that its borders have not been violated, and at least one little country has survived, even flourished, without an army.

Yet it would be hard to recommend Costa Rica as a model for most nations. Across the Atlantic, there are two other small democracies that yearn for peace but have had to deal with neighbours so hostile that there can be no question of doing away with their armies. Small as they are (Switzerland has under six million people, Israel under five million), both are armed to the teeth. Switzerland is surrounded by powerful neighbours who used to invade it at will, and Israel is opposed by hostile antagonists who sometimes deny its right to exist. Switzerland has had no major war in hundreds of years, Israel has been almost perpetually at war, or under the threat of war. Neither has ever been able to afford the luxury of demobilization. Yet both have developed strong democracies in the face of their own powerful military establishments. They share a crucial secret of democratic survival: that to protect democracy from the army, you have to have an army composed of democratic citizens. This means universal military conscription, an army involving all men (in Israel, Israeli men and women both), where the interests of the people and the interests of the military remain identical. Both Athens and Sparta taught this essential lesson. Both Machiavelli and Rousseau celebrated it as civic theory. And it was a key idea of the American revolutionaries, who favoured local militias over standing professional armies. Indeed, right up through the Second World War the United States demobilized its armies at the end of each war.

In Switzerland, we witnessed (see Chapter Seven) the intimate connection between military service and citizenship. There, a vigilant citizenry armed and ready to fight, yet dedicated to principles of neutrality and sustained by a tiny professional (standing) military staff, has managed to stay out of war for several centuries. Nor is Switzerland's neutrality something that can be taken for granted. "Neutral" Belgium quickly fell to the Germans in the First World War, and Hitler had invasion plans for Switzerland in the Second World War; he was dissuaded from attack in no small part because his general staff told him that it would take at least twelve German divisions six months or more to crack Switzerland's formidable citizen-manned defences, and the military installations that honeycomb its formidable mountains. If its national defence force was born of military necessity, Switzerland has managed over the centuries to turn it into an extraordinary civic virtue. Today, when the external threat seems minimal, and when some are urging a national referendum to abolish national service, many others continue to regard the Swiss army as the soul of Swiss democracy.

Israel: Armed Democracy and Perpetual War

Where the Swiss have waged perpetual peace with a well-armed citizen army and an uncompromising policy of neutrality, Israel has waged frequent if not perpetual war; given its hostile neighbours, neither peace nor neutrality seems to be an option.

We come upon Israel at one of the most perplexed moments of its history. When its most steadfast friends abroad and thousands of its citizens at home are appalled at the spectacle of its youthful armed forces retaliating against young rock-throwing Palestinian Arabs rioting in the occupied territories. We are trying to understand what is going on here, with an army composed of "ordinary" Israeli citizens, an army that is almost identical with "the People", an army whose soldiers are the citizens of the democracy, and from whom much of the world expects an extraordinarily high level of conduct.

It is a complicated story.

Israel has all the insignia of democracy: a lively and (mostly) uncensored press, free elections with a broad range of political parties from far left and to far right, vigorous public debate, and elaborate institutions for protecting human rights. Yet it faces daunting problems that imperil its democracy at every turn. The people who are the players in this civic tragedy are a contrary lot—Arabs who would destroy Israel by force of arms if they could, aggressive Jewish settlers who regard the territories taken in the 1967 war as part of a biblical Israel that can never be turned over to the one million Palestinians who live there, religious zealots who are more concerned with Jewish orthodoxy than with democracy, young conscripts whose military training consists of protecting themselves against Palestinian youths who despise them and whom they learn to despise in return, Israeli Arabs increasingly frustrated by their own second-class citizenship and the abuse of their Palestinian comrades on the West Bank, and an international community fixated on Israel's infractions but blind to Israel's dilemmas. That a democracy should survive at all in this sea of violence, anger, and guns is remarkable.

The success of Israel's citizen army, both as a military force and as the common denominator that touches all its people, has certainly contributed to democracy's endurance. Israel's modern founders were seeking to ensure that the horrors of the Europe they had left behind would never recur. Never again a Captain Dreyfus persecuted by an anti-Semitic officer corps as a scapegoat for its failures. Never again laws confiscating Jewish property. Never again Buchenwald.

The Jewish state would provide a homeland for Jews from throughout the world, and it would be a homeland capable of defending itself. Homeland first, defence second, and then democracy—the last a priority of many Jews, but hardly the *raison d'être* of the state of Israel. The democratic state of Israel was born out of war in 1948, when the British abandoned their controversial mandate over the area and the Arabs rejected the United Nations' partition of Palestine into separate Jewish and Arab states. Its birth in war and in terrorism—the underground, anti-British Irgun was run by Jews who did not shy away from terror—created a siege mentality, and helped prepare it for a permanent state of war which might have undone a people less imbued with a sense of the power of liberty and citizenship.

But since then, Israel has faced dilemmas that have turned its citizen army into part of the problem. Its Arab citizens (currently more than a million, out of four million) are not really welcome in the army—not to be trusted! And now there are a million non-citizens who live in smouldering resentment under Israeli military rule in the "greater Israel" created after the 1967 war (including East Jerusalem, the West Bank of the Jordan River that formerly belonged to Jordan, the Golan Heights on the frontier of Syria, and Gaza—the teeming refugee camp on the Mediterranean). In 1987, this resentment exploded into open rebellion—the Palestinians call it *intifada*—that threatens not only Israel's security, but the morale of its army and the integrity of its democracy.

The threat of war is often more costly to democracy than war itself, and Israel has had to pay this price for forty years. The country is preoccupied with terrorism, security, and defence costs—which take up 30 per cent of its Gross National Product and are heavily subsidized by the United States—and its internal politics are fractious, even fratricidal, with extremist political and religious parties proliferating in the volatile political climate. Newer and poorer Oriental Jewish immigrants from the Arab states have little in common with the Ashkenazim from Europe who founded the kibbutz movement and the Israeli state. And even when Israel is at peace, its economy is often in disarray. Its foreign debt is crippling. Inflation can double the price of a refrigerator almost overnight, and currency fluctuations usually bar vacations outside of Israel to all but the richest. Yet despite all this—some might even argue, *because* of all this—Israeli democracy has manifested an extraordinary resilience, making this nation-as-army no less formidable as a democracy than it is as a military power. The nation torn apart within is held together by the external threat to its survival, its people finding a common bond in their military service.

Why this is so can perhaps be better gleaned from the stories of individual Israelis than from the welter of paradoxes that constitute Israel as a nation. Yorom Yair, Shaulin Shimon, and Zeev Weiler are three reservists in Israel's army in whom all of the strengths and not a few of the difficulties of modern Israel are embodied. The three come from vastly different backgrounds, hold different jobs, and agree politically on very little. They have almost nothing in common—except their service in the army. But this turns out to mean more than all the things that divide them.

As reservists, once a year these three men and thousands like them leave their families and their jobs and their everyday lives behind. Exchanging civilian clothes for military fatigues, they spend a month marching, parachuting from planes, engaging in mock battles, and practising for the next war—which everyone is certain *will* come, if not this year, then the next, or the year after. Although reserve service has its pleasures, few do it eagerly. Yet it would not occur to them not to do it. "We don't do it because somebody twists our arm," explains Yorom, thirty-two, an orchard farmer and co-op manager on a kibbutz with an English wife and two young children; "It's because we have to if we want to keep our houses, if we want a chance for our families to live."

David Ben-Gurion, Israel's first prime minister and a kibbutznik like Yorom, liked to say that every Israeli was a soldier with eleven months of leave. In fact much of the population aged between eighteen and fifty-five is in the Israeli defence forces. Until the age of forty men spend thirty-one days a year in military training. Single women serve in the reserves until they are thirty-four. In this unique citizens' army, an egalitarian spirit reigns. Relations between officers and their troops are easygoing; dress is eccentric, with checked windvests or blue pullovers supplementing regular army dress. Trousers are unpressed and nobody ever salutes. Officers can be recognized by discreet epaulettes, but there are neither brass buttons nor bellowing sergeants.

Like so many communards, Yorom retains relatively liberal views. Doctor Zeev Weiler, only a few years older, is his opposite. Zeev and his wife, also a doctor, moved in 1979 to Ariel, near Nablus, on the West Bank, and he supports the right's program for its annexation. Zeev and Yorom are both idealists, one of the left, the other of the right, but Yorom is embarrassed by the occupation of the land on which Zeev has chosen to live. Zeev is there to stay, his body on the line; Yorom wants to give the Palestinians a homeland in exchange for security. Zeev thinks that the West Bank belongs to Israel and that the Arabs who live there are lucky—or at least he thought that before they began to stone his fellow settlers and toss Molotov cocktails at the border police who have been harassing them. Yet, for all of this, when they are thrown together in the same parachute battalion for their annual manoeuvres they are on the same side and they speak as one man. "I feel that everybody should contribute to the maximum," Zeev insists. "That's my duty. If it takes me to the front lines, I'll be there."

Shaulin Shimon is no idealist, just an ordinary citizen struggling to make a success of his small Tel Aviv restaurant. Like many Israelis, he emigrated to America in search of fortune, but he returned to fight in the Lebanon War of 1982—"I came back because Israel is my country and I felt I should do my duty," he says—and he has no intention of leaving again. He employs Arabs in his restaurant, he does his reserve service without making it an occasion for celebration or complaint, and he wishes for peace.

In Israel, military service is an ordinary necessity for ordinary citizens, and war does not seem to have created an extraordinary threat to democracy. Unlike coup-prone Argentina or traditional Nigeria, Israel has no distinct military class. Officers come from the conscript pool rather than from a military academy, and they are as ideologically varied as the rest of the citizenry. Officers retired from the small professional corps may play a prominent role in Israeli politics after they leave the service, but they are far more likely to berate each other in public than to conspire behind closed doors. Yitzhak Rabin and Ezer Weizman were both war heroes, but as politicians they were in full agreement only on the health of their democracy. Weizman said, "In thirty-five years in key positions in the military and the government, I can't think of a single case where our being a democracy hampered me. It certainly didn't prevent us from going to war when we had to." Rabin said, "There's no tolerance for generals who play about with politics while they're serving as generals."

Despite his success as leader in the Haganah, the clandestine militia, during the War of Independence in 1948, Rabin had a hard time being appointed chief of staff in the 1950s. Rabin himself saw no contradiction between the citizen and the general: "The essence of the spirit of Israel is the fact that we are a democracy. People can say whatever they want to say.

The army is the people's army because the people are the army and the army is the people."

Israel has inoculated itself against military coups and military rule through its citizen army. If its democracy succumbs it will not be to the army, but to civilians—such as Yorom, Shimon, and Zeev—who allow security, the occupation of the West Bank, and the deep political ambivalences of Zionism to undermine their commitment to democracy. If the high command continues to reverse a long tradition of openness and close the occupied territories to journalists as it did for a while in the winter of 1988, if a defence minister insists that this army of whose democratic character he has boasted must also be ready to beat the Palestinian protesters until they behave (as he did in the same winter), then perhaps this means that Israeli democracy is broken and needs mending, and it is the Zeevs and Yoroms and Shimons who are going to have to fix it. Unlike the professional French soldiers who staged the Algerian coup, unlike the colonels in Argentina who thought they knew better than the citizens how to run the country, these three soldiers and thousands like them *are* the citizens; they are Israel, and its democracy is in their hands.

In the long run, because their problems are fairly typical of the confrontation of democracy and war, the Swiss and Israeli response to the need for national defence may be more telling than Costa Rica's. For Israel and Switzerland teach us that to survive the fire of war, democratic nations need to nurture armies in which the principles of democracy—equality, participation, mutual tolerance, and respect—are extended to the army itself. A civilian army is a powerful bulwark against potential military abuses by civilians as well as professional military elites. It was the resistance, the reluctance, the debates of American conscripts that helped bring an end to the disaster of America's war in Vietnam, it was French conscripts who prevented the Algerian tragedy from becoming France's graveyard, Filipino conscripts who helped President Aquino to power in 1987 by refusing to fire on civilians, and it was Israeli conscripts who spearheaded the Peace Now campaign that led to Israel's withdrawal from its disastrous incursion into Lebanon and may yet spread a little oil on the troubled waters of the occupied territories. Citizen republics have little to fear and much to gain from citizen armies.

Democracy is never safe from subversion, and a democracy under fire from external enemies or a too zealous internal military establishment runs special risks. In 1960, as he left the presidency, Dwight Eisenhower warned that even as secure a democracy as the United States risked corruption by what he called a growing "military-industrial complex". He spoke of "an almost insidious penetration of our own minds that the only thing this country is engaged in is weapons and missiles [*sic*]." Thirty years earlier, the great American political scientist Harold Laswell had warned against the dangers of the garrison state: democracies at war falling prey—in their pursuit of efficiency, national cohesion, and internal security—to a mentality wholly incompatible with the open and tolerant spirit of democracy. He might have been prophesying what happened to those Canadians and Americans of Japanese ancestry whose story in the Second World War we still remember with sadness.

Whither Democracy?
XI

IN THE DOZEN YEARS SINCE *THE STRUGGLE FOR Democracy* was first screened, there have been three fundamental historical changes that have impacted on democracy's prospects. They do not change the contours of the struggle to achieve freedom and equality, for it is as old as the Athenian Assembly and as entrenched in history as Magna Carta; but they do inflect the struggle with new dilemmas and choices not quite the same as the ones faced in the era defined by Reagan and Thatcher, and Gorbachev and Trudeau, that were the backdrop for the original Series. Communism, which played such a crucial role as the mirror of democracy's struggle in the post-war world, collapsed precipitously a year after we completed our project with consequences still significant into the new millennium. Technology, which already appeared in our work as a crucible for modern democracy, leapt ahead with the dramatic development of computers and the Internet during the 1990s, and began to change the face of capitalism and move us from an industrial to an information economy. And, as a direct consequence of the first two developments, the capitalist economy itself has witnessed a dramatic globalization of markets that had eroded national sovereignty and changed the relationship between politics and the economy.

There are of course many other developments that impact on democracy. These include the growing polarization of the haves and have-nots around these new axes—the so-called digital divide separating the information rich and the information poor. For example: the growing exploitation and abuse of children that, even in the First World, has become an issue as one in five children in the United States find themselves born into poverty; a speculative bubble in the economy that has created an unparalleled economic boon in the West and a volatile stock market, especially around technology stocks, that has transformed (and democratized) investment strategies; and the explosion of ethnic, racial, and tribal conflict in many parts of the world that have thrown a shadow over democratization efforts in places like ex-Yugoslavia, Chechnya, Indonesia, Rwanda, and Afghanistan. No doubt these would have been new leitmotifs in our work, had we being making our film now.

Yet, in fact, these and many other innovative challenges are to a large extent features of, or entailed by, the three major sets of interdependent changes embodied by the fall of communism, the maturation of the information society and the economics of globalization. As we look forward to this new century in democracy's struggles, we can learn a great deal by focusing on these three.

If the collapse of communism proves anything, it is perhaps that democracy is always a struggle, even under (particularly under) conditions of apparent "triumph". The collapse of communism contradicted every theory of totalitarianism that had insisted internal disintegration was not an option, and that the hold of communism over the "minds and hearts" of its subjects meant they could never free themselves from within. At the same time, it signalled a rhetorical victory for "democracy" to which there are today almost no exceptions. Who at the beginning of the twenty-first century would boast to wanting to be other than democratic? Yet victory and the sudden vanishing of democracy's primary opponent (though even the communists had claimed the mantle of "peoples' democracies"!) may actually make the life of the citizen more complicated. Democracy's prospects have improved dramatically in the abstract, but in practice specific democracies have become vulnerable to new challenges that are the more implacable for being the less obvious. The new technology and globalization hardly seemed pernicious in the way communism was—quite the contrary. Yet their challenges were formidable.

Not that communism's threat had been less than formidable. Much of the twentieth-century history of democracy unfolded under the shadow of the experiments of Lenin, Stalin, and Mao, and the often costly wars, both hot and cold, against communism. This reality was reflected in our own approach in the television series to democracy's struggles in the 1980s. Our encounters with China, Russia, Algeria, Libya, and many other countries influenced by social democracy and communism, and our emphasis on the tensions between democratic politics and capitalist economics, all were shadowed by the Cold War and debates about the viability of socialism, state planning, and even egalitarianism itself (as against libertarianism). For that reason, the precipitous collapse of communism just a year after we completed our film is the most striking change we have to confront here.

The collapse of a corrupt version of socialism's bastard stepchild, statist communism, should not of course have spelled the end of the debate between socialists and free market liberals (or "libertarians") over the heart of democracy. Yet for all practical effects, that has been its consequence. The triumphalism represented by books like Francis Fukayama's *The End of History* and the emergence of the United States as the world's only remaining superpower changed the character of international relations. It removed the last barriers to the ubiquity of capitalist markets in labour, currency, goods, and services in a fashion that made democracy the "only" option for nations in transition, even though "market democracy" is not very democratic! Indeed, in Russia and much of the former Soviet empire, for example, many observers have been content to call corrupt regimes "democratic" simply because they are associated with free, even anarchic, markets. Shopping often seems to have become more important than voting as a signature for post-Communist "democracies".

There is little reason to believe that democratic politics and free markets are synonymous, however. As *The Struggle for Democracy* made clear, in nations like Korea and Chile in the seventies (as well as in China or Pakistan today), we find odd and sundry combinations of authoritarian government and free markets that suggest capitalism has no particular preferences when it comes to political systems. Indeed, the orderliness and predictability of authoritarian governments may appear as advantages to those wishing to develop capitalist markets. Hence, if the most dangerous myth of the earlier epoch insisted that a state economy was the same thing as an egalitarian regime, the most dangerous myth of this era insists that a free market is the same thing as a democratic regime.

As James Madison wrote in *Federalist 63*, "liberty may be endangered by the abuses of liberty as well as by the abuses of power." Which is to say, liberty can be jeopardized from the "private" side by monopolistic, irresponsible business, no less than from the side of the state sector. To be sure, in earlier centuries, the state presented liberty with multiple threats; and certainly under "state communism", the primary danger to liberty came from the public side. But wholly liberated, unregulated markets faced only with a weak and flaccid state sector turn out to present dangers of their own, especially in the new age of information technology, where private monopolies over "infotainment" are increasingly the rule. In short, as the monopoly state under communism has lost its grip on our lives, the monopoly multimedia corporation in the age of technology has strengthened its own firm grip.

Technology's impact has not been deterministic, however. Historically, it has mirrored the society in which it evolves. Gunpowder and movable type certainly helped democratize Europe (as we pointed out in Chapter Eight), but gunpowder also reinforced tyranny in the Orient, while literacy—so conducive to Protestant Reformation—also became a condition of totalitarian propaganda in the West. Nowadays, it is often assumed that computers and the Net are wholly democratizing technologies, but while they can be put to democratic purposes, they can also become vehicles for continued commercialization and privatization. Digitalized media have certainly provided a high-speed, increasingly transparent, unmediated, point-to-point, interactive communication medium that erodes traditional boundaries, hierarchies, and hegemonies. Yet not even the "ancient" technology of the telephone is universal, and the new technologies of computers, fibre optics, satellites, and digital media serve less than one half of America's population and a far smaller percentage of the world.

Yet the new technologies do introduce forms of social relations and communication rooted in *speed* (the new, digitalized, computer-based technologies are fast); *simplicity* or simple-mindedness (the new technologies can become reductive, binary); *solitude* (the new technologies can isolate and atomize us); *pictoriality* (the new technologies privilege images and sounds over text even though today they are primarily text-based); *lateralness* (the new technologies offer a horizontal or lateral medium of communication, point to point rather than vertical); *informational* (the new technology privileges raw data, information over knowledge); *segmentation* (the new technologies divide audiences into segments, pieces, and groups, instead of encompassing them as a national or communal whole, as the traditional broadcast networks once did). And these features of new technology have a profound impact on how we practice social, civic and political relations, some beneficial to democracy, others more insidious.

Let me start with what is electronic technology's chief virtue—and vice—its speed. With computer communications we are communicating at the speed of light. When the American Revolution was fought, it took six weeks or more for information to travel between America and England. One might speculate America gained its independence in part because of the slowness of communications; for, with rapid reporting, the British might have responded far more efficiently to the rebellion than they did, and possibly "saved" their colony.

By the same token, the instantaneous transmission of news and data today can undermine authoritarianism and penetrate the most closed societies. Sky Television, Rupert Murdoch's satellite broadcast company, has done more to open China than a hundred years of diplomatic efforts. Yet while the speed of today's media permits instant communication, we may ask whether speed is really appropriate to civic education and democratic deliberation. While the Net is screaming "Hurry up!" deliberative democracy enjoins us to "Slow down!" Because democracy requires time, patience, consideration, and deliberation, the challenge of democracy in the electronic age is how to put speed bumps on the electronic highway. Chat rooms on the Net invite instant thinking, which often means the venting of unfiltered prejudice and unconsidered opinions.

The new technologies can be seen as friendly to speed, then, whereas democracy is friendly to deliberativeness and patience. Technology is supportive of instant opinion polling and elite manipulation of the kind that can reinforce plebiscitary democracy, but it undermines more participatory and deliberative forms of democracy.

The new technologies also tend towards reductive simplicity—towards binary dualisms that, in political terms, facilitate polarization and make the search for common ground more difficult—and they can also divide, isolate and atomize people. A major study by Norman Nie, published in the United States at the beginning of 2000, suggested that the Internet could breeding solitude and loneliness. Friendship and community may be *extended* and preserved virtually, but it is very hard to *create* them virtually. There has been some experimentation with Net voting, but this puts democratic decision-making into a private venue where there is no pressure to consider others or their common goods. J.S. Mill argued that to render decision-making responsible it had to be made public (Mill opposed the secret ballot for that reason). Yet there is no more private space than cyberspace, and to make it a primary venue for voting could privatize the electoral process.

Clicking a yea or nay icon on the computer screen to register and tabulate unreflective private prejudices is not democracy: imagine, at one moment choosing between music tracks on an MTV web site—do you watch Madonna or Garth Brooks?—and the next moment deciding whether to bomb Serbia back into the Stone Age ... or not! Moving around among choices and agendas that are at times trivial and utterly private and at other times deeply consequential and wholly public cannot be a prudent way to pursue democratic decision-making.

On the positive side, there may be some potential in the new technology to bridge time and space in ways that finally transcend Aristotle's notion that community is limited to the land you can traverse in a single day. The quest for transnational democratic institutions to offset transnational economic systems that dominate the globe is crucial to the survival of democracy in the new millennium. The Internet holds the promise to enhance transnational civic communication and help build virtual international communities. New international civic associations like Civicus and Civitas have made effective use of the Net to bring together groups that might otherwise remain geographically segregated.

Finally, though the Net today is dominated by scrolling text that makes it little more than a jet-powered telegraph, it is in its essence a pictorial medium, and digitalization and streaming video will permit it to realize its pictorial potential. The generation that has grown up with computers and the Net is a television-educated, picture-inundated generation that prefers "moving pictures" (i.e., movies or cinema) to stolid letters and words. Yet democracy is word-based and wedded to the deliberative languour of speech. From this perspective, the Net could in the long term undermine the word-based character of democratic political institutions.

Democracy starts quite necessarily as the delicate politics of words against the brutal politics of force and the irrational politics of feeling. As the politics of reason and of promising, democracy demands the currency of words. That is why Aristotle believed that "logos" was the essence both of human being and of politics. Our own politics is rooted in the social contract, and the social contract depends upon the reliability and integrity of promising. Promising depends in turn on the sanctity of words. We do not promise with pictures!

Democracy must find its way today in an information society. Democracy depends, however, on knowledge and wisdom, for which information is a poor substitute. Information is raw, unmediated, undigested, data … meaningless noise. Human civilization and human intellect depend *not* on information but on making sense of information, on converting information into knowledge and (on rare occasions) converting knowledge into wisdom. It is only that end product, wisdom, that serves culture, education, and democracy. Democracy will flourish when citizens have converted the information society into the knowledge society. Indeed, the problem of many developed societies is not too little information or too little access to information, but too much information out of which people often make far too little sense. Schools in the United States are being hardwired. Throughout the world access to computers and the Net has become a benchmark of civic literacy. Yet literacy precedes and cannot arise out of hardware or software. Democracy depends on educated and wise citizens rather than people swimming in a sea of unfiltered raw information. The deficit in developed nations' schools is not an information deficit but a knowledge deficit, a deficit in critical thinking. Too much information can be as devastating to judgment as too little.

Whatever the democratic potential of the Net, it has in reality reflected the larger society, becoming both fragmented in content, monopolistic in ownership (the Disney/ABC merger and the takeover of Time-Warner by AOL in 2000 are examples), and commercialized in its content (more than 90 per cent of Net traffic in the year 1999 was commercial). Distribution certainly remains fragmented, but the ownership of software and portals is monopolistic and tends to be homogenizing as well as commercializing. There has been a palpable "malling" of cyberspace that has made '.com' far more important than ".org" or ".edu". Nearly one-quarter of the commercial traffic on the Net goes to pornography. The Net's "pull" virtues (you get what you go looking for) are being displaced by high-pressured "push" technology devoted to the hard sell (you get what we sell you). Free Net access as well as free hardware (including computers) are available to those who are willing to live with endless scrolling advertising on their screens. A world where everything is for sale is not a world hospitable to democracy.

The real challenge is political not technological, and if democracy is to benefit from technology those who would be democrats will have to start not with technology but with politics. Having a voice, demanding a voice in the making of science and technology policy is the first step that citizens can take in assuring a genuinely, democratic, technology. The new technology is only an instrument of communication. It cannot determine what we will say and to whom we will say it.

Marconi, one of the inventors of twentieth-century communications technology, is reputed to have exclaimed when told his new telegraph had succeeded and he could now talk to Florida, "And do we have anything to say to Florida?" Cyber-enthusiasts around the world are excited by the fact that Stockholm can talk to Hanoi, and Hanoi to Tokyo, and Tokyo to Florida, and Florida to Göteborg. But while folks can talk to strangers around the world, it is not clear that they can talk to their neighbours, or husbands, or fellow citizens. Can democracy's communicative blockages, local incivilities and neighbourhood conflicts be overcome by the miracles of long-distance, computer-based communication? Will virtual community heal the ruptures of real community? Does the Net offer a solution to Kosovo or Rwanda? It seems unlikely. People are not likely to solve on their little keyboards and pixilated screens all the difficult problems they have created with one another face to face. If in this new, remarkable millennium we are about enter—a millennium in which these new technologies will dominate our lives as never before—we want democracy to be served, then the bitter-sweet fruits of science will have to be subordinated to democratic ends and made to serve as a facilitator, rather than a corrupter, of democracy's precious liberty. Whether this happens or not, will depend not on the quality and the character of technology, but on the quality of political institutions and on the character of citizens.

Technology has not only transformed democracy's challenges directly, it has also set the context for the third challenge to democracy's fortunes that had emerged since the 1980s: globalization. In Europe, America, and throughout the world, the nation-state has lost much of the sovereignty upon which democracy traditionally depended, while global markets have become dominant, if not quite "sovereign", forces in everyday lives. This has meant nothing less than a literal passing of sovereignty—in a democracy, the right of the people to decide the collective destiny of the nation—from public to private hands, from transparent and representative political institutions to opaque and unrepresentative economic institutions. It means that in certain ways Bill Gates of Microsoft and Michael Eisner of the Disney Corporation are more "sovereign" in the modern world than President Clinton of the United States and Chancellor Schroeder of the Federal Republic of Germany.

Moreover, the globalization process has created a radical asymmetry that alters traditional relationships. It privileges the economic and market sectors and marginalizes the political sector. It prefers the private to the public, and it associates liberty with the corporate sector, however monopolistic it may be, while it associates coercion and dependency with the government sector, however democratic it may be. It treats crucial democratic values as so many relics of a pre-virtual civilization. Finally, it points to fundamental changes in the relationship between capitalism and democracy brought about by the new information economy—changes that have remained almost entirely outside the debate.

The asymmetry of the new globalism is evident in mergers like Disney/ABC, Viacom/CBS, MCI/Worldcom/Sprint, and now AOL/Time-

Warner/EMI. These mergers present a challenge not just to economic competition in the domain of goods, labour, and capital, but to democracy and its defining virtues: free and autonomous information (guaranteed by the independent existence of plural, discretely owned media); social and political diversity (guaranteed by genuine pluralism in society); and full participation by citizens in deciding public policies and securing public goods (guaranteed by a robust public domain in which public goods and the nature of the society in which we live are democratically chosen).

In fact, the economic vices of nations have been globalized while civic virtues have remained parochial. There has been a globalization of crime, drugs, terror, hate, the weapons trade, pornography, and financial speculation. But civil society, citizenship, and civic virtue remain properties of the democratic nation-state. National boundaries have become too porous to hold the economy in, but remain sufficiently dense to prevent democracy from getting out and civilizing the larger world.

The tendency of globalization to neglect the public sphere is reinforced by tendencies within democratic states. Ideological changes that began in the 1980s with Reagan and Thatcher and made privatization the predominant political philosophy of the era have continued to grow in influence, with leftist and progressive parties in North America and Europe now as devoted to assaults on government "bureaucracy" as parties on the right.

When President Clinton announced what he called the "end the era of big government" in 1996, he signalled a shift that since then is also evident in the Labour and social democratic governments of England, Germany, and even France—if to a lesser degree. The market anarchy of the global economy finds its mirror image within nations in this privatization ideology. The objective of privatization is greater liberty, but its actual consequence has often been greater concentration of private power. This accelerating merger mania in the infotainment telesector is effectively destroying the autonomy, diversity, and integrity of the civic sector so essential to democracy. It would seem odd to nineteenth-century theorists of democracy to observe how today people label democratic government's control over information and news "totalitarian", but when monopolistic corporations exercise a similar control, call it free market "synergy".

Economists will argue that the new international monopolies are not an accidental outcome but a necessary condition of doing business in the new information economy. Vertical integration is not an economic strategy but a condition of synergy. Hence, Microsoft chair Bill Gates has argued in opposing the anti-trust suit brought by the American Justice Department that his integration of an Internet browser into his Windows computer operating system is a "natural" extension of the nature of his original product. Technological convergence entails monopoly, while synergy demands vertical integration. These new developments may suggest that the rules thought to govern classical capitalism—diversity, genuine competition, differential markets, and multiple firms—become anachronistic in a global economy dominated by information technology and a surfeit of goods.

Put differently, the information economy would seem to engender a new and powerful logic that dictates its own imperatives. What this means for democracy, however, has not been sufficiently analysed. If monopoly has become a new necessity of post-modern capitalism, what was once understood as a public "bad" now appears as a public good. Can democracy survive the domination of its public logic by a new private economic logic? The implication of the globalization business of firms is that unelected CEOs and Board members like those who run AOL/Time-Warner and Deutsche Telecom become appropriate representatives to shape the world's destiny as an information society. Corporate decisions become de facto legislation for whole nations. Is this democracy? And if it is not, how can one struggle against it, when it appears in the guise of market freedom?

It would appear then that the new challenge to democracy is how it can re-create the conditions for popular sovereignty and public choice in an international setting where multinational corporations and banks have assumed many of the insignia of sovereignty, and where power is concentrated in the private sector, beyond the control of sovereign peoples. What can traditional "international organizations" like the United Nations and the International Monetary Fund do when they are themselves hopelessly divided, and tainted by divisions among nations, or susceptible to the influence of money and corporations through the governments that ostensibly control them?

Yet the struggle for democracy continues. Citizens have begun to look for ways to influence matters beyond their national boundaries. There is an emerging international alternative to global markets. The world seems out of control because the instruments of control—democratic governing institutions—do not yet exist in the international setting where markets in currency, labour, and goods run like engines without governors. So citizens are moving to create them. There are signs of an emerging internationalism around transnational civic institutions, global social movements and a world "public opinion" yoked to the human rights movement, that promise a degree of countervailing power in the international arena. For a long time, when protesters would cry "no globalization without representation," one would look in vain for a global "we the people" to be represented. That is now changing. There is another internationalism growing today, a forming crystal from which a global "we the people" can grow. No protest can roll back market globalization, but people who care about public goods are working to create on a global scale the civic balance found within nations. Five years ago there was almost nothing. But in Seattle, Washington, during the meeting of the International Monetary Fund there in the autumn of 1999, unions, green organizations, civic associations, and a great many unaffiliated citizens gathered to protest the faceless injustices of the international economy. The struggle for democracy has in fact today become global. Here are some examples of the new global initiatives aimed at democratizing international relations:

- A young woman named Jody Williams, with celebrity help from the late Princess Diana, creates a worldwide civic movement for a ban on land mines, and helps gets a treaty enacted signed by a majority of the world's nations (though not the United States).

- A Bangladeshi visionary named Muhammad Yunus establishes a "bank" devoted to "microfinancing" small businesses in the Third World; the "Grameen" banks micro-credit enables women in Third World societies to jump-start enterprise, liberating them from traditional forms of patriarchy and servitude.

- Striking fear into retired tyrants everywhere, European public opinion and spirited English law lords make possible the arrest in England of a Chilean ex-dictator to be tried in Spain, where he has been charged for his crimes; ill health gets Pinochet off the hook, but the tocsin has sounded: dictators are no longer safe in their retirement havens.

- Women's groups from around the world meet in Beijing without the blessing of their governments in a demonstration of international solidarity that asks nothing of states and everything of civic institutions that are powerfully reinforced by their action.

- Citizen groups use "Good Housekeeping Seal" methods to underwrite safe fisheries ("Dolphin-Safe Tuna") and rug manufacturing without child labour ("Rugmark"), while students at Duke University in the

United States lead a movement to assure that campus sports apparel is not manufactured in child-exploiting sweat shops.

- The stealth Multilateral Agreement on Investment that would have further eroded national attempts to regulate foreign investment is subjected to broad citizen scrutiny, above all in Canada, and indefinitely deferred.

- Hundreds of NGOs gather in new international organizations like CIVICUS and CIVITAS and begin to develop the kind of civic networking across nations that corporations have enjoyed for decades courtesy of the World Economic Forum at Davos.

- Global Internet communication among groups facilitated by organizations like Peter Armstrong's Oneworld.org and Globalvision's new Media Channel.org supersite are diverting the new telecommunications from pure commerce to the public interests of global civil society.

- President Clinton offers the corporate leaders at the 2000 Davos World Economic Forum a "wake-up call" reminding them that there are "new forces seeking to be heard in the global dialogue", progressive forces that want to democratize rather than withdraw from the new world order.

- "Europe" reacts as "Europe" to coalition talks between Austria's traditional parties and Eric Haider's reactionary "Freedom Party," again signalling the potency of an emerging transnational public opinion operating across state boundaries.

These civic efforts—the work of citizens rather than governments, or of governments reacting to citizens (and not just their own)—embody a global public opinion in the making, a global civic engagement that can alone give the abstraction of international rights political weight, a natural outreach of citizens and civic groups that make entities like "Europe" more than a mere function of economic and security concerns. Coteries of NGOs, the shifting voice of global public opinion, and unsteady hand of the international rights movement may not be the equal of multinational corporations or international banks, but they represent a significant starting place for countervailing power. They put flesh on the bare bones of legalistic doctrines of universal rights. James Madison noted that a declaration of rights is a paper fortress from which it is impossible to defend real rights. Rights depend on engaged citizens and a civic space where their activities are possible. These emerging transnational civic spaces offer possibilities for transnational citizenship and hence an anchor for global rights.

Democrats can also continue to utilize national state strategies to strengthen internationalism, as European states do in their support for the E.E.C. Amnesty International and Médicins sans Frontières are obviously not the equivalent in clout of AOL-Time Warner or the IMF. Equality requires the weight and power of government. After all, like the United Nations, the WTO is itself a creature of nation-states and, like the IMF and many other market institutions, could be regarded as the exoskeleton of an international governance organism.

By remaining vigilant (critics say stubborn) in confronting the pressures of privatization, France has in fact held open the possibility of exerting political control of the international arena through international institutions. Indeed, unlike the United Nations, most of the global trade organizations can be controlled by smaller numbers of powerful states. Were they to agree on policy, the G-8 nations could probably work their will at the IMF and the WTO. Currently, the WTO treats national "boycotts" of imported goods, even when they are motivated by safety or environmental or child-labour concerns, as illegal. Its members can change these provisions.

Currently, Third World nations worry with reason that First World environmental and safety and minimum-wage concerns are a way of putting a human face on protectionism. By imposing impossible-to-meet standards, the First World may steal back jobs from developing nations in the name of protecting their peoples. One possible approach to a remedy might be to redistribute the financial costs of environmental and safety speed bumps on the road to development. If the First World asks Brazil not to turn its tropical rain forests into parking lots, it needs to compensate Brazil.

National sovereignty may be a dying concept, but it is a long way from dead. Sovereign nations remain the only true countervailing powers capable of opposing, subduing, and civilizing the anarchic forces of the global economy. The emerging global alternative to world markets is international civil society, but it needs the active support of sovereign states for its fragile new institutions to have even a modest impact. Working together, however, democratic forces within traditional nation-states can make league with democratic forces active in the international arena. Between them, they can guarantee that democracy and civil society will have a voice in how the world is organized and governed.

The struggle for democracy continues. It still begins at the level of the neighbourhood—the ancient Athenian demos—and it certainly remains crucial to politics at the national or federal level of sovereign nations. But it now plays out in a global arena as well. Indeed, the future of democracy today depends as never before on how well it can adjust to the globalization of markets and the growth of the information society that has made globalization seem inevitable. Ultimately, human freedom will depend on the capacity of citizens around the world to make democracy as expansive and encompassing as the global economy. And to bring to the world arena, the robust institutions of self-government first introduced in the polises of ancient Attica.

Appendix

The Making of the Television Series

IN MY FOURTY-FOUR YEARS OF TELEVISION JOURNALISM I have been repeatedly struck by the fact that some of the most corrosive cynicism about democracy and some of the most leaden indifference towards it are expressed by people who live comfortably in prosperous democratic countries. Their own achievements would probably have been impossible without the democratic freedoms they have come to take for granted. Yet I met so many people in the West who were disappointed in their own democratic systems and as a result not contributing to them (or was it the other way around?) that I began to wonder if the story of democracy could be retold in a concentrated and dramatic way—a way that might re-engage the cynics and excite a new generation.

And then, thirty years ago, one particular incident helped to galvanize me: in the early predawn of October 16, 1970, police and uniformed officers fanned out across a sleeping city. Armed with extraordinary powers, they broke into homes, ransacked apartments, confiscated what they wanted, and seized people at will; over 450 were arrested. The police had orders to bring in the suspects, and bring in the suspects they did, holding them without charge or bail and refusing to provide reasons for their arrest.

Where did this happen? Not in some remote military dictatorship or totalitarian people's government in Eastern Europe, but in my own country, Canada—one of the world's most peaceable and stable democracies. A shadowy Liberation Front had appeared in Quebec, claiming responsibility for a series of petty "terrorist" incidents and communiqués and for two political kidnappings (one of which would end in a brutal murder). This had panicked and then paralysed Quebec's provincial government and had given the federal government a motive for dramatic extra-parliamentary action. Amid rumours of arms caches and insurgents, the government had dusted off an old and half-forgotten legislative bludgeon called the War Measures Act—an act which had last been used to incarcerate Japanese Canadians during the Second World War. Astonishingly, the government's move to suspend civil liberties aroused no significant protest from the Official Opposition, from the press, or from the public at large. Opinion polls taken at the time showed that four out of five Canadians approved of these frightening and wholly undemocratic measures. Canada's much-vaunted commitment to democratic rights and liberties seemed to have vanished overnight.

This casual disowning of freedom—so precious, and so long in the making—troubled me deeply. Hence the television series and the book that accompanies it.

The constricting tragedies in our democratic societies exist cheek by jowl with the liberties and opportunities. A woman said to me in Dublin, where she worked in a women's clinic, "There's no democracy in this bloody country! When they can tell a poor girl she can't have an abortion after she's been gang-raped. When you can't get birth control. When women are treated like slaves." A black American said to me, "There's no democracy in this country, man! Look at the jails. Look at the slums." Again and again I have been confronted—by native people in my own country, by women in almost every democratic country I have visited, by scientists who can't get grants, by victims who see the courts let their assailants go free, by poor people in rich countries, and by rich people enraged at the incursions of the state: millionaires complaining about taxes, and prosperous farmers vilifying marketing boards. Freedoms collide. Over and over I have heard from people hurt in these collisions that there is no democracy, or that it doesn't work, that it is messy and chaotic. "Democracy says that ninety-nine half-wits make a better decision than one man who knows all the facts," said an Australian.

But the struggle for democracy has nevertheless driven the human race for thousands of years. The story of the blood that has been shed to win democratic freedoms is the great ongoing epic in history. There is no civilization that does not bear the mark of democracy; few countries today do not describe themselves by that name. Why?, we asked, as we considered the extraordinary and difficult task of conveying democracy on film. And we began the search for those human stories—stories of self-sacrifice and idealism, of power and invention—that would make sense out of the perplexities of democracy, would celebrate the heroes and heroines of democracy. We set out on a quest for democracy.

In June 1984 I assembled a panel of scholars and filmmakers to consider how a television series might actually be made on the subject of democracy. Their thoughts propelled me for the next two and a half years—working with as many as three film crews at one time, and filming in some thirty countries. As film came back to Toronto and was processed and screened, the shape of the series, and of this book, began to grow. Early on I met and joined forces with Benjamin Barber, the most satisfying modern thinker about democracy I know, who began as consultant to the series and found himself swept in with us to write the book as well.

I think together we must have accumulated in our travels a total of 500,000 miles. But more striking is the fact that in six months in 1987 I travelled to Britain, Libya, Israel, the United States, Nigeria, Botswana, Zimbabwe, South Africa, Australia, Papua New Guinea, New Zealand, Switzerland, Japan, Holland, Belgium, and France. We were thrown out of Papua New Guinea on a visa technicality and could not get permission to film in South Africa, but in most countries, from Libya to Peru, we found people helpful, if not always easy to deal with. We were especially pleased by the courtesy shown us by armed forces.

Democracy is built upon communication. Television and books both play a vital role in exposing us to the ways of life of people in every part of the globe, to their political aspirations and their personal needs. It is my belief that all this exposure slowly, cumulatively, prepares the ground for accommodations among peoples that will make peace a more achievable objective and democratic forms of social organization inevitable. Not automatically: it will take acts of faith and determination, labours of construction and devising, resources of patience and good will. But it is communication that will both pave the way for these acts and labours and resources, and allow them to become functional. This is the faith of the communicator. It is not a blind faith.

Patrick Watson
Toronto, September 1988

Authors' Acknowledgements

THE EXPERIENCE AND INSIGHT OF THE MANY SCHOLARS and politicians and the hundreds of citizens and active practitioners of democracy we encountered all over the world are often reflected explicitly in the television series and in these chapters, but there are many wise voices we heard, and learned from, whose wisdom is reflected but not seen. (The opinions and arguments, and the mistakes, are of course our own.)

Our invaluable researcher in New York, Dr. John Samples, made sure that our facts were straight, and provided crucial research and organization of data as well as important bibliographic material. In Canada, Dr. Helen Hatton read the manuscript and drew many historical points to our attention. At Lester & Orpen Dennys, Dean Cooke, Anne Fullerton, and Victoria Foote offered their careful editorial and production assistance, and Louise Dennys, a truly inspiring editor, kept the entire project not just afloat but on an even keel. Juliet Mannock was our indefatigable picture editor. Caroline Furey Bamford was the liason with the TV series took many of the photographs on location. And with his fine sense of design, John Lee gave the book its stamp of distinction and helped stimulate our own imaginations.

But if we were to choose one to whom we would dedicate the book, it would be the late Sir Moses Finley, whose contribution to the study of democratic life and ideas has left a lasting mark on our understanding of western civilization.

Patrick Watson and Benjamin Barber
Toronto and New York, September 1988

Television Series

Acknowledgements

HUNDREDS OF PEOPLE WHO WORK WITH CAMERAS and lights, pens and keyboards, microphones and consoles—colleagues and companions who have been associated with the television series since the beginning—contributed to the series in one way or another. It's been quite a collaboration. There are, though, some specific people who deserve particular thanks. Executive producer Michael A. Levine, Bill Hopper at Petro-Canada, Bill Morgan and Denis Harvey at the CBC, and Richard Creasey at Central Independent Television in England made the series possible. Ted Remerowski, filmmaker and scholar, kept the series honest and would not let us get away with anything other than our best work. Nancy Button kept us organized and marvellously supported the whole project. Caroline Furey Bamford, ensured that we all remembered that democracy was primarily a struggle of ordinary citizens. Filmmakers Michael Gerard, George James, and George Mitchell, cinematographers Neville Ottey, Nikos Evdemon, Mike Boland, and Bob Bolt, soundmen Ian Challis, Gerry King, and Dennis Fitch, and editors John Gareau, David Leighton, Duncan Smith, and Fred Gauthier contributed especially to the power of the series. The work and thoughtful contributions of many people—far too many to name them all, unfortunately—helped bring the series and the book to life.

Patrick Watson
Toronto, September 1988

Bibliography

Democracy as an idea—some classical books

Acton, Lord. *Essays in the History of Liberty*. Indianapolis: Liberty Press, 1985.
    Acton's belief in freedom led him to the famous conclusion that "All power corrupts and absolute power corrupts absolutely." These historical essays trace his understanding of liberty across the modern period with particular focus on Great Britain.

Adams, Henry. *Democracy: An American Novel*. American Biography Service, 1985.
    A classic novel from the early years of this century.

Aristotle. *The Politics*. Trans. Ernest Barker. New York: Oxford University Press, 1946.
    Aristotle was a qualified supporter of democracy and an excellent observer of the politics of ancient Greece. Barker's comments and notes are helpful to the neophyte.

De Tocqueville, Alexis. *Democracy in America*. Ed. Richard Heffner. New York: New American Library, 1984.
    De Tocqueville visited the United States in the 1830s and returned to France to write this classic that probed the egalitarian nature of American self-government. This abridged edition provides the essential analysis of his two volumes.

Dewey, John. *The Public and Its Problems*. Columbus: Ohio State University Press, 1954.

This book presents democracy as a political expression of the pragmatic spirit in philosophy and culture.

Hartz, Louis M. *The Liberal Tradition in America*. New York: Harcourt, Brace, 1955.

A classic history of American political thought that emphasizes the enduring consensus in the United States around the ideas of limited government and individualism.

Jefferson, Thomas. *Democracy*. Ed. Saul K. Padover. Bethesda: Greenwood Press, 1985.

A useful compendium of Jefferson's hopes for democracy in the West.

Locke, John. *Two Treatises of Government*. New York: New American Library, 1965.

Locke's Second Treatise of Government is the most influential defence of limited government in Western history.

Madison, James, Alexander Hamilton, and John Jay. *The Federalist Papers*. Ed. Clinton Rossiter. New York: New American Library, 1961.

These essays written in defence of the American Constitution of 1789 make up the most representative and influential single work of political theory in the United States. An essential guide to the spirit of American political institutions.

Michels, Robert. *Political Parties*. New York: Free Press, 1966.

Having studied the socialist parties of Imperial Germany, Michels concluded that an "iron law of oligarchy" governing organizations would always frustrate democracy in the modern era.

Mill, John Stuart. *Considerations on Representative Government*. London: J.M. Dent & Sons, 1910.

The classic defence of liberal democracy.

————. "On Liberty" in *Essential Works*. Ed. Max Lerner. New York: Bantam Books, 1961.

A classic essay dedicated to defending the principle that the state may not interfere with the individual's freedom except to prevent harm to another. A superb and timeless defence of political liberalism.

Paine, Thomas. *The Rights of Man*. Garden City: Doubleday, 1973.

Plato. *The Republic*. Trans. Allan Bloom. New York: Basic Books, 1968.
Plato's critique of democracy in classical Athens has enjoyed enormous influence over the centuries. The translator of this volume extends Plato's views to current politics and culture.

Rousseau, Jean Jacques. *The Social Contract*. Trans. by Judith Masters. New York: St. Martin's Press, 1978.
A profound and engaging exposition of the theory of direct democracy that has influenced virtually all political and intellectual trends since Rousseau's death.

Schumpeter, Joseph. *Capitalism, Socialism, and Democracy*. New York: Harper & Row, 1981.
The classic exposition of the view that competition for leadership among elites is the essence of democracy.

Whitman, Walt. *Democratic Vistas*. St. Clair Shores, Mich. Scholarly, 1970.
A classical essay on democracy in America, by America's greatest democratic poet.

Democracy as an idea—recent books

Bachrach, Peter. *The Theory of Democratic Elitism: A Critique*. Boston: Little, Brown & Co., 1967.

Banks, Arthur S., ed. *Political Handbook of the World 1984–1985*. Binghamton: CSA Publications, 1986.

Barber, Benjamin R. *Strong Democracy: Participatory Politics for a New Age*. Berkeley: University of California Press, 1984.

A leading study of the philosophical roots and practical possibilities of radical democracy in the current period.

Bell, Daniel. *The Coming of Postindustrial Society*. New York: Basic Books, 1973.
A look into the future by a sociologist who was once voted America's most respected intellectual by his peers.

Bowles, Samuel, and Herbert Gintis. *Democracy and Capitalism: Property, Community, and the Contradictions of Modern Thought*. New York: Basic Books, 1986.
A critique of liberal democracy from a Marxist viewpoint.

Crozier, Michel J., Samuel P. Huntington, and Joji Watanuki. *The Crisis of Democracy*. New York: New York University Press, 1975.

Dahl, Robert. *A Preface to Democratic Theory*. Chicago: University of Chicago Press, 1963.
Dahl has been a leading theorist of pluralist democracy in the West. This book shows his debt to and his modifications of Madisonian democracy.

De Sola Pool, Ithiel. *Technologies of Freedom*. Cambridge, Mass.: Harvard University Press, 1983.
Pool examines the new electronic technology that is just now beginning to emerge in modern societies and questions whether it will advance or retard freedom of speech and ideas.

Finley, M.I. *Democracy: Ancient and Modern*. London: Hogarth Press, 1973.

Friedman, Milton. *Capitalism and Freedom*. Chicago: University of Chicago Press, 1981.
The modern argument for *laissez-faire* capitalism and limited government.

Gorbachev, Mikhail. *Perestroika*. New York: Harper & Row, 1987.

Keohane, Robert O. *After Hegemony: Cooperation and Discord in the World Political Economy*. Princeton: Princeton University Press, 1984.
Questions about the future will turn more than in the past on international politics. Keohane, a leading student of international political econ-

omy, provides a masterful discussion of the ethics and realities of international economic co-operation.

Lowi, Theodore J. *The End of Liberalism*. Second Edition. New York: Norton, 1979.
    Perhaps the most important book written in the last two decades by an American political scientist. Lowi traces the decline of the rule of law in the United States and a loss of democratic control by the national legislature. A troubling work.

Macpherson, C.B. *The Life and Times of Liberal Democracy*. Toronto: Oxford University Press, 1977.
    This distinguished Canadian theorist provides an accessible critique of liberal democracy in this short volume.

Offe, Claus. *Contradictions of the Welfare State*. Cambridge, Mass.: MIT Press, 1984.
    Offe is an important and thoughtful critic of contemporary capitalism and its effects on the state.

Pateman, Carole. *Participation and Democratic Theory*. New York: Cambridge University Press, 1970.
    A response to critics of direct democracy.

Zwerdling, Daniel. *Workplace Democracy*. Magnolia, Mass.: Peter Smith.
    A blueprint for extending democracy to the factory floor.

The practice of democracy in the West

General

Franck, Thomas. *Judging the World Court*. New York: Priority, 1986.
    Franck, a professor of law, provides in this slim volume an excellent overview of the history and working of the World Court.

Kennedy, Paul. *The Rise and Fall of the Great Powers: Economic Change and Military Conflict from 1500 to 2000*. New York: Random House, 1988.

Kennedy argues that great powers in the course of Western history have brought on their own decline by taking on security obligations that weakened their economies.

Australia

Horne, Donald. *The Australian People*. Sydney: Angus Robertson, 1972.

Hughes, Robert. *The Fatal Shore*. New York: Knopf, 1987.
Hughes, an art critic, provides here a popular history of the country that began as a distant prison for Great Britain.

Keneally, Thomas. *Outback*. London: Hodder & Stoughton, 1983.

Terrill, Ross. *The Australians*. New York: Simon & Schuster, 1987.
A provocative and engaging consideration of the distinctive traits of the Australian people.

Canada

Fox, P.W. *Politics: Canada*. Fifth Edition. McGraw-Hill Ryerson, 1982.
A broad overview of the politics and institutions of Canada.

Glassford, Larry A., Robert J. Clark, and Larry Chud. *The Challenge of Democracy*. Toronto: Nelson, 1984.

Miles, Angela, and Geraldine Finn, eds. *Feminism in Canada: From Pressure to Politics*. Montreal: Black Rose Books, 1982.

Taylor, Charles. *Radical Tories: The Conservative Tradition in Canada*. Toronto: University of Toronto Press, 1982.

Van Loon, Richard, and Michael S. Whittington. *The Canadian Political System*. Toronto: McGraw-Hill Ryerson, 1981.
An introduction to Canadian politics that also informs the general reader about the Canadian constitution and its courts.

France

Birnbaum, Pierre. *The Heights of Power: An Essay on the Power Elite in France*. Chicago: University of Chicago Press, 1982.

The French governing caste is here examined by one of its own, a leading sociologist of that country.

Hanley, David, A.P. Kerr, N.H. Waites, eds. *Contemporary France: Politics and Society since 1945*. New York: Methuen, 1984.
This collection of essays is a lively and interesting account of contemporary France.

Greece

Aeschylus. *The Oresteia*. Trans. Robert Fagles. New York: Penguin, 1966.
Aeschylus provides in these plays the first great defence of democracy, the rule of law, and the idea of progress. The introduction by Fagles is especially useful.

Aristotle. *The Constitution of Athens and Related Texts*. Trans. Kurt von Fritz and Ernst Kapp. New York: Hafner Press, 1974.
Aristotle's account of the early history and political development of Athens was lost until the nineteenth century. In this century, classical scholars have raised doubts about the accuracy of his history. None the less, Aristotle's short book on his city is a good starting place for understanding the Greeks.

Finley, M.I. *Politics in the Ancient World*. New York: Cambridge University Press, 1983.
A general overview of the institutions and economics of political life in classical Greece by a leading scholar in the field.

Hamilton, Edith. *The Greek Way*. New York: Avon, 1973.
Hamilton provides a readable and lively account of ancient Greek culture and politics. This volume would serve the general reader admirably as an introduction to the subject.

Herodotus. *Histories*. Trans. Aubrey de Selincourt. New York: Penguin, 1954.
Herodotus is often called the first historian. This is the standard account of the Persian wars that paved the way for the golden age of classical Greece.

Jones, A.H. *Athenian Democracy*. Baltimore: Johns Hopkins University Press, 1986.

Legon, Ronald. *The Political History of the Greek City State to 336 B.C.* Ithaca, N.Y.: Cornell University Press, 1981.

Plutarch. *Lives of the Noble Greeks*. New York: Dell, 1959.
   Plutarch set out to compare the great men and women of ancient Greece and Rome. His accounts of various statesmen and thinkers provide both knowledge and entertainment for contemporary readers.

Stone, I.F. *The Trial of Socrates*. New York: Simon & Schuster, 1987.
   Stone, a journalist for the last half century, offers here an investigative report of the trial and death of Socrates of Athens. His report is the latest brief against Socrates and his student Plato.

Thucydides. *The Peloponnesian War*. Trans. Rex Warner. New York: Penguin, 1954.
   Thucydides witnessed the great war between Athens and Sparta that brought the golden age of classical Greece to an end. His reflections on the irony and futility of war remain instructive.

Iceland

Njardvík, Njördur. *Birth of a Nation*. Reykjavik: Iceland Review, 1978.

Tomasson, Richard A. *Iceland: The First New Society*. Minneapolis: University of Minnesota Press, 1980.
   Tomasson offers a sociological study of the history and structure of Icelandic society.

Ireland

Shannon, William V. *A Quiet Broker?: A Way Out of the Irish Question*. New York: Priority, 1986.
   A solid if short history of the conflict in Northern Ireland together with a clear exposition of the political issues at stake. Shannon is a syndicated columnist in the United States.

Israel

Frankel, William, ed. *Israel: The First Forty Years*. London: Thames & Hudson, 1987.
   The years since Israel came into being are traced here with candour and objectivity.

O'Brien, Conor Cruise. *The Siege: The Saga of Israel and Zionism*. New York: Simon & Schuster, 1986.

The author has made controversy his forte, and here the reader will find a contentious view of the Jewish state.

Shipler, David. *Arab and Jew: Wounded Spirits in a Promised Land*. New York: Penguin, 1987.

The well-travelled correspondent of *The New York Times* has produced a remarkable, balanced volume that never loses sight of the human factor in political conflict.

United Kingdom

Churchill, Winston. *A History of the English-Speaking Peoples*. Four Volumes. New York: Dodd, Mead, 1983.

A valuable account of the growth of democratic institutions in Great Britain.

Sampson, Anthony. *The Changing Anatomy of Britain*. New York: Vintage, 1984.

A lucid and interesting portrait of who runs Britain and its institutions.

United States

Chafee, Zechariah, Jr. *Free Speech in the United States*. New York: Atheneum, 1969.

An older work that runs only to the middle of this century. Chafee does an excellent job, however, of connecting the development of freedom in the U.S.A. to earlier victories in Great Britain.

————, ed. *Documents on Fundamental Human Rights*. Two volumes. New York: Atheneum, 1963.

A representative collection of constitutions, judicial opinions, and political manifestos essential to understanding the development of freedom in the West.

Farmer, James. *Lay Bare the Heart. An Autobiography of the Civil Rights Movement*. New York: Arbor House, 1985.

Farmer was a leader of the civil rights movement in the United States as far back as the 1940s. This recollection of his life from a childhood in Texas, through the freedom rides, to service in Richard Nixon's administration, provides a comprehensive and yet personal account of the movement.

Garrow, David J. *Beating the Cross: Martin Luther King Jr. and the Southern Christian Leadership Conference*. New York: Morrow, 1987.

This extensive biography of the life and times of King emphasizes his religious faith. This work will probably endure as the leading piece of scholarship on its subject.

McCloskey, Robert G. *The American Supreme Court*. Chicago: University of Chicago Press, 1960.

Although dated, this work remains a useful analysis of the history and powers of the American high court.

Malcolm X. *The Autobiography of Malcolm X*. New York: Ballantine, 1973.

A classic autobiography by a leader of the American black Muslims, assassinated in the sixties.

Novak, Michael. *The Spirit of Democratic Capitalism*. New York: Simon & Schuster, 1982.

Smead, Howard. *Blood Justice: The Lynching of Mark Charles Parker*. New York: Oxford University Press, 1988.

In 1959, a white mob in Poplarville, Mississippi, abducted Parker from his jail cell, killed him, and threw his body into the nearby Pearl River. This narrative of the murder and its aftermath provides a glimpse of the American South at its worst, just before the civil rights revolution.

The practice of democracy in the Third World

Africa

Davidson, Basil. *Africa in History*. London: Paladin Books, 1984.

This history places the emergent Africa of the present within its own perspective of time and circumstances.

Lamb, David. *The Africans*. New York: Random House, 1983.

This is a readable overview of the politics and culture of the entire continent.

McEvedy, Colin. *The Penguin Atlas of African History*. New York: Penguin, 1980.

This small volume provides maps of the continent that indicate political and cultural changes. The text accompanying the maps may serve as a concise introduction to the history of Africa.

Ungar, Sanford J. *Africa: The People and Politics of an Emerging Continent*. New York: Simon & Schuster, 1978.

This immensely readable introduction to Africa shows Ungar to be a fair-minded and astute judge of modern politics. He devotes considerable attention to U.S. policy towards the continent.

Argentina

Crawley, Eduardo. *Argentina, A House Divided, 1880–1980*. London: Hurst, 1984.

A general history of the period.

Naipaul, V.S. *The Return of Eva Perón*. New York: Vintage, 1980.

Naipaul must be counted among the foremost authors writing in English at the moment. This essay on the politics and culture of Argentina is a harrowing and powerful view of the obstacles to democracy in that country.

National Committee on Disappeared Persons. *Nunca Mas (Never Again)*. London: Faber & Faber, 1985.

After military rule ended in 1983, an official commission in Argentina investigated the horrors of the army's "dirty war" against leftist guerrillas. Their report makes gruesome but involving reading.

Poneman, Daniel. *Argentina: Democracy on Trial*. New York: Paragon House, 1987.

Poneman provides a lively account of the history of the struggle for democracy in Argentina. The book is particularly strong on the cultural aspects of the difficulties faced by Alfonsín.

Timerman, Jacobo. *Prisoner without a Name, Cell without a Number*. New York: Vintage, 1981.

Timerman was a leading newspaper publisher in Argentina prior to the military rule of the late 1970s and early 1980s. He was taken prisoner and tortured but lived to provide testimony of the brutality and racism of the Argentine junta.

Costa Rica

Ameringer, Charles D. *Democracy in Costa Rica*. New York: Praeger, 1982.

This volume provides a useful introduction to the history and institutions of this remarkable country.

India

Brown, Judith M. *Modern India: The Origins of an Asian Democracy*. Oxford: Oxford University Press, 1984.

A brief and intelligent retrospective of the creation and evolution of the Indian state. This volume may serve as an introduction to the subject.

Gandhi, Mohandas. *Gandhi on Non-Violence*. Ed. Thomas Merton. New York: New Directions, 1965.

A useful representation of Gandhi's thinking on non-violence and its application to the Indian struggle for independence.

Naipaul, V.S. *India: A Wounded Civilization*. New York: Random House, 1978.

An account of a journey to the land of his ancestors by the well-known novelist.

Libya

Ayoub, Mahmoud M. *Islam and the Third Universal Theory: The Religious Thought of Mu'ammar al Qadhdhafi*. New York: Methuen, 1987.

This American scholar provides a sympathetic view of the thought and actions of the Libyan leader. The volume is most useful in elucidating the Islamic origins of Qaddafi's political thought.

al-Qaddafi, Muammar. *The Green Book*. Three volumes. New York: Libyan Consulate to the United Nations, 1987.

The Libyan leader's vision for politics, economics, and society.

Mexico

Johnson, Kenneth F. *Mexican Democracy: A Critical View*. New York: Praeger, 1984.

The one-party state was until recently viewed favourably by many outsiders. This book is an antidote to such optimism.

Riding, Alan. *Distant Neighbors*. New York: Knopf, 1984.

An excellent, readable volume designed to educate its readers about the huge democracy south of the United States.

Nigeria

Jacobs, Dan. *The Brutality of Nations*. New York: Knopf, 1987.

This account of the Nigerian civil war maintains that the U.S., the United Nations, and other international powers prevented aid from reaching starving Biafrans. A controversial history of the period.

Zimbabwe

Blake, Robert. *A History of Rhodesia*. London: Methuen, 1977.

Index